POWER
SHIFT

ON THE NEW
GLOBAL ORDER

RICHARD FALK

ZED

Zed Books

LONDON

Power Shift: On the New Global Order was first published in 2016 by
Zed Books Ltd, The Foundry, 17 Oval Way, London SE11 5RR, UK.

www.zedbooks.net

Typeset in Haarlemmer by seagulls.net
Index by John Barker
Cover design by Kika Sroka-Miller

A catalogue record for this book is available from the British Library.

ISBN 978-1-78360-794-5 hb
ISBN 978-1-78360-793-8 pb
ISBN 978-1-78360-795-2 pdf
ISBN 978-1-78360-796-9 epub
ISBN 978-1-78360-797-6 mobi

Printed and bound by CPI Group (UK) Ltd, Croydon, CR0 4YY

ABOUT THE AUTHOR

Richard Falk is Albert G. Milbank professor emeritus of international law at Princeton University, the author of over thirty books and a specialist on the role of international law in global politics. The United Nations Human Rights Council appointed Falk as the United Nations special rapporteur on the situation of human rights in Palestine from 2008 to 2014.

In memory of Burns Weston
Exemplary Friend, Scholar, Humanist, Citizen Pilgrim

CONTENTS

ACKNOWLEDGEMENTS

Seeking to depict the changes and challenges affecting world order is a daunting undertaking, and is crucially reliant upon direct and indirect collaborative contact that can be only partially identified.

I have long benefitted from scholarly affinities and interaction with talented students of global politics and international law. Among those who have been especially influential in my own work, although no longer alive, I would single out Eqbal Ahmed, Burns Weston, Rajni Kothari, Yoshikazu Sakamoto, Ali Mazrui, Hedley Bull, and James Rosenau. Others who have been influential in the past, or more recently, include Saul Mendlovitz, Yasuaki Onuma, Georges Abi-Saab, Tom Farer, Marjorie Cohn, Ashis Nandy, Mary Kaldor, David Krieger, Hilal Elver, and Paul Wapner.

During work on this book, reflecting shared participation in academic conferences and projects, the ideas set forth here were particularly responsive to the thinking of Fred Dallmayr and Stephen Gill.

I am grateful to the Orfalea Center of Global and International Studies at the University of California, Santa Barbara for providing facilities and support while much of this book was being written, and thank particularly its executive director, Victor Faessel, for being invariably helpful to me.

I thank Kim Walker of Zed Books for her steady encouragement of my work, Dominic Fagan for efficiently managing the production process, and Jakob Horstmann for graciously and skillfully overseeing the two rounds of proofs.

This book is dedicated to recently deceased Burns Weston, whose long distinguished career as an engaged scholar has been inspirational for many of us. We shared a common jurisprudential outlook and mentoring background that derived from the work and vision of Myres S. McDougal, a giant of twentieth-century global public order studies. We also shared the belief, as actively expressed, that to be a scholar of integrity is inseparable from being a citizen of conscience. We believed this realization can only be authentically enacted in the twenty-first century by extending the circle of identification beyond the border of sovereign nations to encompass the whole of humanity, and as well, by coupling preoccupations about present concerns with a dedication to achieving a better future.

Some material was drawn from my chapters in previously published work, although it appears here altered and updated . I wish to acknowledge the following sources: Marjorie Cohn, ed., *Drones and Targeted Killing* (Olive Branch Press, 2015); Stephen Gill and A. Claire Cutler, eds., *New Constitutionalism and World Order* (Cambridge University Press, 2014); Amin Saikal, ed., *Weak States, Strong Societies: Power and Authority in the New World Order* (I.B. Tauris, 2016); Luca Mavelli and Fabio Petito, eds., *Towards a Postsecular Politics: New Forms of Community Identity, and Power* (Palgrave Macmillan, 2014); Stephen Gill, ed., *Critical Perspectives on the Crisis of Global Governance: Reimagining the Future* (Palgrave Macmillan, 2015). Also *Kosmos: A Journal for Global Transformation* (Fall/Winter 2014) and *Great Transition Initiative: Toward a Transformative Vision and Practice* (online publication, 2015).

As in the past, my wife and partner, Hilal Elver, has abundantly provided the basic necessities of a good life: love, patience, and affirmation. Considering that she was formed by the feverish intensities of Istanbul, such a satisfying combination of qualities is rarely encountered.

INTRODUCTION

Globalism and globalization: terrorism and state terror

The central theme of this collection of essays is an assessment of the subversion of the traditional hard power frameworks of statist world order. This process is giving rise to an ongoing and destabilizing struggle to shape an alternative soft power framework of a world responsive to changing conditions, challenges, actors, technologies, and goals. This struggle is carried on amid a bewildering array of contradictory local, national, regional, and global tendencies that are creating intellectual, ethical, and political confusion and frustration on levels of policy and social action, as well as public understanding. The outcome of this epic struggle will exert a great influence on the human condition as it evolves in the twenty-first century and is already reshaping the political imagination as it interprets this unfolding of world history.

There are many dangers and opportunities present in this atmosphere of foundational tension and innovation. The dangers include the intensification by the managers of old militarist patterns long relied upon to achieve order to overcome the decline in the effectiveness of traditional methods of solving problems and meeting security challenges in world society. This intensification of outmoded forms of geopolitics pose a variety of grave risks, which are to a varying extent accepted, acknowledged, evaded, denied by both political leaders and the public. In this way, risks are magnified, and a great deal of unnecessary human suffering takes place.

Among the greatest of these dangers are the responsive siren calls of political extremism often accompanied by regressive anti-modernist thinking that points the finger of blame at some vulnerable segment of the social or even cultural order, at enemies of the stability, civic order, and virtuous living that must be exterminated or walled out. Against the weight of such pressures governments and a compliant media even resort to reassurances of deliverance by divine intervention. There are an additional set of associated dangers that can be attributed to the rise of non-state political actors with large ambitions and a purist agenda directed at reshaping the social and political order, often by the most brutal imaginable means, accompanied by tactics seeking to disrupt normalcy by inflicting shocking harm and delivering threats of impending societal catastrophe. Such non-state movements have the audacity to declare a war on the established order and modernity itself as the sheltering and decadent edifice of values and ideas with fanatical fury. Governments respond by recourse to extreme securitization of public policy, rationalized by blaming minorities or immigrants for societal unrest and using the occasion to mobilize for perpetual war against "terrorist" enemies within and without, and preparing through prayer and diversionary politics awaiting "a second coming" or "messaiah," debilitating the political order from acting prudently, humanely, and creatively in the face of unprecedented risks.

The core of the challenge being presented is that modernity is at once the problem and the solution. It is the problem because a state-centric world order cannot find prudent responses to threats of global scope, nor can the political will be mobilized to deal with dangers arising from the natural surroundings of human activity because of an abiding belief in the innovative capacity of science, technology, and rationality to find the best answers when the necessity is clearly present. Modernity has cultivated a cult of progress by means of technological innovation and continuous economic growth that is politically impossible to challenge frontally. This cult has been given great ideological strength by being tied to neoliberal capitalist priorities associated with profit margins and the efficiency of capital. Such an orientation refuses to set, or even acknowledge, limits on consumerism, economic growth, and population expansion, and either denies or minimizes the challenges posed by human-induced climate change.

In this regard, the modernist consensus among public and private sector leaders holds firm in its refusal to shake the confidence of ordinary people in the problem-solving prowess of technology and growth. In the domain of geopolitics, in an analogous spirit, nuclear war is avoided, not by sensibly eliminating this apocalyptic weaponry, but by relying on elaborate mechanisms of control to prevent supposedly less responsible political actors from ever acquiring the weaponry. Climate change, to the extent that it is understood as a real threat, is to be addressed when it becomes necessary by ingenious and profit-making geo-engineering fixes. Underneath these "fixes" is confidence that military and ideological dominance of the West will protect the forces of order in the world by providing the kind of new tactics and weapons that can maintain a global hierarchy based on the disparity of economic, military, and diplomatic conditions resulting in growing inequality along with a race to the bottom.

Modernity was also the template devised in the West, and serving as the basis for its rise to a position of civilizational dominance through its mastery of technology, especially its application to military capabilities, and its resulting exploitation of the resources of the non-West. Despite being "modern" this is the old geopolitics that is continuously being called into question in recent years by the persistence of unresolved crises, involving global warming, terrorist threats, nuclear weaponry, societal unrest, and strategic rivalry.

Yet modernity is a vital element in any manageable transition to a new geopolitics. Science and technology, despite gross exaggeration by exponents of the established order, remain crucial for the identification of the problems and what needs to be done. This is most obvious with respect to climate change where the scientific consensus helps us to grasp what kinds of adjustment need to be made to avoid a range of catastrophic outcomes, as well as to specify costs and effects of various measures of adaptation and mitigation. This outlook is also true for nuclear disarmament that depends on high confidence techniques for monitoring and verifying compliance with treaty obligations once undertaken.

Modernity offers an ideological framing of our worldview that dysfunctionally conditions the approaches taken to problem solving and policymaking. This framing presupposes a foundation of instrumental rationality that gives no more than lip service to the normative energies associated with law, morality, and peace. As such, its behavioral patterns reflect a reliance on prevalent ideas about capital efficiency and profit margins backed by the iron fist of military might, with a corresponding hostility to "social engineering" intended to subsidize economic and social rights for those who are not able to succeed in the marketplace. This amoral outlook is deficient in the manifestation of empathy towards those on the margins of the social order, and is comfortable with forcibly managing the politics and economics of inequality with suppressive tactics and strategy as necessary.

The state-centric structures of modernity help us grasp the failures of problem solving and policymaking, especially as the state from its earliest European formations in the late Medieval period became a vehicle for protecting and advancing the interests of those inhabiting the political space of a given country. With the rise of nationalism as an effective mobilizing tool the balance between protection by the state in exchange for loyalty to the state became established. As few states could claim to be nations in the full sense due to the presence of religious and ethnic minorities that often existed as nations within nations, both diluting the reality of nationalism and tribalism at the top of the social pyramid while provoking antagonism and subordination at the bottom. These features of a state-centric world add to its complexity, and compound the difficulties of fashioning humane responses to the more profound pressures being exerted on the old geopolitics, creating a variety of irrational obstacles to the effort underway to achieve a smooth transition to the new geopolitics. Among these obstacles is the persisting territorialization of the political imagination in a global setting that should be encouraging various forms of temporalization. What is an especial impediment is the focus by leadership cadres of both governmental and corporate structures on short-run and immediate performance criteria, leaving the future to be addressed when it becomes present!

Despite this bleak overall picture, there are elements of a more encouraging response to this destabilization of the framework of political life that has accompanied the rise of modernity associated historically with the industrial revolution, and its digital aftermath. Major international wars, although still a menacing possibility, are less part of normal geopolitics than in prior centuries. This is partly a consequence of their absurdly destructive effects and partly a result of the universality of nationalist ideology and practice showing the effectiveness of the high endurance of indigenous resistance to attempts at foreign domination. This was not true in the colonial era during which indigenous forces were not mobilized for resistance and intervention was perceived to a cost-effective way to promote the expansion of state power and wealth, usually at the expense of the societies in the global South. The collapse of colonialism and the weakening of the geopolitical infrastructure created by the West have leveled the global playing field to some degree. Instead of Euro-centric organs of regulation for world order, there is a more reliance on inter-governmental policymaking frameworks like the G-20 or private sector arenas like the World Economic Forum to set global policy, especially with respect to trade, investment, and currency. Then there are emerging new initiatives such as the efforts of the Inter Parliamentary Union to create a new more globally situated actor constituted by the legislative representatives each country or of various proposals for Global Peoples Assemblies that have been widely advocated. There is also a more robust transnationalism that is responsive to human rights and environmental protection involving new alignments joining civil society actors to the UN System in various formal and informal ways. These patterns of globalization-from-below are creating a greater balance between the amoral short-termism of governments, corporations, and banks and the longer term and value-laden orientation of autonomous actors representing global civil society. Facing the challenges of constructing an ecologically sustainable civilization is the essence of the new geopolitics that remains at the visionary margins of the forces associated with globalization-from-above, and yet seem to offer the best hope of species survival.

The essays in this volume explore from various angles the interface between the old geopolitics of states and hard power and the new and still inchoate new geopolitics of peoples and soft power. This new geopolitics is inclined toward non-violent conflict resolution and the historical agency of legitimacy wars. It supersedes the Westphalian juridical conception of world order as resting on the horizontal interplay of territorial sovereign states, which was always deceptive to the extent that it distracted attention from the vertical interplay that shaped behavior by the hierarchies resulting from gross inequalities of material conditions. The new geopolitics is far more complex, as it introduces important non-territorial actors outside the state system and challenges ideas of sovereignty and territoriality from a variety of ethnic, religious, and political angles.

The various regions of the world are displaying different patterns of interaction between the old and new. Perhaps, the most frightening of these regional configurations are evident in the Middle East and sub-Saharan Africa where the colonial era deliberately established artificial political communities for purposes of control and exploitation, and with the collapse of colonialism left a normative and political vacuum that is being filled by new types of control, corruption, conflict, and exploitation. In these regions we witness the erosion of the old geopolitics without any real emergence of the new geopolitics, and so the worst features of oppression and chaos are shockingly manifest. What most epitomizes the downfall of the old geopolitics are the waves of migrants seeking safe haven mainly in Europe and North America, the affluent gated communities of the Westphalian era. While the technocrats of the old geopolitics seeks walls, exclusions, and the criminalization of human traffickers, the advocates of the new geopolitics emphasize the root

causes of migration, and view a constructive response as dependent on overcoming the conditions of desperation that lead
people to leave their homelands and take the huge risks of death
and disease that accompany migration. In this sense the policy
focus should shift from stopping the migrants to eliminating the
killing fields of conflict and impoverishment that are responsible
for coercing migration.

These essays combine an assessment of these dangerous
tendencies with a conviction that the potentialities of the new
geopolitics offer some hope for a better human future. It is a
hope that is ultimately grounded in the mobilization of people
to challenge the death tremors of the old geopolitics and guided
by the strength of an engaged planetary vision of post-nationalist
citizenship and a belief in the transformative potency of nonviolent political activism.

1

TOWARD A NEW GEOPOLITICS

Let me begin this commentary on a new geopolitics by making two more or less irreverent remarks about how best to think about this dialogic approach to political transformation. To begin with, I would encourage a greater emphasis on what I would call to the vertical dimensions of dialogue. Let me try to clarify this observation. It is, of course, important to have eminent people drawn from different civilizational and religious orientations speaking to one another in civil tones. But part of the ethos of humane dialogue at this time in world history is to realize that *all* voices are relevant and deserving of recognition. In this spirit, it may be especially important to arrange for the participation in the future of those who are habitually excluded from such interaction. We need to listen carefully to youth, to oppressed peoples, and to women, that is, to those whose voices are typically not heard at all at high-profile gatherings, and if represented at all, then only nominally. I believe that a proper vertically conceived dialogic process would certainly include representatives of indigenous and minority peoples whose ancient wisdom is urgently needed by the world at this ecologically and normatively troubled time. And all of us must learn to listen in ways that are not characteristic of the manner in which the elites of the Western world are accustomed to heed the complaints and concerns of those who have been marginalized and oppressed. As the wave of migrants from the killing fields of the contemporary world suggests, the response of Western publics is increasingly exhibited by barbed wire, police brutality, and mob xenophobia.

The second irreverent suggestion that I would make underscores the importance – because of the urgency of some of the challenges facing humanity – that one move toward a politics of dialogue. It is not enough, it seems to me, to talk to one another. One has to imagine political projects that can move dialogic reflections on what needs to be done into the life world of change and struggle. I wish to critique the old geopolitics which is based on the primacy of hard power, essentially conceived of as military power and its accompanying diplomatic clout, as the essential agent of historical change in the affairs of sovereign states. It seems appropriate at this stage of history to contrast this old geopolitics with an emerging but yet not emergent new geopolitics that relies on soft power and grasps the limits of the role of force in achieving the goals of peoples and the objectives of national governments and international institutions. We are in the messy midst of an indispensable process of replacing this old geopolitics with a new geopolitics. As such, it is a perilous period of contradictory pressures.

This transition will not go forward very far unless reinforced by a dramatic enlarging of the political imagination of leaders and of citizens. This mutation of the imagination must reinterpret its core understanding of what is best for the promotion of national interests. The reigning idea of the national interest must be reinterpreted to include within its compass deference to global interests and human interests. Without this enlargement of the political imagination, the problems that beset the planet at the present time will not be resolved in effective and equitable ways. The current political leadership of states, particularly in the dominant countries, continues to be enmeshed in a dysfunctional ideology of realism that is premised on the effectiveness and necessity for relying on hard power and a national interest orientation to promote the wellbeing of established political communities comprising sovereign states without much concern for adverse implications for the world or the future.

If we bother to look around at the issues that confront the world, starting with climate change, we see the inability of either states on their own or states operating within the framework of the United Nations to address the problem in a manner that responsibly responds to the most dire warnings the world has ever received from the scientific community. Such a consensus has rarely existed among scientists, and yet its policy implications continue to be ignored. We creatures of modernity pride ourselves as belonging to a scientific civilization that flourishes within the ample confines of a temple of reason, and yet we fail so far to heed these warnings because they collide with perceived short-term national and private sector interests. The result is a very dangerous failure to live up to the challenges that are increasingly confronting the world and the human species in currently harmful and potentially disastrous forms.

At the other end of the policy agenda from ecological rebalancing is the kind of interference without constructive results that is exhibited by attempts to shape the outcome of the ongoing bloody conflict in Syria and, to some extent, the earlier conflict in Libya. In other words, the world community lacks the wisdom and capacity to address effectively the war/peace issues of the day at either end of the policy spectrum, that is, either within states or of global scope. There is no current prospect, I believe, that a world structured as ours is, will have that capacity or even the knowledge and wisdom in the foreseeable future to solve the major problems confronting the peoples of the world. A major shift in political consciousness is needed and hopefully can come about voluntarily and through the development of a more cosmopolitan and wiser public and a leadership better attuned to the world historical situation. The unhappy main alternative is for such a shift to result from a traumatic shock administered by a catastrophic breakdown in basic order or through the rise of a dialectic of terrorism (extremist movements and counterinsurgency responses) of the sort undoing the social order of the Middle East.

We are currently experiencing the failures of the old geopolitics, which is producing feelings of helplessness and policies of evasions as the world community tries vainly to cope with a variety of humanly desperate challenges. None is more disturbing ethically and more revealing of the shortcomings of the old geopolitics than is the prolonged failure to end the ordeal of the Palestinian people that has lasted since 1948. The Palestinians are now either disposed from or captive in their own historic homeland, and the remnant left to them after Israeli military expansion is a mere 22 percent of historic Palestine. This remnant has been further reduced by Israeli settlements, the unlawful construction of a separation wall, and through the construction of a network of settlers-only roads linked to Israel. The Palestinians of the West Bank, East Jerusalem, and Gaza have endured this stateless condition of apartheid occupation, an oppressive occupation for more than 45 years following the early dispossession in 1948 known as the *nakba*. And because of the old geopolitics and the way in which the American hegemony operates there is no capacity to address this Palestinian litmus test of human suffering and its indications of the unwillingness and inability of the world system to promote minimal justice in instances of this type.

Despite this generally bleak picture of the existing global setting, of the existing global political landscape, I believe that a new geopolitics is struggling to be born and assert itself. It is forging a different global politics that will incorporate by stages the global and human interest and make our understanding of what it means to be a citizen of a political community have an existential planetary dimension and no longer be confined to the geographic national space of sovereign states, and within that, to short-term concerns.

We have been recently witnessing the extent to which a new series of political actors are emerging around the world. Notwithstanding recent economic roadblocks, China's rise is the most spectacular example of this phenomenon. This ascent of China is not, as in the old politics, through hard power territorial expansion but takes the form of an exemplary instance of sustained soft power success, a success so great that it is almost beyond our capacity to comprehend it, and can only be made evident by pointing to the unprecedented rate of economic progress, the rapidity of modernization and the wholly transformed experience of self-understanding that dominates the country. There are several other countries, Brazil and India being the leading examples of this, with Russia having the opportunity also to be part of this group, that are rising to global preeminence through soft power, although precariously, with rising risks of regression as a result of the backlashes inflicted by the old geopolitics. There is more to this argument than the fact that these states have emerged without relying on more than developing their defensive military capability to offset their vulnerabilities to the waning, yet still dangerous forces of the old geopolitics. Given the current statist structure of world order these states deal with their immediate territorial border and maritime disputes in ways that illustrate the uncertain overlap between the old and the new, with the outcome still shadowed by many doubts.

What has not been sufficiently appreciated, incredibly in my view given the outcome of conflicts since 1945, is the declining capability of hard power to achieve the security goals of major sovereign states that have invested heavily in possessing the best attainable military weaponry. If we reflect upon the collapse of colonialism it becomes evident that military superiority, unlike in the prior colonial era, did not control the outcome of the various struggles of a colonized people against its colonial masters. In all the important colonial wars, perhaps most clearly evident in India, the stronger side from a hard power perspective could not control the political outcome, and in fact abandoned the field of battle. It has been difficult for the opinion makers of the world to absorb the shocking news that global history was increasingly being shaped by the weaker side militarily. The collapse of the Soviet system is another example where an internal set of contradictions led to a completely unanticipated transformation of international relations that had a momentous historical impact that continues to reverberate up to the present time. In analogous fashion, the collapse of apartheid in South Africa as a partial consequence of a global anti-apartheid campaign rested on the moral rejection of racism and was reinforced by militant soft power tactics including boycotts, divestment, and sanctions. The recent upheavals in the Arab World optimistically greeted as the Arab Spring again suggested the limits of hard power as a means of permanently oppressing people, but also the strength of counterrevolutionary tendencies to restore the established political and economic order, no matter how corrupted, unfair, and ineffective it had become.

This pattern is even more general than this if proper note is taken of how often the outcome of international conflicts reflects the failure of hard power, that is, military superiority, especially if the weaker adversary is buoyed by the legitimacy of nationalist credentials. The Soviet Union failed in Afghanistan as has the United States despite the overwhelming military power of both of these gigantic states. Prior to Afghanistan, and more significantly in my view, the United States failed to prevail in Vietnam despite making a prodigious effort over the course of a decade. The U.S. was defeated in Vietnam although it won every battle in the war and exerted uncontested control over air, sea, and land operations due to its military dominance. Two military commanders on opposite sides of the conflict spoke revealingly after the war. The American colonel declared: "You know you never defeated us on the battlefield." And his Vietnamese counterpart, also a colonel, responded: "Yes, you are correct, but it is irrelevant." Not understanding the real meaning of this "irrelevance" precludes the adjustment to nonviolent forms of global governance that takes full account of this declining role of hard power as an agent of historical change and historical control.

In recent decades there have been many demonstrations of this declining leverage of hard power. Trillions of dollars were spent on the wars in Iraq and Afghanistan. Despite American control of the battlefields when we ask the question, "Who was the winner in Iraq?" we get a strange answer. It is not the United States, but Iran. This is hardly the result that the strategic planners in Washington had in mind. In Afghanistan it is not yet fully clear what will happen as American combat forces leave the country, but what is already plain to see is that the vision of what Afghanistan should be like as held in the White House by successive presidents will certainly not be the unfolding Afghan experience. So we see that over and over again military power can no longer control political outcomes in crucial struggles going on in various parts of the world.

Yet the continued American embrace of old geopolitics offers insight into the assessment being made of the decline of the United States as a hegemonic power. There are few present signs that the United States is capable of learning from its hard power failures, which is one of the most discouraging aspects of this whole picture as it inclines dangerously toward further violent encounters in the Middle East. Even the nuclear agreement with Iran is a velvet glove covering the iron fist of a militarist *diktat*. To wage war against Iran would be crazy, perhaps the craziest of all of these violent hard power efforts to hold back the tides of history. We must ask ourselves and each other why is it that the United States is incapable of learning from these experiences of frustration and failure? Why does each failure lead to a reformulation of military intervention thinking and counterinsurgency doctrine to convey an impression that the outcome of the next encounter will be different because new weaponry and different tactics will restore hard power supremacy, and with it historical agency to the political actor that achieves military superiority.

The attack drone is the most recent weapons system that is being touted as restoring hard power capabilities. It is supposed to be capable of changing the balance of forces in conflicts and supposedly enables military power again to become a rational and effective instrument of foreign policy. We cannot yet evaluate the accuracy of such a claim. But it is not too soon to take note of the degree to which the governing process in the United States has itself become militarized by adopting the new tactics and weaponry of conflict. The country has for too long been sustained by a war economy. It has been preoccupied with enemies for almost 80 years, and never allowed itself the benefits and serenity of peace. World War II came, then the Cold War, then the war on terror, and now engagement in the turmoil following the Arab uprisings. All of these wars have given a new credibility internally in the United States to a militarized blinkering of the political and moral imagination, making the leadership, opposition, and public incapable of thinking outside the military box. The Obama presidency faces increasing criticism because it has sought to diminish its dependence on militarism by a pragmatic recourse to diplomacy.

We see this dynamic of self-limitation in the context of the Iranian encounter. Clearly the logical, reasonable solution would be for the United States to use its leverage to get rid of nuclear weapons in the entire region. What would make more sense from the perspective of regional stability than a nuclear-free zone in the Middle East? And yet the American government, despite its hegemonic status, seems unable even to suggest discussion and appraisal of such a sensible solution. This partly reflects the militarization of the American imagination and partly the unhealthy degree to which Israel is capable of blocking consideration of even the most sensible rational proposals of American foreign policy if these clash with Israel's preferences. This is a perverse expression of declining American hegemony that allows a secondary state to acquire sufficient political leverage to manipulate the policy choices of the supposedly dominant political actor on the world scene in ways that make regional chaos and violence more likely.

The foregoing analysis supports the view that strong incentives exist to explore the prospects for world order based on the theory and practice of nonviolent geopolitics. I think it is clear to the leadership of countries like China, and Japan, Germany, India, Brazil that the road toward their success is a road that avoids major war and destabilizing and costly arms races. It is also notable that one of the achievements of the European Union – which is still not as widely acknowledged as it should be – is the degree to which an internal culture of peace has been, at least provisionally, established in Europe after centuries of warfare on the continent. At this stage it is not yet an external culture of peace as the European enthusiasm for the Libyan intervention in 2011 made evident. This experience of the last 75 years in which hard power has produced so much suffering, imposed such heavy economic burdens, and encroached on political freedoms and democracy, and yet has little to show for it hopefully will lead to an upsurge of anti-militarism. The old geopolitics is increasingly ineffective historically and politically and actually harms those that rely upon it, a pattern frequently identified as "blowback." Of course, hardened militarists will continue to argue, until engulfed by catastrophe, that political failures result from an insufficient political resolve and either wrong tactics or inadequate battlefield capabilities.

It will be a step forward if we incorporate these developments into the thinking of those who are influential in this overall dialogic process, which I am hopeful will prove helpful in producing an understanding that there now exists a tangible concrete human interest that must gradually complement traditional preoccupations with defining the national interest from hard power territorial perspectives. In this spirit, we need to educate our students to understand that engaged cosmopolitan citizenship has become the only sensible way of being a member of any political community. Furthermore, that we agree that becoming citizen pilgrims is about giving our attention to the wellbeing of the whole planet, but also about being attentive to its future. The debt to future generations involves a citizenship that has a temporal dimension as well as a spatial one. The human species has been given this incredible opportunity at this point in human history, but we are made anxious by the sound of a ticking clock, and it hardly matters whether we believe the ticking clock is associated with climate change or associated with nuclear weapons that could destroy human civilization in a matter of minutes. These contingencies make precarious present methods of governing the planet and solving its problems. The most daunting challenge is how can the human species be awakened to the dangers and the opportunities to meet the threats. I strongly believe that at the core of a cosmopolitan dialogic process must be convergent transnational commitments to global justice, as linked to the imperatives of civilizational, species survival, and ecological balance.

2

THE POST-SECULAR
DIVIDE

PRELIMINARY CONSIDERATIONS

What we mean when addressing "the post-secular in international politics" is not at all settled, and there are diverse interpretations responding to a variety of understandings that relate back to the plural renderings of "the secular."[1] This chapter attempts to gain a footing on this slippery terrain. It seems important to provide a context for the post-secular beyond positing the obvious, yet highly unexpected, return of religion to an increasingly globalized public space of world politics. I will presume that explaining and assessing the twists and turns of this return to a political and cultural milieu that is more infused with identities that are self-consciously associated with the religious and cultural legacies of the major world civilizations is the core significance of the post-secular moment. Religion was a dormant presence throughout the period of secular hegemony, but its resurfacing as an often crucial element in war/peace settings and in a variety of postcolonial settings is what has made this preoccupation with the post-secular seem such a significant challenge to the conceptualization of international relations in the early twenty-first century.[2]

In this respect, post-secularism fundamentally challenges in different forms the previously dominant idea of a *universalizing* modernity that is forever linked to science, instrumental rationality, and the Enlightenment tradition, a worldview that is perceived increasingly instead as a turn that evolved specifically in Western civilization before being selectively exported to the rest of the world, which seemed more receptive than it truly was. This anchoring and privileging of modernity in the Western experience is being critically reevaluated from many distinct perspectives, including in the West itself. In the non-West there are two strands of post-secularism: the partial rejection of modernity in its Western embodiments, and the reconciliation of modernity with a newly inclusive attitude towards religion and non-Western thought in the organized political and cultural life of society.[3] At the same time the West itself is interrogating its fusion of secularism and materialist modernity from a number of angles: first of all, especially in the United States, the reassertion of religious and spiritual values and interpretations into debates about national policy in a manner that challenges deference to scientific rationality that had previously shaped ideas about political leadership in governmental spaces; a spiritually grounded questioning of materialism and consumerism from the perspectives of ecological sustainability and the quality of life, which generates a sharp critique of neoliberal forms of capitalism as the basis for national economic life and a globalizing world economy.[4]

An initial trap for this kind of inquiry is to conceive of secularism as having been altogether superseded by post-secularism or to think that the relationship between these two labels of convenience can be presented as a choice between alternative sequential constructions of international politics. The position taken here is that the emergent post-secular needs to be taken into account in depicting and evaluating current world order, but that it should not be done at the expense of repudiating the positive legacies of the secular or overlooking the persistence of its negative features, most especially war and political fragmentation. The relationship between the secular and the post-secular should be understood as being both/and, as well as past/present/future, and not conceived as before/after or either/or. Some additional account needs to be taken of what might be called "the pathological" in political life, whether it assumes a deformed embodiment in the governing process associated with a state as in totalitarian regimes of Hitler's Germany or Stalin's Soviet Union or a kind of crazed extremism as in al-Qaeda or ISIS.

There are at least six overlapping reasons why it is useful to talk about "post-secularism" when interpreting international politics, provided it is done with the caveat of the prior paragraph in mind. First, to register the claim that the return of religion as a force in public spaces is a development of sufficient weight to establish a discontinuity in the way we study and practice international politics. In this regard, prior to the Iranian Revolution of 1978–1979 the relevance of religion to politics was misleadingly interpreted in the West as of principally historical interest and private devotion, with the main storyline of world politics being told as one of the rise of a Cartesian science-based modernity superseding by stages a religion imbued with the medieval ethos.[5] Such a story had several components, including the establishment and evolution in Europe of the modern state that no longer rested its legitimacy on a religious identity and mandate, but on the authority of the ruler and the repressive stability effectively imposed by a territorial government ideally providing order within, and protection against, external enemies. Another leading component of this Western modernity was the linkage of human well-being and progress with the liberating impacts of technological innovations made possible by applying the results of scientific inquiry, a dynamic that was explained as originating in the Industrial Revolution enacted initially in the United Kingdom in the first third of through the eighteenth century.[6] The prevailing ideologies of recent times, capitalism and Marxism, both treated religion as marginal to their standard operating procedures, and essentially irrelevant for the making of a desirable human future.[7] Yet Western institutional religions generally adapted to capitalism, at times even rationalizing its inequities, while adopting a hostile and unconditionally critical approach to Marxism in all its forms, although "liberation theology" as articulated and practiced in Latin America reflected the essential features of the Marxist critique of capitalism, and its adherents were labeled as "Communists" by the defenders of the established order.

Second, the epistemological and geopolitical realization that the consensus that previously affirmed the Enlightenment privileging of rationality and liberalism as the universal foundation of political legitimacy in world politics is no longer capable of dominating political space. Whether it be the voice of religious leaders as to the ethical consequences of public policy choices or the pronouncements as to good and evil made by political leaders, there has emerged a post-secular discourse that needs to be acknowledged as reshaping political identity. In some respects, the encounter between Osama bin Laden and George W. Bush personified the manner in which the grand issues of strategy and security were being symmetrically restructured in political consciousness at opposite ends of the ideological spectrum.[8]

Third, a focus on the rise of secularism helps us to appreciate the degree to which secularism was socially constructed to address distinctively Western political crises provoked by the breakup of Christian unity in Europe several centuries ago, and has both weaker and different impacts on the moral and political imagination in non-Western parts of the world. I would note in passing the somewhat Orientalist attempt by Habermas to reclaim this normative hegemony for the West by contending that only the Judeo-Christian foundations of being in the world possessed a capacity to generate a universally valid framework of values. To a similar effect is the significant attempt by John Rawls to postulate a "law of peoples" derived from Western liberalism that is both sensitive to the postcolonial moment and constitutes a futile effort to reclaim primacy for liberal values if observed in practice by even illiberal forms of political governance.[9] This means that "the law of peoples" is not dependent on the adoption of constitutional governments of the sort associated with the liberal democracies of the West. That is, the ideas about every individual having an entitlement to human dignity, the foundational ethical affirmation of the Western human rights tradition, can be understood as a secularization and further elaboration of religious ideas about right conduct towards neighbors and strangers.[10] The reverse is actualized in the post-secular: the secularly inscribed values of international human rights standards are read back into political life through the prisms of "correctly" interpreted religious and cultural tradition.

Fourth, and perhaps least obviously, post-secularist thought helps us to assess the degree to which the roles of the territorial state are shifting under the impact of globalization and resistance to globalization, giving rise to tensions and contradictions that define the originality of this historical period. In the secular epoch the sovereign state was treated as the only candidate for full membership in international society. This questioning began to be taken seriously while remaining within a secularist framework in the worldwide uproar created by Samuel Huntington's thesis of "a clash of civilizations."[11] Often overlooked in the uproar generated by Huntington's positing "the West against the rest" was his influential post-secular assertion that global political life was returning to its premodern emphasis on "civilization" as the most illuminating way to comprehend configurations of conflict and community on a world scale. In a more positive vein the United Nations has sponsored a continuing project on "Alliance of Civilizations," co-chaired by Spain and Turkey, and treating religion as the core identity of each distinct civilization.

Fifth, the secular context was increasingly defined during the prior century in ideological terms, creating the impression that the future of world history would be shaped by the outcome of ideological rivalry. Since the end of World War I, and the triumph of communism in the Russian Revolution, and the subsequent ascendancy of fascism in Germany, Italy, Spain, and Portugal, the essence of international conflict was portrayed as a struggle between antagonistic ideologies, liberalism and socialism contra fascism in World War II, followed by liberalism versus socialism in the Cold War.[12] It was the triumph of Western market-oriented liberalism fused with Westcentric myopia and the Chinese buy-in under the impetus of Deng Xiaoping's modernization approach that lent an aura of superficial and temporary credibility to Fukuyama's ridiculously triumphalist assertion that with the collapse of the Soviet Union the world has reached "the end of history." What does seem to be the case is that the end of colonialism combined with the evaporation of ideological rivalry within the West has produced a resurgence of religious influence on the formation of public policy even in the West as well as elsewhere. It has also subverted the claims put forward on behalf of Western civilization as offering the exclusive model for modernity and development, opening political space for non-Western conceptions of modernity, which in fact were always part of the evolving reality on the part of close observers, as well as for the rise of several anti-modernist cults of which ISIS is the most prominent and challenging.[13]

And sixth, an appreciation of the multidimensional and interactive contextuality of secularism and post-secularism that radically destabilizes the meaning of this labeling of the distinct events and processes that constitute political life, raising questions about whether the convenience of their usage outweighs the confusions generated. There is, for instance, a sharp difference between the American emphasis on religious freedom and the French laïcité with its tendency to impose restrictions on religious expression and to exhibit a broader hostility to any public role given to religion. Similarly, Indian secularism is basically a commitment of tolerance toward non-Hindu religions, and a related assurance of proportionate representation in governmental decision-making bodies, employment opportunities, and other facets of societal life. Turkish secularism in the Ataturk period tended to follow the French lead, but since the AKP (Justice and Development Party) assumed political control of the country in 2002, there has been a notable shift towards the American approach, that is, making Turkish public life more hospitable for the religiously devout, although there are residues of the stricter kind of secular orientation as expressed by formal and informal restrictions imposed on women wearing a headscarf in public spaces that restrict employment of women in government and certain professions, and make women feel unwelcome in certain social spaces, especially, up-scale stores, hotels, and restaurants.

Against this background it follows that religion needs to be taken into explicit account in the study and practice of international politics, although this should not be interpreted to mean that secular conceptions of political legitimacy with respect to the sovereign state are becoming obsolete, or even that a persuasive case is being made for their declining relevance. I have adopted the view that secularism and post-secularism are best understood as overlapping, using as a reference point Derrida's profound commentary on the conditions pertaining to what is implied when we speak about living *well* together in the world rather than, as is inescapable, which is the purely descriptive matter of living together.[14] This perspective offers us a normative compass that is at odds with the realist paradigm that has long dominated Western thinking about international politics and foreign policy. The focus of this chapter is on how this Derridean way of seeing is needed for a complex evaluation of the evolution of the sovereign state and economic market as the principal providers of legitimacy and order in the international politics of the early twenty-first century, although subject to challenges from a human rights orientation or on the basis of cultural tradition. The understanding proposed is not only complex; it is also contradictory. We need to admit that the state, state system, and market neoliberalism continue to provide the basic optics for interpreting international political life despite changing parameters that make territoriality less central and the emergence of various forms of limits far more critical, for example limits on greenhouse gas emissions, on population, on warmaking, on consumerism, and on governmental abuses of authority. That is, living well together presupposes the creation of appropriate regimes of global scope that are sufficiently sensitive to these limit conditions, and take account of the human interest, and not just the national interest. Such undertakings are not easily reconciled with either the allocation of effective control on the basis state boundaries or the imposition of limits on economic growth that regulate production and consumption for the sake of sustainability and the rights of future generations.[15]

This transition to a world order scheme that stresses limits is bound to be hazardous and beset by obstacles. There are many powerful vested interests embedded in state, market, and culture that are resistant to such adaptive changes. The challenge to post-secularism is to make this transition without repudiating secularism or succumbing to absolutisms additional to nationalism, statism, and market fundamentalism.

As I hope to make clear, it is highly desirable that the "secular" dimension, however denominated, is allowed to persist despite the necessity to take the fullest advantage of the opportunities afforded by post-secularity. It is probably annoyingly obvious to point out there are so many relevant varieties and gradations of the secular and the post-secular that it becomes deeply misleading to pretend that anything meaningful can result from a straightforward conceptual contrast, choice, and interplay between these two postures towards political reality, each of which has an extremely unstable meaning. To underscore the sequential aspects of the relationship between secularism and post-secularism would overstate the discontinuity of the significant shift in international politics occasioned by the rise and renewed relevance of religion, as well as implying that the secular project has lost its relevance for living well together on this planet. This rise of religion, and the rediscovery of limits in everyday life, in the last few decades does establish a new phase in world order that seems crucially different than the preceding Cold War phase, the peak historical interval for the marginalization of religion, a time during which international conflict was preeminently an encounter between two forms of materialism: on the one side, Soviet state socialism, and on the other, American market-oriented constitutionalism, although affirming its identity by referring to "the other" as "godless Communism."

Both of these -isms that were dedicated to maximizing technologically driven forms of materialism that were equally inattentive to according limit conditions to ensure sustainability. I would also note in passing that "secularism without secularism" offers a useful way to combine the quest for inclusive governance with the de-Westernization of the language, adapting the conceptual apparatus of political theory and international relations to civilizational and religious identities, and globalizing tendencies that were approaching extraordinarily important limit conditions.[16]

"SECULARISM" AS AN UNWELCOME IDENTITY IN THE AFTERMATH OF THE ARAB SPRING

The non-Western milieu of these concerns is illuminated in unexpected ways by the experience of the Turkish prime minister's 2011 visit to Cairo where he uttered the following unexpected words to a somewhat startled Egyptian audience: "Do not be wary of secularism. I hope there will be a secular state in Egypt." Mr. Recep Tayyip Erdoğan clarified this remark by pointing out that "'a secular state' does not mean 'an irreligious state.'" Of course, what raised eyebrows in Egypt and elsewhere, what made the advice so surprising and evocative, and nowhere more than in Turkey, was that this plea on behalf of secularism came from a political leader who had been widely regarded, with apprehension from some and admiration by others, as a post-secular champion of a political outlook infused with religious beliefs, practices, and values drawn from his Muslim faith. Subsequent developments in Egypt, especially the failed leadership of the Muslim Brotherhood, and even more, the bloody coup in 2013 and its aftermath lend a retroactive stamp of approval to Erdogan's unsolicited advice to the Egyptian people.

In Turkey, Erdoğan is anxiously viewed with a mixture of contempt and suspicion by the polarizing Kemalist CHP opposition. Erdoğan's AKP party is angrily accused by urban cadres of self-proclaimed unyielding secularists in Turkey of pursuing a hidden agenda that has as its nefarious goal the imposition of an Iran-style theocracy on Turkey, and Erdoğan is himself alleged to be seeking authoritarian powers. In effect, the opposition insists that the political path taken by Erdoğan is in the process of repudiating Kemal Ataturk's secular legacy that has hitherto served as the unshakeable pillar of legitimacy in republican Turkey. It is of more than passing interest that Erdoğan throughout his political career has been targeted by what might be called "coercive secularism" in Turkey, which relied on its governmental and societal power prior to the ascent of AKP in 2002 to impose undue restrictions on political parties deemed to be religiously oriented, as well as on the free practice of religion in the country, especially with respect to women and free speech, all in the name of secularism.

The events in Cairo need also to take account of the reality of Erdoğan's charisma and prestige. He was at the time the most popular political figure in the region, and far more so than any Egyptian aspiring leader back in 2011. Such an unusual stature, especially for a Turkish leader given the many unhappy Arab memories of Ottoman rule, gave his words a weight that would not be accorded in this period to the views of any other foreign leader. At the same time, there was a pushback that should have been anticipated, partly because at this time of revolutionary enthusiasm in Egypt and throughout the region, there was bound to be a negative reaction to a Turkish leader telling a proud foreign country how it should shape its future. Also, the national context was entirely different. In Turkey, Erdoğan when assuming leadership realized that if he wanted to govern effectively, he needed first to reassure the Turkish public of his genuine acceptance of the secular framework of governance. The situation in Egypt is entirely different. Egypt is an essentially conservative society, it lacks the Turkish legacy of an indigenous embrace of secularism by the still revered founder of modern Turkey. The early post-Tahrir mood in Egypt seemed determined to move at least nominally in the direction of affirming Shari'a as the foundation of its political legitimacy, and there were no longer inhibitions in Egypt based on prohibiting the political participation of avowedly Islamic movements such as the Muslim Brotherhood. To be sure as a result of the 2013 coup these prohibitions directed at political Islam in Egypt have been restored, and intensified, as one aspect of shifting power back to the supposedly highly secularized and anti-democratic elites that had run the country prior to the upheaval of 2011. Although the Sisi regime is careful to seek the blessing of the conservative Egyptian religious establishment in making his repressive moves against the Muslim Brotherhood.

My reason for dwelling on this incident is not to comment upon the complex ideological encounter in Egypt or in Turkey. It is rather to reflect upon such unexpected secularist advocacy by this leading world statesman known for his devoutness as a Muslim, and by so doing grasp its relevance to the uncertainties embedded in post-secular circumstances. In effect, we need to ask ourselves why it should be deemed desirable to endorse "secularism" and secular values in a post-secular world, especially in the unstable political atmosphere prevailing in Egypt where such comments by an outsider of Erdoğan's stature were bound to be provocative and controversial, especially among the formidable societal forces that were intent on achieving an influential role for Islam on state and law. An international reading of this Turkish "intervention" in Egyptian politics would emphasize, I think, Erdoğan's view that a benevolent future for Egypt depended on sustaining the religious neutrality of the state, and the only clear way to express such a sentiment was by invoking the language and outlook of secularism. This was a mistake in 2011, but perhaps it would be less so in 2013, as during the interval the Muslim Brotherhood has won the presidency, and has governed in a manner that has enraged the nonreligious constituencies in Egypt and made Erdoğan's advocacy of secularism seem in retrospect to be words of sage guidance, which if followed, might have avoided renewed turmoil in the country that has prevented economic recovery, the establishment of a stable and humane political atmosphere, and has led to a counterrevolutionary restoration of governmental control by the old authoritarian establishment. Maybe the real lesson here is that the discourse of secularism and post-secularism does not communicate effectively in many non-Western settings, first, because it is a Western discourse, and second, because such advocacy can be understood as a sign of disrespect towards political independence. Perhaps Erdoğan's talk would have been received more favorably if he had spoken of the virtues of "inclusive democracy" and the need to affirm the religious and spiritual heritage of the country. It is notable, of course, that Turkey's modernizing successes of the past decade have not been as yet able to overcome its reputation for exclusionary democracy in relation to the Kurdish and Alevi minorities in its own country, and so it might, after all, not seem credible to urge Egypt to achieve what Turkey has failed to do after almost a century of secular governance.

In effect, if the goal is to avoid internal strife and regional conflict, then no state should ever proclaim itself overtly Islamic or Jewish or Christian. A precondition for political legitimacy and stability in the twenty-first century crucially depends on ensuring "the rights of others," particularly those entrapped within the borders of sovereign states, which in cases of antagonistic relations might be identified as "captive nations." Erdoğan made this form of rationale clear when he associated his advocacy of secularism with "religious freedom," stating that only a secular state can be credibly dedicated to a show of "respect for all the religions and giving all individuals the freedom to practice religion as they please." Significantly, I suppose, it was deemed either unnecessary or uncongenial for Erdoğan to extend overtly this freedom to atheists, that is, those who reject religion altogether, although notably, Pope Francis departed from his Catholic forebears by affirming the lives of atheists to the extent of their good works. Erdoğan's message also seemed, in this vein, indirectly critical of the Islamic Republic of Iran as well as of the insistence on the part of Israel to be formally acknowledged as "a Jewish state," which privileges ethnic Jews as compared to its large Palestinian minority, which itself is composed of a mixture of Muslims and Christians. In effect, the legitimacy of the state requires that its identity transcend its societal roots associated with a given ethnicity or religion. To accept this stricture even in a religiously homogeneous country such as Turkey is impressive, although it has yet to be implemented. A secular orientation for the state is particularly compelling in Egypt where a significant Coptic minority has credible fears recently substantiated about its security and freedom given the character and behavior of the Egyptian leadership, including its promotion of a constitution and state identity that seems inclined towards institutionalizing a new form of exclusionary authoritarianism, thus betraying the essential promise made by the 2011 gathering in Tahrir Square.[17] Threading the needle of cultural sensitivity depends on reflecting societal values without invalidating or threatening the dignity of those adhering to minority and diverse religious identities. Reverting to a political discourse that is built upon this ethos of inclusion, there is a rejection both of antireligious secularism that is a kind of fundamentalism and of theocratic structures of governance that are inherently exclusionary and discriminatory toward "others."

While making his defense of secularism clear in relation to the protection of religious diversity, Erdoğan failed to affirm the importance attributed by secularist thinking to protecting liberty of conscience for the individual, and this oversight should not surprise us. After all, Erdoğan's political leadership in Turkey, impressive in so many respects, has not shown much sensitivity to this core liberal idea of upholding the autonomy of the individual. That is, the dignity of individuals and groups requires more from the state than neutrality on matters of religious and ethnic identity, but also needs to address characteristic secularist concerns about the autonomy of thought, rights of dissent, and free association rights of individuals and collectivities. These issues draw somewhat on a specifically Western heritage, but the imperative is open textured enough to allow ample space for non-Western views on responsibility and community sentiments to be given priority in the rewriting of human rights for a postcolonial world order. In effect, I am trying to formulate an agenda for "secularism without secularism," which also amounts to devising a formula for positing a successful transition to "post-secularism." As has been pointed out, affixing "post" to secularism is evasive in relation to the features of the present milieu that constitute the discontinuity with the past.

RELIGION AND POLITICS IN IRAN

Let me refer to another revealing instance of the revived relevance of religion to the politics of our time as confirmed even by those who are wary of religious influence, having been victimized. In commenting on Mir Hossein Mosavi, the leader of the Green Movement of opposition in Iran, Muhammed Sahimi, a respected and influential Iranian journalist committed to the reform struggle taking place in his country, took critical note of the reluctance of the green reformist leaders to abandon in their advocacy the Islamic part of the Islamic Republic despite couching all their demands and grievances in relation to "the republican deficit" of the Ahmedinejad/Khamenei governing process. Sahimi expresses this secularist concern about the approach taken by Mosavi in a sentence with revealingly tortured wording: "No one can expect Mosavi to put aside his religious thinking and system of belief, but is it not unreasonable to expect him not to emphasize a 'true religious government,' even if he thinks it can be democratic."[18] With sentiments parallel to those of Erdoğan, despite sharp private differences and an entirely different political challenge, Sahimi insists that his only motivation is to engender maximum unity within the Green Movement, which means making it more receptive "to different schools of thought." And this search for inclusiveness is meant to raise the comfort level of those many Iranians who now believe that an Islamic Republic can never, contrary to Mousavi, be reconciled with real democracy, including equality of participation in the public sphere. Sahimi speculates that adherents of this more skeptical view "probably outnumber" those who, like Mousavi, believe reconciliation is possible and desirable. In effect, the conviction present here is that a movement to democratize the state must do two things to attain twenty-first-century legitimacy: first, ensure the participatory rights of religious and ethnic others by symbolically endorsing and rigorously practicing pluralism; second, reinforcing this orientation by refraining from ever characterizing the state by reference to a dominant religious or ethnic identity, or in fact, by endowing it with any formal religious role or function.

The paradoxical reflection is that *in certain circumstances* the recognition of "secularism" has become more vital to political legitimacy of the state and movements for change during these early stages of post-secular emergence than it had been in the latter stages of secular preeminence in the West where it became taken for granted, and need not even be mentioned. Because religion has become so significant for identity within political communities that define rights and duties, it is necessary to avoid hierarchical and exclusivist implications that are incompatible with the protection of human rights and the realization of democratic values, a project as yet unfulfilled, what Derrida referred to from time to time as "the democracy to come." In this regard, forebodings were generated when Mustafa Abdel-Jalil, the chair of the Libyan Transitional National Council, said at a victory rally in Benghazi on January 24, 2011: "We are an Islamic country. We take Islamic values as the core of our new government. The constitution will be based on our Islamic religion." Such a statement seems to be starting a new chapter in the unfolding story of the rise of religion as a political force in the world and reminds us of the importance of renewing the secularist project in a language that non-Western ears can hear without dismissing such sentiments as a combination of Orientalism and neocolonialism. The objective in Libya should be to accomplish the seemingly impossible task of building sustainable democracy, interethnic harmony, tribal autonomy, and societal peace for the country. An aspect of this politics of impossibility is to embrace religion inclusively and in a manner that gives the state a spiritual sense of belonging to the whole of humanity without compromising the rights and dignity of the nonreligious or negating identities associated with territorial nationalism.

Of course insisting on this secularist trapping for the post-secular state should not be allowed to serve as a vehicle for the suppression of Islam or to further the contradictory ambitions of those promoting various forms of Islamophobia in Europe and North America. If the secularized state, for instance, abandons the ethos of neutrality and validates suppressive regulation of human activity as with imposing restrictions regarding wearing a headscarf or takes an overly permissive approach to religiously tinged hate speech, then "the secular state" compromises its legitimacy by operating under the banner of what can be described as "coercive secularism," and sometimes labeled as "militant secularism." In other words, the post-secular discourse on legitimacy pertaining to the state must be contextually framed in relation to specific state/society relations. The nominally neutral state that is led by or under the influence of Islamophobes poses a severe danger to minority rights in several European and North American countries at the present time.[19]

With this in mind, it would be as inappropriate for Erdoğan to urge the American or French governments to be as vigilant in protecting their secular identity at the present time as it seemed constructive to make his suggestions to the Egyptians, however ill-considered it was to deliver that particular message in such blunt language. Also, involved here are the varieties of secularism, making the American tradition of concern for diverse religions a more desirable referent for secularism than French laicism that tends to reveal its antireligious roots whenever applied to controversial behavior of religious believers, although each variant is nuanced in relation to its interpretation by history, tradition, political context, and cultural setting. The further confusing irony here is that Turkish secularism as developed in the Kemalist form was premised on laicism yet Erdoğan chose to project an understanding of secularism that was protective of religious freedom while expressly disavowing the political option of a theocratically administered sovereign state.

Such a view of political legitimacy is not intended to appease the mainly neurotic Western anxiety about the Islamic resurgence, and the inflammatory claims of violence and extremism being intrinsic to Islam that have been commonplace in the West since 9/11. This opposition to a religious or ethnic state that has been articulated is directly relevant to the strenuous efforts of Israel to be formally acknowledged as "a Jewish state" despite the fact that over 20 percent of its population possesses a Palestinian Arab identity, mainly Muslim, but also Christian.[20] This is a very unreasonable demand on the part of Israel, especially considering that it comes on top of the realization that the Israeli state has long been operating as a de facto Jewish state, and with that identification in mind has enacted a series of discriminatory laws and exhibits a variety of societal norms that are punitive towards the Palestinian minority, imposing burdens based on citizens with a non-Jewish nationality and conferring privileges on those considered to be of Jewish nationality. This Israeli experience shows why the ethnoreligious neutralization of the state is an essential precondition for the attainment of an inclusive political community based upon equality of opportunity and participation, as well as dignity for all. This debate about the political future of Iran, as of Egypt, is so salient because religion has for better and worse become an integral ingredient of political identity and reflects the dynamics of political self-determination, displacing in many instances the earlier ethnically and religiously homogenizing impact of nationalism. In an important respect, what is at stake is a reinterpretation of the fundamental human rights collective norm of self-determination, acknowledging its primacy with respect to struggles against alien or foreign rule, but accepting its subordination to the requirements of protecting individual and group human rights once political independence is achieved. This is an indirect way of expressing strictures on the exercise of majoritarian democracy when it comes to the architecture and mission of the governmental structures of a sovereign state, importing secularism without secularism. In effect, prescribing inclusiveness as a constraint on the political will of the citizenry.[21]

THE GLOBAL DIMENSIONS OF THE TRANSITION TO A POST-SECULAR WORLD

Considering briefly the international implications of this controversy relating to superseding of secularism calls our attention to the structures that frame global political activity. The Westphalian orientation shaped modernity in two central respects: by the emergence of territorially bounded European political communities endowed with sovereignty as a juridical foundation of their international status and by globally projecting a hierarchy of states based on West-centric ideological and political hegemony.[22] The success of the anticolonial movement has had the formal effect of universalizing the Westphalian approach to statehood, but without overcoming its existential hierarchical character exhibited in the practice of geopolitics. The recent interventions in Iraq, Afghanistan, and Libya, as well as the threats directed at Iran and Syria, are all expressive of this unfinished resistance to Western encroachments on the autonomy, freedom, and resources of the non-West.

There is no doubt that starting with the 1978–1979 revolution in Iran religion played an increasingly strategic role in mobilizing national publics worldwide for resistance to Western forms of direct and indirect intervention and occupation of ancestral lands. But there was also a secondary effect: the weakening of statist forms of identity, and thus the weakening of the bonds between state and society, a process also reinforced by neoliberal globalization. I recall a meeting with Ayatollah Ruhollah Khomeini shortly before he left Paris for a triumphal return to Iran in February 1979, he several times insisted that what was happening in Iran was an "Islamic Revolution" and not merely an "Iranian Revolution." What this religious leader meant was not that the Iranian state would necessarily be Islamic, although he obviously hoped that it would, but rather that the revolution was a normative process that needed to be replicated wherever Islamic societies were to be found. His outlook was clearly one that regarded boundaries circumscribing religious communities as more significant than the sovereign boundaries of states that appear on a standard map of the world. Such a reconfiguring of community generates a new politics that is a direct challenge aimed at the European conception of the modern state and the individualist presuppositions embedded in liberalism and articulated in an international legal form in leading human rights instruments. This reconfiguring is most evident, often in tragically destructive forms, throughout the Middle East and sub-Saharan Africa, which are also the regions where territorial allocations to colonial powers overlooked the natural boundaries of political community.

In this regard, the religious resurgence by replacing assimilationist ideologies such as "the melting pot" in the United States with multiculturalist orientations is undermining from within the state as a political actor just as globalization in its many dimensions is undermining the state from without.

The one feature of Samuel Huntington's otherwise notorious "clash of civilizations" thesis that deserves enduring critical appreciation is his assertion that civilizational identities are resuming some of their traditional prominence in the wider domains of world politics, and that statism is a relatively recent phenomenon that departs from the mainsprings of human experience and history. This assertion is more radical than it may appear at first hearing, and is, if you will, part of the signature of the post-secular. In this formulation the secular is best understood as that by-product of modernity that gave rise to the Westphalian framework of territorially bounded sovereign states as the foundation of a legitimate world order. This understanding initially territorialized religion in accord with the particular wishes and affiliations of an autocratic ruler, and minorities were treated as outsiders and tended to be abused and subjugated by the state. Consistent with the rise of political democracy in Europe, especially in response to the French Revolution and its proclamation of "the right of man," there was an accompanying strong impulse to curb both monarchical rule and the Catholic Church as a political actor, giving law a positivist jurisprudence that operates within an autonomous zone of governance without interference by insinuation of influence on behalf of institutionalized religion.[23] This pattern of political evolution culminated in the rise of the secular state, which in America took the form of making a society safe for diverse religious beliefs while at the same time encoding slavery and the dispossession of indigenous people within its foundational claim of constitutional legitimacy. That is, there was no humanist or ethical content associated with the secular commitment, although there were some pretensions to this effect summarized in the pretensions of being "a city on the hill," even "a new Jerusalem," conveying the sense that being secular could still mean valuing and embodying religious ideals.

Undoubtedly our interest in the post-secular is predominantly a tribute to the return of religion as a political force that is viewed either as a promising antidote to the crass materialism of the capitalist mentality or as a dire threat to ideas of moderation, tolerance, and the rule of law that are the greatest achievements of modern constitutional democracy. On the one side is the spiritualized identity of those who adhere to a faith tradition, whether institutionalized or not, and on the other side is the dual presence of the suicidal extremist determined to shake the foundations of modernity and the secular fundamentalist who perceives religion as the root of most evil.[24]

In geopolitical language, the post-9/11 world order is beset by this issue, as vividly expressed by Benyamin Netanyahu in his address to the General Assembly on September 23, 2011. He declared "a malignancy is growing between East and West that threatens the peace of all. It seeks not to liberate, but to enslave, not to build, but to destroy. That malignancy is militant Islam."

In the Cold War the malignancy that mobilized the capitalist West during those decades was, of course, militant communism, a form of materialism that suppressed religion as a matter of ideological dogma. In one sense, then, the post-secular imperative is the rescripting of world politics to focus on an epic struggle between the Judeo-Christian West and the Islamic East, although unlike the Cold War, there is a strong resistance as yet to defining the core conflict in such grandiose terms, and hence a tendency to focus on extremism as a distorted expression of religious identity.

The rescripting is structural as well as ideological – the adversary of the West is no longer associated with state power (although Netanyahu tries hard to make Iran into the ideological equivalent of the Soviet Union) as it is in the nonterritorial "long war" fought between the American nonterritorial world polity and the networks of extremists dedicated to violent struggle against the established order. This structural side of the post-secular has to do with a fundamental development: the borderlessness of the new geopolitics, as well as its disassociation from territorial sovereign states. Putting the issue in very simplistic terms, neither the United States nor al-Qaeda are territorial sovereign actors. The nomadic hunter in the twenty-first century is the Predator Drone roaming the planet in search of its prey much like premodern hunters roamed the forest without any notion of territorial limits. President Barack Obama offered a set of mild assurances in a much heralded speech to the National Defense University on May 23, 2013, that there were risks that the War on Terror had become a perpetual war, and that this must not be allowed to happen.[25]

The modern secular reality as it emerged in the West was as concerned with establishing and securing boundaries as it was with religion. Modernity, whether at the level of the state, the individual, and the company was very concerned with fixing proper boundaries on who owned what, but its views of the future were unconstrained by limits or sustainability concerns. It was this Western sense of enclosing space that gave rise to the identities that shaped secularist consciousness. It is the urgently necessary shift under way from a defense of boundaries to the multidimensional quest for sustainability that shares with religion the core sense of an emergent post-secularism.

3

WHY DRONES ARE MORE DANGEROUS THAN NUCLEAR WEAPONS

THREATS TO INTERNATIONAL LAW AND WORLD ORDER

Weaponized drones are probably the most troublesome weapon added to the arsenal of war making since the atomic bomb, and from the perspective of world order, may turn out to be even more dangerous in their implications. This may seem an odd, alarmist, and inflated statement of concern. After all, the atomic bomb in its initial use showed itself capable of destroying entire cities, threatening the future of civilization, and even apocalyptically menacing the survival of the species. It changed drastically the nature of strategic warfare, and will continue to haunt the human future until the end of time. Yet, despite the irrationality and war mentality that explains the diabolical unwillingness of political leaders to work conscientiously toward the elimination of nuclear weapons, it is a weapon that has not been used in the intervening 69 years since it was first unleashed on the hapless residents of Hiroshima and Nagasaki, and achieving non-use has been a constant legal, moral, and prudential priority of leaders and war planners ever since the first bomb inflicted unspeakable horror and suffering on the ill-fated Japanese who happened to be present on that day in those doomed cities.

The *second order constraints* imposed over the intervening decades to avoid nuclear war, or at least to minimize the risk of its occurrence, although far from foolproof, and likely not sustainable over the long term, were at least compatible with a world order system that has evolved to serve the principal shared interests of territorial states.[1] Instead of reserving this ultimate weaponry of mass destruction for battlefield advantage and military victory, nuclear weapons have been confined in their roles to deterrence and coercive diplomacy, which although unlawful, morally problematic, and militarily dubious, presupposes that the framework of major international conflict is limited to the belligerent interaction of territorial sovereign states.[2]

Reinforcing these constraints are the complementary adjustments achieved by way of arms control agreements and nonproliferation. Arms control based on the mutual interests of the principal nuclear weapons states, the United States and Russia, seek increased stability by restricting the number of nuclear weapons, foregoing some destabilizing and expensive innovations, and avoiding costly weapons systems that do not confer any major deterrent or strategic advantage.[3] In contrast to arms control, nonproliferation presupposes and reinforces the vertical dimension of world order, legitimating a dual legal structure superimposed on the juridical and horizontal notion of the equality of states. The nonproliferation regime has allowed a small, slowly expanding group of states to possess and develop nuclear weapons, and even make nuclear threats, while forbidding the remaining 186 or so states from acquiring them, or even acquiring the threshold capacity to produce nuclear weaponry.[4] This nonproliferation ethos is further compromised by linkages to geopolitics, giving rise to double standards, selective enforcement, and arbitrary membership procedures, as is evident by the preventive war rationale relied upon in relation to Iraq and now Iran, and the comfort zone of silence accorded to Israel's known, yet unacknowledged, arsenal of nuclear weapons.

This experience with nuclear weaponry discloses several aspect of international law and world order that establishes a helpful background for considering the quite different array of challenges and frightening temptations arising from the rapid evolution of military drones. First of all, the unwillingness and/or inability of dominant governments — the vertical Westphalian states — to eliminate these ultimate weapons of mass destruction and achieve a world without nuclear weapons despite their apocalyptic implications. The requisite political will has never formed, and has over time actually receded.[5] There have been many explanations given for this inability to rid humanity of this Achilles Heel of world order, ranging from the fear of cheating, the inability to disinvent the technology, the claim of superior security when deterrence and strategic dominance is compared to disarmament, a hedge against the emergence of an evil and suicidal enemy, an intoxicating sense of ultimate power, the confidence to sustain the global domination project, and the prestige that comes with belonging to the most exclusive club joining together dominant sovereign states.[6]

Secondly, ideas of deterrence and nonproliferation can be reconciled with the virtues and thinking that has dominated the tradition of political realism that remains descriptive of the manner in which governmental elites think and act throughout the history of state-centric world order.[7] International law is not effective in regulating the strategic ambitions and behavior of stronger states, but can often be coercively imposed on the rest of states for the sake of geopolitical goals, which include systemic stability. Thirdly, the international law of war has consistently accommodated new weapons and tactics that confer significant military advantages on a sovereign state, being rationalized by invoking "security" and "military necessity" to move aside whatever legal and moral obstacles stand in the way.[8] Fourthly, due to the pervasiveness of distrust, security is calibrated to deal with worst-case or near worst-case scenarios, which is itself a major cause of *insecurity* and international crises. These four sets of generalizations, although lacking nuance and example, provide a background understanding as to why the efforts over the centuries to regulate the recourse to war, weaponry, and the conduct of hostility have had such disappointing results, despite highly persuasive prudential and normative arguments supportive of much stricter limitations on the war system.[9]

CONTRADICTORY NARRATIVES: CHIAROSCURO GEOPOLITICS[10]

Drones, as new weapons systems responding to contemporary security threats, have a number of features that make them seem particularly difficult to regulate, given the shape of contemporary political conflict. This especially includes the threats posed by non-state actors, development of terrorist tactics that threaten the capability of even the largest states to uphold territorial security, and the inability or unwillingness of many governments to prevent their territory from being used to launch transnational terrorist attacks on even the most powerful country. From the standpoint of a state considering its military alternatives within the present global setting, drones appear particularly attractive, and the practical incentives for possession, development, and use is far greater than in relation to nuclear weaponry. Drones are relatively inexpensive in their current forms as compared to manned fighter aircraft, they almost totally eliminate any risk of casualties to the attacker, especially in relation to warfare against non-state actors, they have the capacity to launch strikes with precision in even the most remote hiding places difficult for ground forces to access, they can target accurately on the basis of reliable information gathered through the use of surveillance drones with increasingly acute sensing abilities, their use can be politically controlled to ensure restraint and a new version of due process that vets the appropriateness of targets in procedures of assessments carried on behind closed doors, and the casualties inflicted by drones are miniscule as compared to other methods of counter-terrorist warfare. In effect, why should not the use of drones by a morally sensitive, prudent, and legitimate leadership of the sort that controls American counter-terrorist policy be endorsed rather than criticized and lamented?[11]

There are two contradictory narratives, with many variations for each, analyzing the essential normative (law, morality) quality of drone warfare, and its dominant recent role in implementing the tactics of targeted killing of designated persons. On the one side of the dialogue, are the "children of light" who claim to be doing their very best to minimize the costs and scale of war while protecting American society against the violence of extremists whose mission is to use violence to kill as many civilians as possible. On the other side, are the "children of darkness" who are critically portrayed as engaged in criminal behavior of the most reprehensible kind to kill specific individuals, including American citizens, without any pretense of accountability for errors of judgment and excesses of attack. In effect, both narratives present warfare as a discretionary form of serial killing under state auspices, officially sanctioned summary executions without charges or with no explanation or accountability even when the target is an American citizen.[12]

The comparison of drone use with nuclear weapons is revealing in this setting, as well. There never was an attempt to endorse the civilizing role that could be enacted through threats and uses of nuclear weapons, beyond the provocative contention, which can never be demonstrated, that their mere existence had prevented the Cold War from becoming World War III. Such a claim, to be credible at all, rested on the amoral belief that their actual use would be catastrophic for both sides, including the users, while the threat of use was justifiable to discourage risk taking and provocation by an adversary.[13] In contrast, with drones, the positive case for legitimating the weaponry is associated exclusively with actual use as compared to the alternatives of conventional war tactics of aerial bombardment or ground attack.

"CHILDREN OF LIGHT"

The children of light version of drone warfare was given canonical status by President Barack Obama's speech delivered, appropriately enough, at the National Defense University, on May 23, 2013.[14] Obama anchored his remarks on the guidance provided to the government over the course of two centuries in which the nature of war has changed dramatically on several occasions but supposedly never undermining fidelity to the founding principles of the republic enshrined in the Constitution, which "served as our compass through every type of change. ... Constitutional principles has weathered every war, and every war has come to an end."

Against this background, Obama continues the unfortunate discourse inherited from the Bush presidency, that the 9/11 attacks initiated a *war* rather than constituted a massive *crime*. In his words, "This was a different kind of war. No armies came to our shores, and our military was not the principal target. Instead, a group of terrorists came to kill as many civilians as they could." There is no attempt to confront the question of why this provocation might have better been treated as a crime, which would have worked against launching the disastrous post-9/11 wars against Afghanistan and Iraq. Instead, Obama offers the bland, and rather disingenuous claim that the challenge was to "align our policies with the rule of law."

According to Obama, the threat posed by al-Qaeda a decade ago has greatly diminished, although not disappeared, making it "the moment to ask ourselves hard questions – about the nature of today's threats and how we should meet them." Of course, it is revealing that the crowning achievement of this type of warfare was not a battlefield victory or territorial occupation, but the execution in 2011 of the iconic al-Qaeda leader, Osama bin Laden, in a non-combat setting that was essentially a hideaway with little operational significance in the broader counterterrorist campaign. Obama expressed this sense of accomplishment in terms of striking names from a kill list: "Today, Osama bin Laden is dead, and so are most of his top lieutenants." This outcome is not a result, as in past wars, of military encounters, but rather a consequence of targeted killing programs and special forces operations.

It is in this setting that the speech turns to the controversy generated by the reliance on drones, which has increased dramatically since Obama came to the White House. He affirms in vague and abstract language that "the decisions that we are making now will define the type of nation – and world – that we leave to our children. ... So America is at a crossroads. We must define the nature and scope of this struggle, or else it will define us." In an effort to refocus the struggle against global terrorism, Obama offers some welcome downsizing language: "... we must define our effort not as a boundless 'global war on terror,' but rather as a series of persistent, targeted efforts to dismantle the specific networks of violent extremists that threaten America." Yet there is no explanation offered as to why the struggles for political control in far-flung places such as Yemen, Somalia, Mali, even the Philippines should be considered combat zones from the perspective of national security unless the global reach of American grand strategy is encompassed. Surely, to introduce American military power in what appear to be struggles to control the internal political life of a series of foreign countries does not create grounds in international law for recourse to war or even for the use of force.

It is not that Obama is rhetorically insensitive to these concerns,[1] but it is his steadfast unwillingness to examine the concrete realities of what is being done in the name of America that makes his rosy picture of drone warfare so disturbing and misleading. Obama asserts that "[a]s was true in previous armed conflicts, this new technology raises profound questions – about who is targeted, and why, about civilian casualties, and the risk of creating new enemies; about the legality of such strikes under U.S. law and international law; about accountability and morality."[16] Yes, these are some of the issues, but the responses given are little better than bland evasions of the legal and moral concerns raised. The basic argument put forward is that drone warfare has been *effective* and *legal*, and that it causes fewer casualties than other military alternatives. These contentions are subject to severe doubts that are never addressed in concrete terms that would be appropriate if Obama really meant what he said about confronting hard questions.[17]

His defense of legality is typical of the overall approach. Congress gave the Executive broad, virtually unrestricted authority to use all necessary force to address the threats unleashed after the 9/11 attacks, thus satisfying domestic constitutional requirements of separation of powers. Internationally, Obama sets forth some arguments about the right of the United States to defend itself before asserting, "So this is a just war – a war waged proportionally, in last resort, and in self-defense." It was here that he could have raised some skeptical questions about the attacks on the World Trade Center and Pentagon as being regarded as "acts of war" rather than crimes of such severity as to be "crimes against humanity." There were alternatives to recourse to war accompanied by a claim of self-defense against the transnational terrorist network that al-Qaeda appeared to be that might have been at least explored, even if not actually adopted, back in 2001. Such a reclassification of the security effort as of 2013 could have re-raised the fundamental question or, more modestly, deescalated the counter-terrorist undertaking from war to a global fight against transnational crime carried forward in a genuinely collaborative inter-governmental spirit.

Obama failed to seize such an opportunity. Instead, he presented a deceptively abstract set of responses to the main public criticisms of drone warfare as concept and practice. Obama claims, despite the growing body of evidence to the contrary, that drone use is constrained by "a framework that governs our use of force against terrorists – insisting upon clear guidelines, oversight and accountability that is now codified in Presidential Policy Guidance." It followed similar lines to those taken by John Brennan in a talk at the Harvard Law School a year or so earlier. Brennan was then serving as Obama's chief counter-terrorism advisor. He stressed the dedication by the U.S. Government to adherence to the rule of law and democratic values that have given American society its distinctive shape: "I've developed a profound appreciation for the role that our values, especially the rule of law, play in keeping our country safe."[18] Brennan, while claiming to do all that can be done to protect the American people against these threats from without and within reassured his law school audience in a manner that includes "adhering to the rule of law" in all undertakings, with explicit mention of "covert actions." But what is meant here is clearly not to refrain from uses of force prohibited by international law, but only that the covert undertakings that have become so much a part of Obama's "war on terror" do not exceed "authorities provided to us by Congress." With a rather sly sleight of mind, Brennan identifies the rule of law only with *domestic* legal authority while seeming to rationalize uses of force in various foreign countries. When it comes to the relevance of international law, Brennan relies on self-serving and unilateral constructions of legal reasonableness to contend that a person can be targeted if viewed as a threat even if far from the so-called "hot battlefield," that is, anywhere in the world is potentially part of the legitimate war zone.[19] Such a claim is deeply deceptive as drone use in countries such as Yemen and Somalia are not only far from the hot battlefield; their conflicts are essentially entirely disconnected, and so-called "signature strikes" treat as proper targets individuals acting suspiciously in their particular foreign setting.

The claim of the Obama presidency is that drones target only those who pose a threat, that great care is taken to avoid collateral civilian damage, and that such a procedure produces less casualties and devastation than would result from prior approaches to such threats that relied on the cruder technologies of manned aircraft and boots on the ground. Obama addressed the awkward question of whether it is within this mandate to target American citizens who are acting politically while resident in a foreign country. Obama used the case of Anwar Awlaki, the Islamic preacher, to explain the rationale underlying the decision to kill him, pointing to his alleged connections with several failed attempted terrorist acts in the United States: "… when a U.S. citizen goes abroad to wage war against America … citizenship should no more serve as a shield than a sniper shooting down on an innocent crowd should be protected from a swat team."[20] Yet such an explanation does not respond to critics as to why prior to the assassination no charges against Awlaki were put before some sort of judicial body, enabling a court-appointed defense, to ensure that "due process" within the group deciding on targets was not just a rubber stamp for CIA and Pentagon recommendations, and certainly why there cannot be a full post-facto disclosure of evidence and rationale.[21]

More disturbing, because it suggests bad faith, was Obama's failure to bring up the even more problematic drone targeting of a group of young people in a different part of Yemen than where the drone struck Anwar Awlaki. The targeted ground included Awlaki's 16-year-old son, Abdulrahman Awlaki, a cousin, and five other children while they were preparing an open air barbecue on October 14, 2011, three weeks after the drone killed Abdulrahman's father. The grandfather of Abdulrahman, an eminent Yemeni who was a former cabinet minister and university president, tells of his frustrating efforts to challenge in American courts the reliance on such hit lists and the absence of accountability even in such extreme cases. It is this sort of incident that highlights why the whole claim of effectiveness of drones is under such a *dark* cloud of incredulity. The younger Awlaki seems to have been the victim of what military jargon labels as a "signature strike," that is, a hit list directed not at designated individuals but at a group that CIA or Pentagon analysts finds sufficiently suspicious to justify their lethal elimination. Notably, Obama never mentioned signature strikes in his talk, much less committed the government to end such targeting. This undermines his whole claim that targeting is responsibly conducted under his personal direction and done in an extremely prudent manner that limited targets to so-called "high value" individuals posing direct threats to U.S. security and to arranging any attack so as to eliminate to the extent possible indirect damage to civilians. This whole line of rationalization is deceptive even if accepted on its own terms as drone strikes and threats by their nature spread deep fears to entire communities, and thus even if only the single targeted individual is killed or wounded, the impact of a strike is felt much more widely in space, and for a long duration in time.

There are two other matters in the Obama speech that warrant assessment. His central logic is one of giving priority to protecting the American people against all threats, including the homegrown ones of the sort illustrated by the Fort Hood shooting and Boston Marathon bombings, and yet he affirms that no American president should ever "deploy armed drones over U.S. soil."[22] First of all, what if there is a protection or enforcement imperative? Secondly, there is a seeming approval given, at least tacitly, to unarmed drones, which means surveillance from the air of domestic activities. Also dubious is Obama's way of acknowledging that American diplomats face security threats that exceed those faced by other countries, explaining that "[t]his is the price of being the world's most powerful nation, particularly as a war of change washes over the Arab world." Again the vague abstraction never yields to the concrete: why are American diplomats singled out? Are there legitimate grievances against the United States, which if removed, would enhance American security even more than by making embassies into fortresses and carrying out drone attacks anywhere on the planet provided only that the president signs off? Are America's imperial claims and global network of military bases and naval presence relevant? What about the global surveillance program disclosed in the government documents released by Edward Snowden?

Again the abstractions are fine, sometimes even clarifying, on their own detached plane of discourse, unless and until compared to the concrete enactments of policies, which are enveloped in darkness, that is, deprived of light. In encouraging tones, after providing a rationale for continuing a wartime approach, Obama does observe at the end of his speech that this war "like all wars, must end. That's what history advises, that's what our democracy demands." He finishes with an obligatory patriotic flourish: "That's who the American people are – determined, and not to be messed with." Brennan chose almost identical words in ending his Harvard Law School speech: "As a people, as a nation, we cannot – and must not – succumb to the temptation to set aside our laws and values when we face threats to our security… We're better than that. We're Americans."[23] The sad point is that the abstractions are decoys. What we have done in the name of security is precisely what Obama and Brennan say we must never do with respect to law and the values of the country.

"CHILDREN OF DARKNESS"

Turning to the counter-narrative in which the reality of drone warfare is presented in an entirely different mode. This does not necessarily imply a total repudiation of drone warfare, but it does insist that such tactics and their current implementation are not fairly or honestly reported, and as such, cannot be readily reconciled with constitutional or international law or with prevailing moral standards. The critics of the mainstream Washington discourse can be faulted for tending to presume that there is no way to scale back reliance on drones in a manner that is sensitive to the limitations of law and morality rather than to dwell only on the abusive and dangerously dysfunctional ways in which drones have been and are being used by the U.S. government. In other words, if the basic fallacy of the pro-drone children of light discourse is to keep the focus on an abstract level that ignores the existential challenges by the actual and potential patterns of use, the complementary fallacy of the children of darkness scenario is to limit their commentary to the concrete level that neglects the legitimate security pressures that motivate reliance on drones and their counterparts in the domain of "special operations" with a lineage that can be traced back to World War II, if not earlier. An appropriate discourse on drones would involve a synthesis that took some account of the security justifications while recognizing the normative tensions of undertaking a borderless war rather than defining the threat as one of borderless crime, as well as worried about the implications of validating reliance on robotic approaches to conflict where the human connection with acts of war is broken or rendered remote.

This is undoubtedly what Dick Cheney was referring to when he said that for the United States to be effective in a post-9/11 world requires actions on "the dark side." The initial disseminators of the "children of darkness" discourse were actually unabashed in their embrace of this imagery and accompanying policies. Indeed, it was Cheney himself who articulated the positive rationale in a September 16, 2001 interview on *Meet the Press*: "We also have to work, though, sort of the dark side, if you will. We've got to spend time in the shadows of the intelligence world ... That's the world these folks operate in, and so it's going to be vital for us to use any means at our disposal, basically, to achieve our objective."[24] What this meant in real time was reliance on torture and kill lists, and either the sidelining of legal constraints or the readiness to warp them out of shape to validate policies.[25] It meant reliance on "black sites" in a series of countries that would allow the CIA to operate their own secret interrogation centers free of national regulatory constraints, and there would be no questions raised. It led to "extraordinary rendition," transferring suspects to governments that would engage in torture beyond what was evidently acceptable as "enhanced interrogation" under direct American auspices. Donald Rumsfeld's motivations in a vast expansion of the Pentagon Special Access Program for Joint Special Operations Command (JSOC) was partly to avoid further dependence on the CIA because dark side initiatives were in his words being "lawyered to death."[26] When the PBS TV documentary *Frontline* presented its depiction of the war on terror associated with the neoconservative presidency of George W. Bush in 2008, it chose the title "The Dark Side," as did Jane Mayer in her searing critique of the tactics employed by the Cheney/Rumsfeld designers of the governmental response to 9/11.[27] It is not surprising that Cheney was even seemingly comfortable with being cast as the personification of evil in the popular culture by way of the *Star Wars* character Darth Vader.[28]

As is well known by now, 9/11 facilitated a prior resolve by Cheney and Rumsfeld to concentrate war powers in the presidency and to project American power globally on the basis of post-Cold War strategic opportunity and priorities without regard for the territorial limitations of sovereignty or the restraints of international law. Their goal was to preside over a revolution in military affairs that would bring warfare into the twenty-first century, which meant minimizing conventional weapons and tactics, which produced casualties and domestic political opposition to an aggressive foreign policy, and relying on technological and tactical innovations that would have surgical capacities to defeat any enemy anywhere on the planet. 9/11 was at first a puzzle as the neocon grand strategy was devised to achieve quick and cheap victories against hostile foreign governments on the model of the Gulf War in 1991, but with an increased willingness to be politically ambitious in imposing the kind of political outcomes that would enhance U.S. global dominance. What had not been anticipated, however, and struck fear in many hearts, was that the main hostile political actors would turn out to be non-state actors whose forces were dispersed in many places and lacked the kind of territorial base that could be targeted in retaliation. Adapting to that kind of security threat is what brought the dark side tactics front and center, as human intelligence was indispensable, the main perpetrators could hide anywhere including within the United States. Because their presence was often intermingled with the civilian population, there would either have to be indiscriminate violence or precision attained through targeted killing. It was here that special operations, such as the killing of Osama bin Laden, are emblematic, and drone warfare becomes the tactics and means of choice. And it is here that the counter-terrorist, despite being shrouded in a cloak of darkness, becomes a deadly officially sanctioned species of terrorist. The political extremist who blows up public buildings is not essentially different from the governmental operative who launches a drone or goes on a kill mission, although the extremist makes no claim of targeting precision and refuses to accept any responsibility for indiscriminate killing.

In reaction to the degree of continuity exhibited by the Obama presidency despite its reliance on the "children of light" discourse, liberal critics have tended to focus on the *behavior* of the state as characterized by its reliance on dark side tactics. Authors such as Jeremy Scahill and Mark Mazetti discuss the degree to which the essential features of the Cheney/Rumsfeld worldview have been sustained, even extended, during the Obama presidency: a war in the shadows; a global battlefield; surveillance of suspects that are defined to include anyone, everywhere; conception of imminent threat as potentially anyone (including American citizens) within or without the country; accelerated reliance on drone strikes as authorized by the president; and targeted killing as "the battlefield" acknowledged by Obama pointing to the execution of Osama bin Laden as the high point of his success in the war against al-Qaeda and its affiliates. There are some refinements in the conduct of the war on terror: the emphasis is placed on non-state adversaries, and the regime-changing warfare against state actors is terminated; torture as a tactic is pushed deeper into the darkness, meaning it is repudiated but not eliminated (e.g. force-feeding controversy at Guantánamo). In other words, the children of darkness still control "the real" conflict, dramatically confirmed by Obama's harsh responses to such whistleblowers as Chelsea Manning and Edward Snowden. The liberal discourse of the children of light calms American society, but evades the fundamental challenges being directed at international law and world order by the ongoing tactics of the Obama approach to a continuing war in response to 9/11 (that is, to date, implicitly sharing the Cheney view that it would be a gross mistake to treat "terrorism" as a crime rather than as "war").

DRONES AND THE FUTURE OF WORLD ORDER

The central debate about drone warfare focuses on issues of style and secrecy, and downplays matters of substance. Both children of light (representing the Obama presidency and liberal supporters) and children of darkness (the Cheney/Rumsfeld cabal) are unapologetic advocates of the military use of drones, ignoring the problematics of such weaponry and tactics from the perspectives of international law and world order. To underscore this contention, the introductory references to nuclear weapons are relevant. For drones, the idea of first order constraints of drones based on unconditional prohibition and disarmament to ensure non-possession seems outside the scope of debate. Given the rise of non-state political actors with transnational agendas, the military utility of drones is so great that any project seeking their prohibition at this stage would be implausible.

The same situation pertains to second-order constraints associated with controls on their dissemination comparable to the nonproliferation approach. Already drones are too widely possessed, the technology too familiar, and the practical uses for a range of states too great to suppose that any significant sovereign state would forego the advantages associated with the possession of drones, although the deployment of attack drones may lag for a period of time depending on the perception of security threats by various governments. Therefore, the best that can be hoped for at this time are certain agreed upon guidelines relating to use, what might be called third-order constraints similar to the way in which the law of war has impacted upon the conduct of hostilities in a manner that gives way to the perceived requirements of "military necessity." The world order issues have also been evaded in the unfolding debate on the use of drones, never being mentioned in the Obama speech of May 23, and only acknowledged indirectly in the Cheney/Rumsfeld view of the post-9/11 terrain of warfare. In short, the treatment of the 9/11 attacks as "acts of war" rather than "crimes" has more enduring significance than the attacks themselves. It leads almost thoughtlessly to viewing the world as a global battlefield, and to a war that has no true end point as has been the case in past wars. In effect, it submits to the logic of perpetual war, and the related acceptance of the idea that everyone, including citizens and residents, are potential enemies. Since the suspicion is fueled by intelligence gathering, which is done secretly, the primacy given to protecting the nation and its population gives to political leaders and unaccountable bureaucracies a license to kill, to impose extra-judicial capital punishment without the intervening due process steps of indictment, prosecution, and trial. As time passes, this authoritarian nexus of governmental power as it becomes normalized undermines both the possibility of "peace" and "democracy," and necessarily institutionalizes "the deep state" as standard operating procedure for contemporary governance. If linked to the consolidation of capital and finance in plutocratic patterns of influence, the advent of new variants of fascism becomes almost inevitable, whatever the shape of the global security system.[29] In other words, drones reinforce other trends in world order that are destructive of human rights, global justice, and the protection of human interests of global scope. These trends include large investments in secret global surveillance systems that scrutinize the private lives of citizens at home, a wide range of persons abroad, and even the diplomatic maneuverings of foreign governments on a basis more extensive and intrusive than traditional espionage.

DRONE WARFARE AND INTERNATIONAL LAW: DIMINISHING RETURNS

There are certain specific effects of drone warfare that exert a strain on the efforts of international law to constrain uses of force and regulate the conduct of war. These have been discussed by some "children of light" critics of the official policies as to scope of permissible use of drones. In effect, drones are not challenged per se, but only their mode of authorization and rules of engagement pertaining to use.

Recourse to war

A prime effort of modern international law has been to discourage recourse to war to resolve international conflicts that emerge between sovereign states. In many respects, that undertaking has been successful in the relations among major states with respect to international wars as distinct from internal wars. The destructiveness of war, the diminishing importance of territorial expansion, and the rise of a globalized economy ensure that this idea of war as a last resort is an important achievement of the latest phase of state-centric world order. Such an achievement is now at risk due to the rise of non-state transnational violence and the response by way of drones and special forces that operate without regard to borders. What this means is that international warfare becomes more and more dysfunctional, and the war mentality is shifted to the new wars waged by a global state against non-state political actors. And these wars, which are largely conducted behind a thick veil of secrecy, and with low risks of casualties on the side relying on drone attacks, make recourse to war much less problematic on the home front: the public does not have to be convinced, Congressional approval can be achieved in secret sessions, and there are no likely U.S. military casualties or vast diversions of resources. These one-sided wars become cheap and easy, although not for civilian populations subject to barbaric violence of extremist political actors.

State terror

There had always been some tendency for the tactics of warfare to involve explicit reliance on state terror, that is, military force directed at the civilian population. The indiscriminate bombing of German and Japanese cities during the last stages of World War II was one of the most extreme instances, but the German blockades of Soviet cities, rockets fired at English cities, and the rise of submarine warfare against ships carrying food and humanitarian supplies to civilian populations were other prominent examples. Yet the type of "dirty wars" undertaken after 9/11 embraced state terror as the essence of the dark side conduct of the effort to destroy the al-Qaeda network, and indeed undertake the destruction of so-called terror networks of global reach. As American operations in Yemen and Somalia suggest, the notion of "global reach" has been replaced by armed movements or groups with a jihadist identity even if the scope of their ambitions is confined to national borders, posing no threat, imminent or otherwise, to American national security if conceived in traditional territorial terms. This tension between treating anti-state "terrorists" as the worst form of criminality that suspends legal protections while claiming to engage in comparable forms of violence is to deprive international law of its normative authority. Until the Cheney/Rumsfeld embrace of secret war by assassination, the United States did not follow Israel' s adoption of terror to fight terror that had evolved from the shadows of Israeli policy to an outright avowal of legality in 2000 (after years of disavowal). In addition to the tactical adoption of a terrorist approach to weakening the enemy, there is the terrorizing of the society as a whole that is the scene of drone attacks. That is, it is not only the targeted individual or group, but the experience of having such drone strikes, that creates acute anxiety and severe disruption within the communities that have been attacked.[30]

Targeted killing

Both the international human rights law and the international law of war prohibit extra-judicial executions. There is insistence that such targeting is legal if the threat is perceived as substantial and imminent, as determined by secret procedures, not subject to post-facto procedures of investigation and potential accountability. The reliance on such a process for the legalization of practices associated with drone warfare and special operations does two types of damage to international law: (1) it situates targeted killing beyond the reach of law, and dependent on the non-reviewable discretion of government officials, including the subjective appreciation of threats (such a rationale is basically one of "trust us"); and (2) it substantially erodes the prohibition on targeting civilians not engaged in combat operations, and at the same time eliminates the due process arguments that those charged with crimes are entitled to a presumption of innocence and right of defense. As a result, both the customary international law and the distinction between military and non-military targets is weakened and the human rights effort to protect civilian innocence is completely disregarded. Also, the underlying contention that extra-judicial targeted killing is done sparingly and in the face of imminent threat as underpinning the claim of "reasonableness" is unreviewable because of the secrecy surrounding these uses of drones, and the critical independent assessments of actual patterns of use by journalists and others do not support government claims of responsible behavior. That is, even if the argument is accepted that the law of war and human rights law must bend in relation to imminent security threats, there is no indication that such constraints have been or will be observed in practice. The criterion of imminence, even if interpreted in good faith, is notoriously subjective.

Expanding self-defense

The most fundamental argument with respect to drone warfare is that given the nature of the threats posed by political extremists pursuing transnational agendas and situated anywhere and everywhere, preemptive tactics must be authorized as components of the inherent right of self-defense. Reactive tactics based on retaliation in the event that deterrence fails are ineffective, and since the destructive capabilities of non-state actors pose credible major threats to peace and security of even the strongest of states, preemptive strikes are necessary and reasonable. Such subjectivity surrounding threat perception, as applied in relation to drone warfare, undermines the entire effort to limit international uses of force, to objectively determine defensive claims that can be reviewed as to reasonableness and in relation to objective criteria such as are embodied in Article 51 of the UN Charter. The central ambition of the Charter was to restrict to the extent possible the scope of self-defense under international law. The abandonment of this effort represents an unacknowledged return to a pre-Charter approach to international uses of force, reverting to an essentially discretionary pre-Charter approach to recourse to war by sovereign states.[31]

The logic of reciprocity

An essential feature of the law of war is the idea of precedent and the acceptance of the reciprocity principle that what is claimed as legal by a dominant state cannot be denied to a weaker state as a central application of the logic of reciprocity.[32] The United States established such a precedent by recourse to atmospheric testing of nuclear weapons, and was not able to complain when other countries, including France, Soviet Union, and China, later tested their own weapons, although by that time the United

States was limiting its own testing to underground sites with less damaging environmental effects. With patterns of drone use, however, the world would be chaotic if what the United States is claiming is lawful for its undertakings with drones is undertaken by other states. It is only a geopolitical claim by the United States in relation to uses of force that can be projected into the future as a sustainable basis of world order, and as such, it implies a repudiation of Westphalian notions of the juridical equality of states. The drone debate has been so far implicitly embedded in a legal culture that takes American exceptionalism for granted.

The global battlefield

In significant respects, the Cold War converted the world into a global battlefield, with the CIA managing covert operations in foreign countries as part of the struggle against the spread of Communist influence ("warriors without borders"). After 9/11 this globalization of conflict was renewed in a more explicit form, and directed particularly at the security threats posed by the al-Qaeda network that was declared to exist in as many as 60 countries. As the threats emanated from non-territorial bases of operations, secret intelligence, sophisticated surveillance, and identification of dangerous individuals living ordinary lives in "sleeper cells" amid civilian society became the prime focus of interest. Foreign governments, most notably Pakistan and Yemen, were induced to give their confidential consent for drone strikes within their own territory, which were the subject of explicit rebuke and protest by the governments in question. Such patterns of "consent" eroded the autonomy of many sovereign states, and generated intense distrust in the relations between the state and the people. It also raises questions about what might be called "representational legitimacy". It is questionable whether this muffled form of consent provides adequate justification for such erosions of the political independence of sovereign states.

The American claim has been that it has the legal option to use drones against targets that pose a threat if the foreign government is unwilling or unable to take action on its own to remove the threat, with the underlying legal presupposition being that a government has an obligation not to allow its territory to be used as a launching pad for transnational violence. What becomes clear, however, is that both the globalizing of conflict, and of threats and responses, are incompatible with a state-centric structure of law and effective global governance. If a legal order is to persist under these conditions, it must be globalized, as well, but there is an insufficient political will to establish and empower truly global procedures and institutions with such effective authority. As a result, the only alternatives seem to be an inchoate geopolitical regime of the sort that presently prevails, or an explicit global imperial regime that repudiates in explicit form the logic of reciprocity and the juridical idea of the equality of sovereign states. To date, neither of these alternatives to Westphalian world order has been established or would be accepted if proclaimed.

One-sided warfare

Drone warfare carries forward various tactics of warfare that are virtually without human risk for the more technologically powerful and sophisticated side in armed conflict, and have assumed recent prominence due to the tactics and weaponry employed by Israel and the United States. A pattern of one-sided warfare has resulted that shifts the burdens of warfare to the adversary to the extent possible. To an extent, such a shift reflects the nature of warfare that seeks to protect one's own side to the extent possible from death and destruction, while inflicting as much damage on the other side. What is distinctive in the recent instances of military intervention and counter-terrorism, the two main theaters of combat, is the one-sidedness of the casualty figures. A series of military operations are illustrative of this pattern: Gulf War (1991); NATO Kosovo War (1999); Iraq Invasion (2003); NATO Libya War (2011); and Israeli military operations against Lebanon and Gaza (2006; 2008–09; 2012; 2014). The increasing use of attack drones in Afghanistan is a culminating example of one-sided warfare, removing the drone operational crew from the battlefield altogether, executing strikes by commands issued from remote operational headquarters (e.g. in Nevada). The repudiation of torture as an acceptable tactic of war or law enforcement partly reflects the one-sidedness of the relationship between the torturer and the victim as morally and legally objectionable aside from liberal arguments contending that torture is ineffective and unlawful.[33] An analogous set of reactions to drone warfare exists, including the liberal contention that the rage and resentment of a population subject to drone attack encourages an expansion of the very kind of political extremism that drones deployed against, as well as alienating foreign governments.

Futuristic drone warfare

While the politicians are preoccupied with responding to immediate threats, the arms makers and Pentagon advance planners are exploring the technological frontiers of drone warfare. These frontiers are synonymous with science fiction accounts of robotic warfare with ultra-sophisticated weaponry, and massive killing machines. There are possibilities of drone fleets that can conduct belligerent operations with minimal human agency, communicating with each other to coordinate lethal strikes on an enemy, which may also be armed with defensive drones. The reliance on drones in current patterns of warfare has the inevitable effect of devoting attention to what can be done to improve performance and to develop new military missions. Whether the technological momentum that has been released can be controlled or confined seems doubtful, and again the comparison with nuclear military technology is instructive. Yet it is important to keep in mind that drones are widely considered to be usable weapons, including for legal and moral reasons, while so far nuclear weapons are treated as non-usable except conceivably in ultimate survival situations.

A CONCLUDING NOTE

Four lines of conclusion emerge from this overall assessment of the impact of drone warfare, as practiced by the United States, on international law and world order. First, it is not plausible to eliminate drones from the warfare so long as the security of states is based on a military self-help system. As a weapons system, given the current threats posed by non-state actors and the memories of 9/11, drones are effective. In any event, the technological momentum and commercial incentives are too great to halt.[34] As a result, such first-order international law constraints as an unconditional prohibition on drones as adopted in relation to biological and chemical weapons, and proposed in relation to nuclear weapons, is not plausible.

Secondly, the debate on the legality of drone warfare has been carried on within an American context in which the risks of setting precedents and the dangers of future technological developments is accorded minimal attention. This debate has been further trivialized by being conducted mainly between those who would cast aside international law and those who stretch it to serve changing national security priorities of American foreign policy.

Thirdly, the debate on drones seems oblivious to the world order dimensions of creating a global battlefield and coercing the consent of foreign governments. The precedents being set are likely to be relied upon by a variety of actors to pursue goals antagonistic to maintaining international legal order.

Fourthly, the embrace of state terror to fight against non-state actors makes war into a species of terror, and tends toward making all limits on force seem arbitrary, if not absurd.

It is against this background that the counter-intuitive argument is put forward seriously to the effect that drone warfare is, and is likely to become, more destructive of international law and world order than is nuclear warfare. Such a contention is not meant to suggest that reliance on nuclear weapons would somehow be better for the human future than the acceptance of the logic of drone use. It is only to say that so far, at any rate, international law and world order have been able to figure out some regimes of relevant constraint for nuclear weapons that have kept the peace, but have not been able to do so for drones, and will be unlikely to do so as long as the military logic of dirty wars is allowed to control the shaping of national security policy in the United States and elsewhere.

4

CONTOURS OF NEW CONSTITUTIONALISM

New Constitutionalism is the complex framework that system-izes the norms, prevailing practices, and institutional procedures designed to produce order favored and generated by dominant economic and political elites, whether presiding over governmental structures or administering a range of non-state actors, especially those that are market based. Stephen Gill articulates this innova-tive and prescriptive orientation toward constitutionalism with a primary reference to the operational logic of the world economy in this era of neoliberal globalization.[1] Here I propose extending the scope of New Constitutionalism to encompass security, criminal accountability, and environment, especially as policy and behavior of others are impacted by the global domination project of the United States in the early twenty-first century.[2] I regard these issue areas to be organically linked, either as an extension of global economic disciplinary policies, procedures, and institutional arrangements designed to liberalize trade, facilitate investment, encourage resource exploitation, and take advantage of commodity markets. These initiatives would have a secondary objective of diverting public attention from alarming evidence that current patterns of globalization are linked to environmental deterioration and widening inequalities. There are also many signs of mounting opposition to any political initiatives that diminish prospects for profitability, capital accumulation, and equitable taxation systems.

Indeed, New Constitutionalism depends heavily on the selective application of global norms and procedures that facilitate the manipulation of the world economy for the benefit of corporate and finance capital. This process also extends to the adaptation of the institutional arrangements set up after World War II under the sway of the Old Constitutionalism, e.g. as associated with the UN Charter, so as to minimize interference with the institutional and policy preferences of neoliberal elites. New Constitutionalism operates on the basis of double standards that exempt geopolitical actors from many mechanisms of accountability for wrongful and criminal acts, and shapes law and its implementation so as to serve these overriding economic interests. As such world order structures combine states, markets, and the geopolitical control mechanisms with a pervasive bias toward either privatization or state capitalism tied to market forces as in China, thereby underpinning the New Constitutionalism. Nonetheless, these top heavy features of globalization are being challenged mainly from below by rising popular forces of resistance dedicated to a more equitable and ecologically sustainable distribution of the benefits of economic development, as well as demanding a more regulated world order in relation to the deployment of political violence to resolve conflict. Such subaltern eruptions of resistance put forward a visionary endorsement of direct and substantive democracy on a global scale as necessary and attainable.

POINTS OF DEPARTURE

It is my contention that the distinctiveness of New Constitutionalism is as a governmentalizing instrument dedicated to promoting private sector market-driven goals and finance capital in a variety of respects additional to, although interconnected with, the subject matter of trade, investment, and markets. For instance, New Constitutionalism has recently exerted its influence in the security domain by way of a large-scale reliance on tendencies toward interventionary diplomacy, the outsourcing of war, and increasing the direct and indirect governmental roles in controlling worldwide energy reserves and trade routes.[3] Paramilitary entrepreneurs such as Blackwater, operating at the interface between the formal military and civilian society, are the sinister mercenary face of war in its privatized facets; the same tasks can often be performed by professional military forces at a fraction of what is paid to a private security firm.[4]

Privatization, aside from considerations of the profitable, deliberately asocial, and environmentally risky or damaging deployments of capital, tends toward a reduced political and moral accountability to the electorate and a diminished oversight by representative institutions, which can constrain non-defensive war making only by a show of concern about mounting casualties and costs. Fully acknowledged battlefield losses and funding is far less politically saleable to a democratic public, even in American society, despite its disposition to support wars of choice so long as they do not last too long and offer reasonable prospects of victorious outcomes. It is also the case that evasions of accountability for these undertakings has frequently been achieved by relying on covert operations, black sites, and secret sources of funding kept off the books, and thus almost totally exempt from legislative and media scrutiny.[5] Some states may rely on transnational security firms to avoid the humiliation of having to give their consent to the presence of foreign troops to manage their security interests, thereby acknowledging an embarrassing lack of governing capacity, which is delegitimizing for countries that recently became formally independent. There has emerged various forms of dependence on neo-colonialist structures, techniques, and even an unsavory reliance on the superior weaponry of the former colonial powers to police ex-colonies, especially in sub-Saharan Africa, the scene of some of the worst colonial atrocities.

Similarly, European moves to regulate carbon emissions by trading mechanisms ("cap and trade") is another example of seeking private sector solutions to collective goods challenges of global scope that should be assessed as costs of production and not passed onto society. It is disappointing, as well, that Barack Obama's expressed concern in his 2013 State of the Union Address about growing threats of global warming was joined to an assurance that responses would rely on market mechanisms, despite their poor and inequitable record with respect to regulating the emissions of greenhouse gasses. There tends to be an uncritical refusal to comprehend the nasty mind game at work: selling rights to pollute does not so much restrict emissions as marketize and commodify the process without a sufficient attentiveness to environmental protection. Whether such an approach provides any confidence about preventing the buildup of greenhouse gasses beyond the safe thresholds of 320–360 ppm (parts per million), or even the internationally embraced more permissive ceiling of 400 ppm, is never seriously addressed. Given what is known, skepticism about such a capitalist approach to global warming seems fully warranted.[6] Private interests have counterattacked, launching their own lavishly funded campaign of climate skepticism that seems designed to avoid putting any burden whatsoever on major emitters of greenhouse gasses mainly by misleadingly claiming, in opposition to an authoritative consensus among climate scientists, that there is no convincing evidence to believe that GHG emissions produce global warming. The result of this campaign has been to confuse public opinion sufficiently as to discourage any meaningful response in the U.S. and elsewhere despite mounting evidence of both present harm and future catastrophic dangers. To ignore this overwhelming scientific consensus that includes a sense of time urgency in fashioning a response is the height of irresponsibility in relation to human wellbeing. The carbon buildup in the atmosphere is already causing present harm (extreme weather events, food insecurities, polar melting, and acidification of the oceans) and poses severe future threats to human wellbeing. Despite this retreat from the responsibilities of global leadership, geopolitical ideologues continue to put forward national claims to the effect that the United States is providing the world with beneficial leadership in relation to the global public good.[7] Leadership appropriate for *human* security presupposes a repudiation of the current ideological bias and agenda of New Constitutionalism, and its replacement by a people-oriented *Just* New Constitutionalism.[8]

A global justice movement that seeks to displace the regimes associated with New Constitutionalism needs to develop an emancipatory understanding of law and its underlying jurisprudence. In this regard, geopolitical manipulation based on links between law and power and the normative insistence on connecting law with morality underscore the relevance of distinguishing between *legality*, as a positivist category of interpretation, and *legitimacy*, as a geopolitical/moral category, thereby clarifying the quest for global justice.

DISTINGUISHING LEGALITY AND LEGITIMACY

Reliance on the distinction between legality and legitimacy subjects the constitutional metaphor to geopolitical and normative scrutiny in an era of neoliberal globalization, and in doing so go beyond the positivist domain of law as rules and procedures generated through the consent of governments acting on behalf of sovereign states.[9] In some respects, this inquiry considers the symbiotic coexistence of Old and New Constitutionalism. By situating concerns about legitimacy within the ambit of New and Just Constitutionalism the intention is to bring to bear ordering and limit notions that derive their authority from a consideration of contextual factors that mandate action or restraint beyond the strict boundaries of law. It purports to act on the basis of moral or humanitarian claims while obscuring the causal significance of geoeconomic and geostrategic factors such as securing energy reserves or protecting military bases. For instance, international uses of force outside of sovereign territory where there is absent an authorization by the UN Security Council may still be justified by a normative argument given the imminence of genocide or in reaction to massive crimes against humanity, and its real motivating explanation may reflect geopolitical considerations. Contrariwise, the unavailability of sufficient forces to carry out a protective mandate on behalf of those being victimized counsels against intervention even if the required political support exists in the Security Council suggests the weakness of the geopolitical motivation, and thus the political will. The legalization of proactive legitimacy considerations has been formalized in recent years by enactment of the Responsibility to Protect (R2P) norm. R2P represents a doctrinal attempt to justify various interventionary responses to internal strife, including military action, which had been previously rationalized as "humanitarian intervention."[10] Situated in a twilight zone, whether R2P reflects a more principled collective response by the international community to alleviate the suffering of the vulnerable and marginal, or is a semantic cover-up for obtaining approval for a disguised geopolitical ploy, must be ascertained by contextual analysis of each particular situation. We must ask in each case whether a disciplinary use of force is an indirect implementation of New Constitutionalism but disguised to conceal such coercive applications of neoliberal discipline. Recent UN practice invoking R2P on humanitarian grounds, particularly the 2011 NATO intervention that was deceptively undertaken to achieve regime change in Libya, seems to support the skeptical view that R2P is the old wine of Western hegemony and energy geopolitics contained in a new bottle with a different label.

To illustrate further, suppose a genocidal sweep was expected to take place internal to a large state, with a population exceeding 100 million, the moral argument for acting to protect the vulnerable population might be very persuasive, even compelling, but if there were insufficient capabilities available to make a protective mission credible, then it would be prudent and "legitimate" to opt for inaction, or to limit action to such humane initiatives (as receiving refugees, supplying medicines for civilian use, and diplomatic good offices seeking a ceasefire). This relative passivity is one of the tragic consequences of geopolitical pluralism, given the hierarchal features of the persisting state system in which dominant states are exempted from interventionary challenges for *practical* reasons associated with the costs and uncertainties of intervention rather than for *legal* reasons associated with conformity to the strict limitations imposed by international law on claims to use force for non-defensive purposes. There may also be present compelling *moral* reasons to circumvent the use of a veto by a permanent member of the Security Council, and enable an emergency undertaking to protect vulnerable people at great risk.

The totality of contextual factors that affect decisions on global policy, which vary depending on the issue area and situation, is embraced by the legality/legitimacy duality, and gives substance and structure to my interpretation of the New Constitutionalism. In effect, law is an ingredient of New Constitutionalism, and is operative at the interface between soft and hard power, and is often manipulated for the benefit of dominant forces, but under the power of insurgent reason may also be invoked due to genuine humanitarian concerns or to further political projects.[11] New Constitutionalism cannot be consistently relied upon to address all geopolitical calls for action in the world of the twenty-first century, given the cross-purposes of major state actors in some settings, e.g. Syria since 2011. Law can also be invoked as a counter-hegemonic soft power instrument by subaltern constituencies, as in the UN and civil society efforts to challenge the legitimacy of Israeli policies in occupied Palestine. The Boycott, Divestment, and Sanctions (BDS) Campaign being mounted globally in protest against Israel's unlawful denial of fundamental Palestinian rights is an illustrative project of Just New Constitutionalism that gives prominence to the disciplinary role of popular movements, transnational activism, and non-state actors.

INTERNATIONAL LAW AND THE "OLD" CONSTITUTIONALISM

The distinction between legality and legitimacy can be constructed in several different ways and its application varies with the substantive context and the global setting in its various temporal phases. The specific articulation of the distinction emerged initially in the course of the policy debate occasioned by the 1999 Kosovo War, then later in articulating the mandate and mission associated with the NATO War in Libya. It also underlies the UN and global debate on how the international community should and can respond to the mayhem that has been experienced in Syria since early 2011. The Kosovo debate concerned whether a non-defensive use of force by NATO was justified by a claim of humanitarian intervention that was rather widely endorsed by public opinion in Europe and North America but never authorized by the UN Security Council and strongly opposed by Russia and China. This opposition was premised on strategic alignments and a reluctance to authorize interventions under UN auspices despite humanitarian justifications. It was derided as opportunistic and cruel, but is different than the American efforts over the decades to shield Israel from adverse consequences of its unlawful oppression of the Palestinian people. Without UN authorization, a use of force other than as self-defense against an armed attack is categorically unlawful even if done under the auspices of a regional arrangement.

Against this background of tension between what was legal and what was widely believed at the time in Europe and North America to be a humanitarian imperative that justified protective action by means of intervention, the Independent International Commission on Kosovo struggled to find a way to evaluate the action taken by NATO. The Commission formally relied upon this distinction between legality and legitimacy, accepting the proposition that the use of force by NATO was unlawful or illegal, but nevertheless legitimate.[12] The role of the distinction was to admit the clear violation of the UN Charter associated with NATO recourse to war without a mandate from the Security Council while accepting the moral and political arguments as justifying preventive action to avoid further Serbian atrocities and threatened ethnic cleansing against the Muslim majority population of Kosovo. The Commission discussion lamented the existence of this gap between the legal and the legitimate, recommending its prompt closure by Charter amendment or interpretative resolution. It concluded that until this gap was closed by formal revision of the interpretation of the legal norms prohibiting the use of force in a manner that was more responsive to humanitarian claims, it was preferable to carve out a zone of privileged exception to the constraints of international law as it presently exists. What was not discussed was the geopolitical double standards that surround the practice, which is used to protect some victimized civilian populations but not others. Why the Kosovars but not the Chechins? Why the Libyans but not the Syrians? The answer my friends is hidden behind the curtain of geopolitical maneuverings. As the prior section discussed, R2P was put forward as an alternative ground for elevating considerations of *legitimacy* to levels of *legality*, thereby legalizing the battleground in which the main contestants are geopolitical rivals or subaltern forces.[13]

By stages, responsibility to protect has emerged as an innovative, if controversial, customary norm of international law due to its adoption by the UN Security Council, but whether this development has really altered the nature of this fundamental difficulty of identifying the proper limits of *legal* authority remains in doubt.[14] We need also to reflect upon the choice between the legality/legitimacy approach and that associated with reliance on R2P.

It is my view that the latter prods the UN to act for the sake of vulnerable peoples but opens wider the loophole for the pursuit of geopolitical projects associated with uses of force. It weakens the domestic jurisdiction inhibitions of Article 2(7) that were an integral component of the political contract embedded in the UN Charter back in 1945 during the reign of Old Constitutionalism. It also evades the injunction of the Preamble to the Charter "to save succeeding generations from the scourge of war," while purporting to take growing account of the emergence of human rights as a challenge to earlier notions of an unconditional sovereign right.[15] R2P also does not explicitly consider whether a proposed course of action is politically feasible or not with respect to the relation of means and ends.

Assuming that unconditional deference to law is not an acceptable resolution of the difficulty posed by states severely abusing their own people by the massive commission of crimes against humanity, some mode of principled reasoning to identify the scope of permissible action is needed. Of course, whenever we dilute the clarity of restraints on force we almost certainly lend encouragement to geopolitically shaped decisions, expressed through the selective application of legitimacy criteria and an acceptance of the implication of double standards. As has been noted there is a greatly different approach taken by the UN to the various popular uprisings and regime responses in Libya, Bahrain, Syria, as well as others that have taken place during 2011–12.[16] The prolonged ordeals of the Palestinians and Kashmiris are illustrative of the geopolitical insistence on foregoing protective action even when it is desperately needed.

The law/legitimacy tension with regard to a contested use of force has been invoked directly and indirectly in two ways with respect to the 2011 NATO role in Libya. Unlike Kosovo there was an initial authorization provided by the UN Security Council for a broadly conceived No Fly Zone framed in language that suggested that the limited goal was civilian protection, especially in and around the besieged city of Benghazi. This mandate by the Security Council, whose authority was diluted by five abstentions from important members, gave the intervention under NATO auspices an initial cover of legality. The military undertaking was then immediately expanded, without further

UN involvement, beyond the intended scope of UN authorization with the obvious intention of helping the rebels prevail in a civil war, which depended on the collapse of the Qaddafi regime.[17] The Libyan debate concerns whether the expansion of the No Fly Zone beyond its initial mandate subsequently made the NATO operations unlawful *and* illegitimate, as well as creating a controversial precedent that precluded a more vigorous international response a few months later that might have averted, or at least mitigated, the slaughter of civilians in Syria. Some supporters of the Libyan operations, despite the failure to abide by the original mandate, nevertheless viewed the actions as legitimate, even as a positive model, because of the desirability of regime change given the oppressive policies and recourse to crimes against humanity by the dictatorial Qaddafi leadership, or from a more sinister viewpoint, considering the relevance of controlling Libyan oil prices and reserves.[18] In effect, the Libyan operation can be subsumed under the heading of New Constitutionalism, its militarist implementation to rein in an outlier from the perspective of neoliberal logic.

The contours of the Libyan debate are more complicated as it could be contended that the intervention was illegitimate from its outset because reliance on airpower to achieve regime change was not an acceptable means to reach such a goal, and therefore the *political* dimension of the undertaking failed the test of legitimacy. It might also have failed the test because of the absence of a credible alternative to the Qaddafi leadership that had reasonable expectations of providing effective governance for the country as a whole, a concern fully justified by the post-intervention failures to establish order and uphold rights of various segments of the civilian population in Libya. Beyond this, even if politically feasible, an intervention in an ongoing civil war challenged the *moral* dimension of legitimacy by its refusal to abide by the logic of self-determination that enjoys normative priority in the post-colonial imaginary, and is integral to subaltern identity. Thus, whether lawful or not, the intervention in Libya could and should be viewed as illegitimate for reason of means, goals, and overall effects, although it was definitely rationalized in the Security Council debate by invoking the R2P norm although even that was invoked to achieve the more modest objective of protecting threatened Libyan civilians, and not regime change. It has been argued by proponents of the Libyan intervention that the authorization of "all necessary means" in the resolution delegated almost unlimited discretion to the intervening NATO forces. This seemed radically inconsistent with the language used, the reasonable expectations of the abstaining governments, and more institutionally, with the constitutional responsibility of the Security Council to do all that it can to avoid war and limit the uses of force in conflict resolution situations and interpret strictly any mandate to use force. It is especially relevant to decide whether the benefit of the doubt should be given to geopolitically governed uses of force that purport humanitarian and restricted aims,[19] especially when their effect, whether acknowledged or not, is to reinforce the disciplinary dimensions of the New Constitutionalism in the service of world capitalist interests.

Despite this, the legality/legitimacy distinction seems discursively useful, however, as pointing to situations where the legal assessment cannot be allowed to end responsible inquiry into preferred action. In this regard, the distinction offers useful, even illuminating, modalities of discourse, although it is only capable of providing exceedingly limited decisional guidance (Independent International Commission on Kosovo, 2000). It does alert us to the possible deficiencies of adopting a legalist posture with respect to global policy debates under conditions of extreme humanitarian challenge or geopolitical manipulation, suggesting that *responsible* global policy needs also to take flexible account of relevant moral and political considerations without being oblivious to geopolitical motivations. This is the case, especially, when exceptional conditions are present, although all the difficulties of granting "a right of exception" in the context of the UN emerge. Such reasoning should also be extended to the application of New and Just Constitutionalism standards to national situations of stress and emergency associated with economic crises and natural disasters, and to assess who favors and who opposes, and discern why in relation to the logics of economic globalization.

In this regard, the law should not be applied mechanically. Put differently, the stability of international interactions strongly favors adherence to legality, especially in war/peace settings, but with the proviso that insurgent and moral appeals to legitimacy are allowable, even encouraged, provided they are rendered transparent, and more controversially, seem credible as a *necessary* right of exception. This insistence on imposing a heavy burden of diplomatic persuasion to uphold a claimed right of exception seems particularly important with respect to second-guessing or diluting legal restraints on the use of force in Old Constitutionalism as these were embodied in the UN Charter and affirmed as also descriptive of contemporary international law in the *Nicaragua* decision of the International Court of Justice,[20] a notable instance of adjudicatory leadership within the understanding given by Upendra Baxi. It is almost always the powerful states, and particularly in recent decades, the United States, that seek to legalize policies that go beyond the supposed limits of legality to validate their controversial behavior; weak states may be as inclined to violate, but recognizing their lack of political leverage, and rarely make an effort to cloak their departure from law in garments of an enlarged legality, but appeal directly to moral justifications or political necessity usually on the basis of a very self-serving rendering of the factual conditions. Insurgent reason also generates its own versions of legitimacy when the pathways of legality seem to block challenges to existential instances of injustice. For instance, the Istanbul Tribunal on the Iraq War (2005), a pure global civil society initiative, provided a comprehensive "legal" accounting of war crimes committed by invading forces led by the United States and the United Kingdom.[21] The entire undertaking, including calls for boycotts and sanctions, and imposition of criminal accountability on political leaders, can be viewed as a symbolic assertion of legal authority issued by the parallel institutional structure being constructed on behalf of a subaltern global imaginary, a counter-hegemonic move that is intended in part to discredit New Constitutionalism.

The legality/legitimacy distinction also has security applications in the context of counterterrorism and counter-proliferation, two other aspects of the New Constitutional world order that has been unfolding in recent decades, especially since the end of the Cold War, with some bearing on the global political economy. What is consistently excluded from mainstream discourse is multiple connections between geopolitical patterns invoking humanitarian and world order rationalizations and protection of the property interests of a neoliberal world economy. Such protection includes opposing insurgent movements of resistance that are motivated by global justice. It has become important for critics of New Constitutionalism to connect these dots, and thereby delegitimizing the new rationales for Western uses of force in non-Western countries in the altered discursive setting of the post-colonial milieu, but with operational continuities with the colonial era: safeguarding favorable trade relations and opposing all trends that weaken the rights and benefits of property holders.

MANAGING NUCLEAR WEAPONRY AND NEW CONSTITUTIONALISM

If we are considering the constitutionalism of hard power at its supreme high end of nuclear weapons we initially take note of the interface between an unequal Nonproliferation Treaty (1968) and its "unlawful" geopolitical enforcement by the United States in the name of counterterrorism.[22] The peak instance of such enforcement was the 2003 attack on and occupation of Iraq on the principal grounds of preventing the regime of Saddam Hussein from acquiring and possessing nuclear and other weapons of mass destruction. In effect, the dubious legality of the NPT was linked via contrived and false intelligence briefings to unabashed aggression to validate recourse to war against Iraq by an American-led "coalition of the willing" despite the prior rejection by the UN Security Council of the American request for authorization.[23]

The tangled structure of the New Constitutionalism in relation to the nuclear weapons regime suggest the contours of the prevailing structural hierarchy: nuclear weapons states possess the weaponry, disregarding their treaty commitment to engage in nuclear disarmament in good faith; some states are allowed to acquire nuclear weaponry without adverse consequences, such as India, Pakistan, and Israel; other states, such as Iraq, North Korea, and Iran, are faced with military threats and economic sanctions if they seek to acquire such weaponry to uphold their national security; the NPT gives every state a legal right to withdraw from the treaty or to refuse to become a party, but this status can be overridden by the means by which the geopolitical goals of counter-proliferation are pursued; in no area of international political life is U.S. diplomacy more evident than in administering this complex and contradictory law/geopolitics regime that has been established to guard dominant political interests with respect to weaponry of mass destruction. And as the case of Iraq illustrates, this is connected to dominant economic interests in control over the substantial Iraqi and Iranian oil deposits and in geopolitical access to Gulf reserves, and more subtly in many other settings where threats and uses of force help stabilize trade and investment profitability, as well as positive connectivity with the capitalist orientation of the world economy, although these New Constitutionalism goals can never be avowed.

We have considered the relationship between law and geopolitics in the setting of counter-proliferation, but what about the connection with legitimacy? Here, again, from a conceptual perspective the issue is rather instructive. Unlike humanitarian interventions where in the background there is agreement among relevant political actors that genocide and crimes against humanity are *global* wrongs, the issue of proliferation gives rise to contradictory legitimacy interpretations. The mainstream Western view argues that proliferation is intrinsically dangerous, increasing the risks of catastrophic war, and hence is illegitimate and should be prevented by all possible means, even if expedient allowances are made for strategic exceptions. U.S. willingness and capabilities to prevent unwanted proliferation adds feasibility to the counter-proliferation undertaking. The contrarian view insists that proliferation goals should be subordinated to the security needs of sovereign states, a position that is reinforced by the unacceptability of a two-tier structure of discrimination that has persisted for decades. Some states are allowed to possess, develop, and threaten the use of these weapons and others are unconditionally prohibited from acquisition. Nowhere are such double standards more prominently exhibited than in the contrast between Western acceptance of Israel's arsenal of nuclear weapons and its reliance on its military superiority to deny other regional actors a comparable nuclear option. The articulation of these policies never admits or discusses New Constitutionalism dimensions. The Just New Constitutionalism view, aligned with the strictures of insurgent reason, argues that nuclear weapons should be abolished, with a Plan B, that so long as hegemonic states purport to be nuclear weapons gatekeepers, non-Western states have a legitimate right to develop a nuclear weapons capability. In the New Constitutionalism geopolitical hierarchy inconvenient contradictions are suppressed, such as allowing Israel to possess an undisclosed nuclear weapons arsenal while imposing hurtful sanctions on Iran and threatening the country with a military attack if it crosses the nuclear threshold. Such patterns of inequality reveal the essential character of New Constitutionalism.

In effect, then, carrying counter-proliferation initiatives beyond the limits of the NPT, and perhaps even disregarding these limits, is tainted with illegitimacy if assessed from the perspectives of Just New Constitutionalism. Additionally, to the extent that counter-proliferation justifications for non-defensive and unlawful uses of force are relied upon their function is also related to geo-economic imperial goals directly linked to control of natural resources as in relation to Iraq and Iran. In effect, counter-proliferation camouflages economically motivated uses of force that are not only unlawful, but also illegitimate, which necessitates inventing ways to protect the global dispersion of capitalist investments and interests that are direct affronts to post-colonial sensibilities. One such way is to invoke humanitarian or world order justifications for uses of disciplinary force in contexts where the principal motivation is geo-economic.[24]

INTERNATIONAL CRIMINAL ACCOUNTABILITY

This same complexity is also present in relation to the emergence of international criminal law as providing mechanisms for holding individually accountable political and military leaders of sovereign states. Such accountability is vital to the existence of a robust global rule of law, which it should be emphasized, is quite at odds with the geopolitically oriented hierarchies of the New Constitutionalism. Let me clarify the distinction: according to the rule of law equals are treated equally, a basic operational principle of what is identified here as "Just New Constitutionalism"; as such, no political actors, whether non-state entities or persons, are practically or conceptually exempt from accountability. By contrast, in New Constitutionalism hard and soft power is used by dominant actors to encode double standards with respect to the implementation of regulatory regimes. The result is a variety of discriminatory and selective applications of the law. In this regard, a given application under the auspices of New Constitutionalism may be procedurally consistent with rule of law and due process standards, giving defendants a fair opportunity for mounting their defense and a decision that reflects a conscientious application of legal norms, while being substantively selective by granting impunity to the criminality of the powerful, and their "friends."[25]

A stark illustration involved the refusal to inquire into the legality of the strategic air attacks on German and Japanese cities during World War II, as well as the atomic bombs used in Japan, during the Nuremberg and Tokyo War Crimes Tribunals set after World War II. Famously, the American prosecutor,

Justice Robert Jackson, promised that in the future the principles of accountability applied to the defendants from defeated Germany would apply to those countries whose representatives were sitting in judgment.[26] This Nuremberg Promise, implicitly designed to facilitate the emergence of a Just New Constitutionalism, has never materialized: the Nuremberg Promise has been broken beyond repair as those states whose representatives sat in judgment in 1945 have committed analogous crimes without being held accountable. It is also relevant to observe that this discriminatory application of law crudely used to encode power relations in Old Constitutionalism provided a template for the more sanitized role of international law in New Constitutionalism, but the primacy of geopolitical goals meant that similar patterns of manipulation would occur ensuring the harmonization of international criminal law with the grand strategies of geopolitical leaders.[27]

THE POST-9/11 COUNTERTERRORIST CHALLENGE

Turning to counterterrorism the complexity and contradictions are somewhat differently situated, but wide ranging in character and impact. There are two primary issues: relying within the state on detention and homeland security practices that exceed permissible international legal limits, and encroaching upon widely shared commitments to democracy and human rights; violently engaging beyond the state, with or without consent of the targeted country, in a number of interventionary practices that violate sovereign rights and international human rights standards. The American domestic scene since 9/11 well illustrates the first cluster of issues that have been extensively examined.[28] It includes the torture debate, the impact of the Patriot Act, the reliance on Guantanamo as a prison enclave beyond the reach of law, and recent legal justifications of targeted killing by drones, including of Americans, anywhere in the world as well as indefinite detention of anyone on mere suspicion of a connection with terrorist activity: instruments of coercive legality that result in pressures upon the legitimate use of governmental authority even in relation to citizens, and exerting a chilling effect on the exercise of normal oppositional rights enjoyed in democratic societies. The cumulative effect of these "emergency" measures is by indirection to bring a new kind of polity into being, especially if combined with the politics associated with growing economic inequality that has transformed the United States: the first global authoritarian democracy.[29] Such a reality is reinforced by the U.S. role as enforcer of the New Constitutionalism, which as a declining empire has few geopolitical assets of prestige and respect to rely upon, and so is induced to rely increasingly on its military machine that is globally situated, but despite its battlefield dominance throughout the world is unable to reach desired political outcomes at acceptable costs. This same militarist mentality also explains moves on the home front to thwart any insurgent anti-capitalist resistance as prefigured by the Battle of Seattle in 1999 and by the Occupy Wall Street Movement in 2011.

When considering the transnational dimensions of counter-terrorism there are obvious tensions between the legal principles of a state-centric or Westphalian world order and the insistence on a borderless global battlefield for counterterrorism operations, which include covert activities by special forces units, black sites for the interrogation of witnesses, transnational drone missions and other operations carried out without respecting territorial sovereignty. The May 1, 2011 execution of Osama bin Laden in his hideout at Abbattobad, not far from the Pakistan capital of

Islamabad, is emblematic of these concerns. The killing of bin Laden by a Navy seal unit was conducted in a foreign country, likely in a manner that violates fundamental human rights with respect to the prohibition of extra-judicial executions, and as such seems both illegal and illegitimate. Thinking otherwise, it is possible to contend that bin Laden alive and at large was a global menace, and that exceptional methods would be justified in killing him. Bin Laden had himself declared war on the West, and arguably his execution was an act of war authorized by the American commander in chief acting in his combat role despite the target person being the beneficiary of a tacit right of sanctuary in Pakistan. Whether the transnational realities of large-scale terrorism are such as to make it legitimate to override the normal constraints of territorial sovereignty is a large hovering question that clouds the nature of global governance, and relates closely in the political imagination to the borderless world preferred by the chief strategists of transnational corporations and banks.

And suppose the security claims are persuasive, are these tactical claims being conferred on a reciprocal basis? That is, if a non-state party to such an asymmetrical war were to manage to execute political leaders of their opponent, would that be treated as an act of war rather than of terror? Are the constraints on the conduct of military or violent operations applicable to both sides in the so-called "long war" or is only the non-state side so constrained? Note that in normal warfare the conduct rules of the law of war apply to aggressor and non-aggressor equally, although as discussed accountability mechanisms tend not to be. Even within a Westphalian framework, it is doubtful that United States', and to a certain extent Israel's, claims to kill their opponents in third countries is seeking to establish a legal precedent available to others similarly situated. Surely, Iran and many other foreign governments and non-state actors would have a strong basis for attacking individuals in Israel or the United States if the contours of permissible behavior are determined by the logic of *reciprocity* rather than by the geopolitical logic of *hierarchy*.

IMPERIAL NEW CONSTITUTIONALISM

The argument here is that these settings pose serious issues involving the non-economic dimensions of the New Constitutionalism, as well as highlighting the relevance of the distinction between legality and legitimacy. Ronnie Lipschutz in his important book, connects these inquiries into the sort of authority structure fashioned in a "constitutional" form by the overall domination project that continues to being pursued by the United States despite the setbacks of recent years: "The constitution for a new hybridized political structure such as Imperium is not an off-the-shelf product, and it most certainly will not be written 'in Congress gathered.' Indeed, as the product of long and constant struggle among various centers of power and authority, the Constitution of Imperium is unlikely ever to appear as a single text. Nevertheless, a hundred years hence it is likely to be as 'real' as any similar document under glass today."[30] Lipschutz' formulation, although concerned with the rewriting of the American Constitution to serve the purposes of administering the New Constitutionalism, is relevant in its realization that a constitution may be composed of diverse elements that cannot be reduced to a text or series of texts, but involves geopolitical norms of action and instrumentalized norms of authority designed to facilitate the maintenance of structures of domination.

It is important to take note of two features of this constitutional restructuring of world order: (1) Domestic authority structures are shaped by a permanent war economy exercising continuing emergency powers in ways inconsistent with human rights and political democracy, bringing about "authoritarian democracy"; (2) New Constitutionalism as applied on behalf of a post-colonial West-centric hegemonic worldview that administers a dualistic legal system, involving unmediated discretion for the dominant power and its allies in crucial spheres of action, is coupled with legal constraints as set forth by international law to regulate the hostile behavior of insurgent forces, some of which are motivated by the precepts of Just New Constitutionalism and others by new hegemonic dreams.

NEOLIBERAL GLOBALIZATION AND THE NEW CONSTITUTIONALISM

In the aftermath of World War II, there was a definite plan to establish a world encompassing legal and economic architecture of institutions and practices that would benefit all, but especially the industrial capitalist countries of the North. This architecture has demonstrated its resilience by continuously being adapted to serve these same interests despite changing global circumstances, especially the collapse of the colonial order. John Ikenberry has emerged as a leading champion of the virtues of this world economic order, contending that it will remain a benevolent framework for the foreseeable future, endorsing New Constitutionalism as the best option for realizing world public goods.[31]

However the clear imbalance between rich and poor was accentuated after the end of the Cold War, commonly referred to as "the Washington consensus," in which neoliberal ideology created a capital-oriented approach to development based on property rights and financial markets that favored the rich and punished the poor and vulnerable, and was especially harsh in relation to the very poor.[32] That is, as Stephen Gill (2008) and others have argued, international law has played a regulatory role that validated financial institutions and markets at the expense of the peoples of the world, premised on promoting ecologically non-sustainable consumerist lifestyles, and undisturbed by impending petroleum and water scarcities, widening income disparities and persisting enclaves of extreme poverty, and even the generalized menace of global warming.

Legitimacy in this setting of globalization needs to be understood primarily in terms of a contrarian people-oriented development, or what I have referred to in the past as globalization from below, and what Gill characterizes as the "post-modern prince."[33] In this respect, Gill points to "the battle of Seattle" as an epic expression of this encounter between the forces of law and the forces of insurgent legitimacy, between the scheduled meetings of bureaucrats and officials within the offices used by the IMF and the demonstrations by citizens in the streets.[34] Such subaltern legitimacy is associated with resistance while legality is an instrument of the established order. It is legitimate resistance because of the failures of the New Constitutionalism to achieve either the appearance or reality of fairness in developmental economics, especially with regard to the distributional benefits of growth, as well as the less emphasized failure to impose ecologically responsible constraints on production and consumption patterns or to manage force in accord with a scrupulous regard for the legal framework set forth in the UN Charter. More specifically, from the perspective of environmental concerns about climate change and sustainability or in relation to poverty eradication, New Constitutionalism is exhibiting a lack of capability and a weakness of political will, to protect the global public good of present and future generations. This is well illustrated by the failure of annual UN conferences on climate change to adopt policies regulating emissions that take responsible account of the authoritative scientific consensus.

Conceptually, then, law and legality are identified with the contradictory mixture of institutions, procedures, norms, and practices associated with the established order and the prevailing ideology associated with neoliberalism. In opposition are a body of ideas that form a coherent sense of legitimacy that draws upon a morally and politically based critique that is premised upon the principles of humane global governance and ideas of global justice, a world order that provides for the needs and dignity of all the peoples and persons living on the planet and is sensitive to the claims of future generations.[35] To a significant degree, prospects for humane global governance rest on the promise of authoritative instruments of international law, especially in the field of human rights, but only if applied without geopolitical selectivity. As with the use of force, however, geopolitics has managed to narrow the effective scope of human rights in such a way as to relegate its more far-reaching norms to the never-never land of utopian aspiration. Populist forces that invoke international law in counter-hegemonic moves are seeking a maximal reappropriation of the global law discourse on behalf of the subaltern agenda.[36] These social forces are mounting on some occasions a law-centered resistance that overlaps with insurgent claims of legitimacy based on considerations of global justice. Although this can be confusing, it is existentially compelling as reflective of contemporary political practice.

Let me illustrate this critical advocacy of a Just New Constitutionalism by reference to some provisions of the Universal Declaration of Human Rights, which amount to a subaltern

Trojan Horse that entered the domain of legality by stealth from the remnants of Old Constitutionalism. Articles 25 and 28 of UDHR are provisions of a formal instrument that is generally treated as expressive of customary international law and, overall, a seminal achievement of human rights, but has been so far effectively neutered with reference to global economic justice by the supervenient operating principles of the New Constitutionalism.

Article 25 posits "the right of a standard of living" adequate for individual and family basic needs, including "the right to security in the event of unemployment, sickness, disability, widowhood, old age or any lack of livelihood in circumstances" beyond control. Article 28 is even more encompassing and radical: "Everyone is entitled to a social and international order in which the rights and freedoms set forth in this Declaration can be fully realized." It is so obvious as to require no exposition that the New Constitutionalism embodying the logic of neoliberalism is dramatically at odds with these provisions of international human rights law, and completely ignores their presence. In this regard, international law as understood from above contradicts the people-oriented law being affirmed from below.[37] This gap can also be explained as establishing a legal order that accommodates hierarchies of power and wealth via New Constitutionalism while a second legal order, a necessary subaltern imaginary or Just New Constitutionalism seeks to transform this exploitative structure so that it more closely corresponds with prevailing ideas of justice, including considerations associated with equality and inequality, in its quest for legitimacy.[38] This struggle concerning the nature of legitimacy has not been adequately theorized and is mainly ignored. Its radical promise of global justice for the poor is obviously at odds with the way the world is being organized both horizontally (inequality among states) and vertically (hierarchical patterns of control), but it underlies, usually implicitly, the imaginary of resistance that adopts such norms of legitimacy as foundational for its hopes and struggles, and reflective of its ethical belief in the unity and eventual ascendancy of people: "the sky has many stars, but the earth has only one human family."Here the legality/legitimacy interplay is used to contrast ideas of what is *lawful* in the sense of being in accord with what "the law" prescribes with ideas about what is *legitimate* in the sense of what accords with ideas of justice and practicality (or political feasibility). There is a fundamental tension between legality and legitimacy in all those settings where the law is aligned with the interests and preferences of the geopolitically dominant political and economic actors. As far as economic globalization has encoded neoliberal ideology, this tension is crucial. Legality constitutes institutional and rule-governed arrangements (most prominently, as enacted by the Bretton Woods institutions) that prescribe rules and procedures that favor investment interests and capital efficiencies regardless of human consequences. Such an approach is manifest in widening disparities between rich and poor within and among states and regions as well as by the failure of the system to satisfy the needs of those living in extreme poverty. The "legality" of neoliberal globalization is sharply contested by a variety of populist insurgent initiatives premised upon the "illegitimacy" of the process and substance (e.g. IMF conditionalities and structural adjustment mechanisms that mandate cuts in debtor governments capacity to give material benefits to the poor and needy) of New Constitutionalism.

A CONCLUDING COMMENT

In conclusion, there are various ways to conceptualize Just New Constitutionalism. It has often in the past been associated with discussions of "humane global governance" or, simply, "global justice." The guiding idea is to find a way to identify the overall outlook of what I have in the past called "horizons of desire," or more tangibly, with what would be the implications of a world order constructed on the principles of a human rights culture based on realizing the aspirations of Articles 25 and 28 of the Universal Declaration of Human Rights. In the end, fulfilling the normative potential of any just form of constitutionalism in the near future will depend on a robust dialectic between functional centralization to meet problems of global scope (e.g. climate change, nuclear weaponry, world poverty, water scarcity, food insecurities, pandemics) and a determined insurrectionary politics of subsidiarity, dispersion, and above all, resistance. The main animating idea would be to shift power from the governmental center in sovereign states to local grassroots arenas of authority and community. This will also involve a struggle to wrest the discourse on legitimacy from the geopolitical manipulators acting on behalf of neoliberal and imperial versions of New Constitutionalism. The overriding goal of global reform must become a Just New Constitutionalism that is guided by the principles of insurgent reason and subaltern visions of global justice.

5

HORIZONS OF GLOBAL GOVERNANCE

CRITIQUING HORIZONS OF FEASIBILITY

An inquiry into horizons of global governance touches upon the core of what we can expect and hope about the future of world order. The future of global governance is well encompassed by a comment made in an essay by Ralph Waldo Emerson, nineteenth-century poet/philosopher, who wrote "the health of the eye seems to demand a horizon. We are never tired so long as we can see far enough."[1] A line from the fellow transcendentalist of Emerson, Henry David Thoreau, complements this call for long-distance visualization: "It is not what you look at that matters, it's what you see." By highlighting such assertions I am expressing my belief that the interpretative gaze crucially informs any discussion of the past, present, and future of global governance. In actuality, it is not peering into the future that makes a consciousness of the future so crucial at the present stage of history. It is taking account of present risks in ways that make a benevolent future more likely.

Perhaps the simplest way of expressing my point of departure from this Emerson/Thoreau perspective is to insist that the world badly needs a geopolitical ophthalmologist. We are not currently able to see clearly the emerging *global* scale risks that confronts and challenges the human future, which if not properly addressed, are highly likely to inflict catastrophic consequences. Among these risks are nuclear warfare, climate change, global economic collapse, declining biodiversity worldwide energy and water scarcities, extreme poverty, the dangerous fissures that arise from transnational waves of migration and extreme societal inequality.[2] Note that during most of human history the social risk agenda was of local or, at most, of a civilizational scale, with collapse a recurrent possibility, but without global or species implications.[3]

We now face threats of collapse at various levels of social organization, but except individually and locally where the dynamics of self-empowerment may generate radical solutions, responses are dependent on nationally bounded mechanisms of decision-making and seem hobbled by self-limiting constraints. For instance, in relation to climate change, a strong scientific consensus exists as to future dangers, but it has been so far impossible to translate this into an appropriate policy consensus because of many intervening obstacles. Among these are the abstractness of the threat, the confusion deliberately wrought by a climate skeptic campaign funded by major emitters, a short-cycle of accountability among political leaders, and the geographic distance between major emitting states and those experiencing the greatest immediate harm due to increases in average temperature.[4] Such an overall context encourages politicians to defer action on longer-term challenges that if met currently would be somewhat burdensome on taxpayers and economic growth, although far less so than in the future if the buildup of greenhouse gasses and predicted trends toward global warming are allowed to unfold relatively unabated.[5]

In my view the academic discipline of international relations, and its policy-related frameworks, are severely handicapped by prevalent forms of horizoning of emergent challenges. Overwhelmingly, academic and policy inquiry are entrapped by what I would call "horizons of feasibility" that depicts the future as essentially confined to an incremental continuation of the past, as most probably reflecting the effects of gradual change, with the single large exception that is encompassed being the restructuring impacts of major wars. This incrementalism that is posited as rationality and normalcy, and from the perspective of the policymaker is an appropriate consequence of a realist orientation toward world politics. Realism presupposes a framework of interpretation based on the interplay of sovereign states of different size, wealth, and military capabilities and political leadership. Limiting perception to these parameters excludes any acknowledgement of the likely intrusion of the unexpected as producing non-incremental effects.[6] The realist is also rarely distracted by a contemplation of the necessary and desirable as these categories of interpretation, which are regarded as normative concerns, irrelevant to serious analysis and recommendation that take their cues from a conception of politics as the art of the possible, that is, the perspectives of the problem-solving decision maker acting on behalf of the sovereign state.

I insist that even the most superficial account of recent world history reinforces the impression that there have occurred many non-incremental shifts in the perception of actual international conditions and the challenges of global political life during the last several decades. These have fundamentally reshaped our understanding of the "real" and significant in international life, but still have not managed to displace the dominant template that restricts itself to the feasible as the sensible limit of useful conjecture and contemplation. Such a confinement of the political imagination, coupled with a suppression of the moral imagination, disables citizens and leaders alike from thinking clearly and benevolently about how to solve existing problems, whose solution requires non-incremental policy responses.

The end of the Cold War, the peaceful transformation of racist South Africa, the 9/11 attacks, the 2008 financial meltdown and more recently the unfolding of the Arab spring and the birth of the Occupy Movement came as complete surprises to the academic community and the policy domain. Despite the many billions annually spent on intelligence activities, including futurist simulations and scenarios depicting the future, which supposedly provide the best available information on the range of plausible expectations, our capacity to anticipate drastic modifications of present circumstances in the political realm is extremely limited. Explanations are retrospectively given of such transformative events but they are after the fact, a reconstruction of unanticipated changes by glancing in the rear view mirror, and trying to fashion sensible reactive approaches. We can interpret the present and explain the past with the cognitive tools at the disposal of adherents of horizons of feasibility but we are unable to grasp the future as a field for action and reaction. In this sense we are captives of the present with very little imaginative space available that is supportive of even an inclination to overcome current problems by proposing non-incremental solutions, which by realist definition will be dismissed as non-feasible. In this regard, the sensibility of political realism is dysfunctionally dominated by logics of feasibility. This orientation (mis)-shapes the governing process and media discourse with the consequence that problem-solving capabilities are disabled in relation to principal contemporary threats to human security, with the decidedly negative implication that the established order if it is to respond sensibly to such threats, must do so only reactively, which seems almost certain to be too late to avert catastrophic harm, and far more costly socially and economically.

There are two conclusions to be drawn: major unlikely and unexpected happenings from the perspective of the present do frequently occur, and give rise to major changes that can be disruptive; our most influential frameworks of public reason are not disposed to take sufficient account of such unlikely or drastic future developments, and even if accorded some marginal notice by way of future scenarios and gaming options, these futuristic conjectures are not allowed to impact directly on policy shaping dynamics or public debate. Upendra Baxi explores such a deficiency of modern governance by way of an enlargement of the domain of public reason to what he usefully labels as "sentimental popular reason" (bringing to bear ethical and reformist proposals emanating from civil society) and "insurgent reason" (proposing transformative projects, including the advocacy of revolutionary challenges to the established order).[7]

In the deservedly influential *The Black Swan* the author convincingly argues that the unfolding of human experience, correctly interpreted, is essentially a narrative of the unexpected, the random, and the implausible.[8] This understanding of historical unfolding is difficult to take into account given the sort of false confidence in policy reasoning that constrains public debate and governmental behavior. The horizon of the feasible (mis)shapes the thinking, not only of the academic community, but especially of those charged with the shaping of foreign policy. Political realism understands the shaping of global history quite differently than Nassim Taleb, reflecting the interplay of sovereign states as interpreted primarily through the prism of hard power. The blind spots of this orthodoxy are likely to have particularly dire consequences for humanity given the existing circumstances of world order. Indeed, so much so that in the early twenty-first century this persisting authority accorded realism to guide policymaking and behavior suggests the discrediting phrase, "crackpot realism," deployed by the influential sociologist, C. Wright Mills, a generation ago when he was critiquing the prevailing thought and policy paradigms of the Cold War era. A gentler way of offering the same critique is to insist that the policy domain limits the consideration of policy alternatives to "thinking within the box," and what is worse within an anachronistic box that wrongly exaggerates the international agency of hard power capabilities in the setting of twenty-first-century realities that favor reliance on soft power approaches to the pursuit of national, regional, and global goals.

HARD POWER FALLACIES

As argued, hard power realism misleadingly presupposes a high degree of continuity between the present and the future. It also adopts a scientific way of encompassing reality that resists giving attention or relevance to unjust and outmoded features of world order. This blinkering of inquiry is also expressed by an unwillingness to reexamine the exaggerated reliance on the agency of hard power diplomacy by leading governments in their construction of policies and capabilities designed to promote "security."[9] The United States exemplifies this heavy investment in hard power capabilities as well as the inability to learn from the gathering evidence of the generally detrimental effects of seeking to resolve political conflicts by imposing a military solution. Instead of learning from failure, the main effort of governmental decision-makers is to redesign weapons and doctrine so as to restore confidence in the military instrument of diplomacy.

This exaggerated reliance on military superiority has been especially pronounced in the United States since the 9/11 attacks. It has expressed itself in the complex effort to address alleged transnational threats of political violence by military interventions in countries such as Afghanistan, Iraq, Somalia, and Libya, and by mounting threats of attack directed at Iran and by a military intervention currently contemplated for Syria. These interventionary undertakings, each proposed in light of its own distinctive circumstances, confer upon the agency of hard power an unjustifiable confidence in the capability of superior military force to sustaining global governance for the benefit of the established order.

Extending the scope of inquiry to include law and legitimacy is treated from this realist perspective as essentially irrelevant or as moralizing propaganda.[10] Henry Kissinger probably remains the most influential exponent of this way of seeing and acting in the world. Kissinger's contempt for law and legitimacy (except when it happens to coincide with American foreign policy objectives) is manifest. In his memoirs he acknowledges his displeasure and impatience whenever his aides presume to suggest that he take some account of the moral or legal dimensions of policy.[11]

NEOLIBERAL FALLACIES

In hegemonic conceptualizations of global governance it is helpful to appreciate the extent to which horizons of feasibility are organically linked to structures of privilege, exploitation, and hierarchy. Those structures, practices, mentalities, and norms serve to perpetuate control over the poor, the weak, and the vulnerable by the rich and powerful.

The policy leadership associated with the promotion of neoliberal globalization as the only worthwhile governance ideology of our time have a definite agenda designed above all to insulate the established order from challenges mounted from below. This leadership is constituted by an assemblage of private and public sector elites that might be identified as "the Lords of Davos" or their G-20 mechanism, and their effective dirty work has taken its human toll: widening disparities of wealth and income within and between countries, stagnant levels of extreme poverty, and massive unemployment especially among youth. This ethical insensitivity has been accompanied by steadfastly ignoring the ticking bombs of unsustainability, especially the imposition of ecological limits on economic growth, as well as developing energy scarcities, water shortages, and insufficient food supplies. It is my contention that these dimensions of an unsustainable world order are not addressed with the urgency that seems prudent given our knowledge and professed values.

This hazardous failure to address anticipated future problems is partly a reflection of myopic greed that is disguised by adopting an orientation toward "reality" that claims to be objective due to its market-guided belief system that has the side effect of marginalizing ethical shortcomings and environmental threats as diversionary "externalities" of market behavior.

DELIMITING HORIZONS OF NECESSITY

From the perspectives of sustainability, as well as law and legitimacy, there is implied a deliberate capacity to serve humanity and promote global public interests. This entails a rejection of the existing global imperium operated for the benefit of a transnational plutocracy and their bureaucratic handmaidens. Their rationalizations of hierarchy and exploitation must be challenged in our thinking and politics by depicting horizons of necessity and conceiving of policy with an appropriate sensitivity to and respect for ecological limits and a dedication to the human dignity of all inhabitants of the planet. That is, a focus on necessity brings before us what must be done to ensure our future viability as a species co-existing on the planet and safeguarding as a sacred trust the opportunities of future generations. Accepting such a reorientation of perspective also suggests the need to combine the functional pursuit of survival and sustainability with the ethical quest for a world order that is grounded in human security, including a far more equitable distribution of the material benefits of economic activity.

Acknowledging the gaps between feasibility and necessity is one means of expressing the crisis of our time: the feasible is insufficient to sustain our future, while the necessary is not now able to achieve policy relevance, and so the prospects for the future fall beneath a darkening shadow. The endeavor to close this gap should unite persons of benevolent intention throughout the planet, but to have success will depend on achieving a global democracy as an operative political framework that transcends the workings of state-centric world order, and offers humanity what appears from the perspective of the present to be a "necessary utopianism."[12]

THE EMERGENCE OF HORIZONS OF DESPERATION

There is another consequence of the growing realization of this persisting, ever widening, gap between the feasible and the necessary, and that is an emerging mood of societal desperation. Putting this observation in the framework of my argument about cognitive identities, we are experiencing in our surroundings the rise of what might be described as horizons of desperation. This set of horizons assume at least two forms: first, recourse to extreme religious and cultic viewpoints that embrace an apocalyptic future, and thereby make the gap not an occasion for worry, but on the contrary a welcome or unavoidable part of a divine plan for the final phase of human existence on earth; secondly, recourse to a variety of escapist and denialist adaptations that ignore the reality of the gap, or put differently, fail to acknowledge the imperative of accommodating policy and behavior to horizons of necessity because of a refusal to accept the practical adjustment in life style, consumptive habits, and various forms of inequality. The presence of horizons of desperation is a symptom of a cultural situation where potentially mortal challenges directed at survival and sustainability are ignored or minimized for as long as possible, but their actuality and neglect appear to prefigure catastrophic outcomes. Such a phenomenon raises questions about whether the species as a biological entity possesses a strong will to survive collectively.

There are strong reasons to believe that the earliest religious impulses were themselves desperate efforts to somehow address the virtually omnipresent threats of flood, famine, disease, and drought in pre-modern times, most often coupled with practical steps to do what was possible to mitigate such threats (storing food, water; caring for soil, migrating), but was never enough to avoid an omni-present sense of dependence on nature. Modernity with its confidence in technology and science has inverted this relationship, subjugating nature to satisfy limitless human wishes for a more abundant life experience. Horizons of desperation have become so relevant because nature is now biting back, imperiling humanity in unprecedented ways, even threatening collapse on a global scale, and giving the lie to modernist pretensions of mastery over nature.

THE ROLE OF HORIZONS OF DESIRE

Introducing horizons of necessity and desperation as an historical reflection as to the inadequacy of horizons of feasibility seems clarifying as to what is to be done, but is not enough. We need to add the idea of horizons of desire as a way of incorporating the familiar Gramscian directive: "optimism of the will, pessimism of the intellect." Horizons of desire refer to the pursuit of what is desirable, which may exceed what is necessary, as well as accord mobilizing energy to the projection of a benevolent future at the level of the individual person, the community, and the world. Horizons of desire combine the essential embodiment of a human rights outlook with an affirmation of the sacredness of life on the planet. Humanistic and ecological orientations inform horizons of desire as a projection of a historically mandated emancipatory politics. Given the challenges of moral globalization, the rule of law and considerations of legitimacy are needed to promote and protect ideals of equality and reciprocity, thereby displacing the present logic of world order, which is tasked with upholding and securing structures of authority based on ideas and practices of sovereignty, inequality, hierarchy, and exploitation. As Baxi points out, "insurgent reason" as a revolutionary challenge seems indispensable to advance the agenda associated with horizons of desire. The established political discourses associated with "public reason" as Baxi explains the disciplinary structures of society are too closely connected with entrenched interests to be swayed by the imperatives of social and ecological necessity.[13]

GEOPOLITICAL MANAGEMENT OF WORLD POLITICS

A more concrete depiction of how this logic of inequality and domination works can be illustrated by referencing several major areas of global public policy where wealth, prestige, and war/peace are at issue. For instance, consider the approach taken over the course of more than six decades to the dangers posed by nuclear weapons that gave rise to a treaty regime of nonproliferation binding most states in the world to forego an option to acquire nuclear weapons in exchange for a promise to have unimpeded access to nuclear technology for peaceful uses. This arrangement amounts to an ingenious geopolitical mind game that rests on the (mis)impression that the real danger of nuclear weapons comes from the countries that don't presently possess these weapons but might acquire them in the future, rather than from the countries that continue to possess, deploy, develop the weaponry, and have strategic plans calling for their threat and even use. It is an extraordinary ongoing diplomacy of deception that the nuclear weapons states, particularly the United States, have used in dealing with the rest of the world ever since 1945 with only minor defections despite its obvious encoding of a world of grossly unequal sovereign states that contradicts the promise of sovereign equality embedded in the UN Charter.

The Nuclear Nonproliferation Treaty that entered into force in 1970 gave rise to a legal regime that was superficially based on a mutuality of rights and duties among the parties that were all sovereign states. The nuclear weapons states pledged in Article VI to get rid of their weapons by immediately entering into good faith nuclear disarmament negotiations in exchange for the commitment by non-nuclear states to forgo their nuclear weapons option, although not unconditionally, as a provision of the treaty explicitly permitted withdrawal from the treaty whenever a party to the treaty believed that its supreme national interests required such a move. In effect, the negotiated treaty seemed like a balanced legal instrument that treated the condition of nuclear "haves" and "have-nots" as a temporary circumstance that was justified as a transitional way of freezing the acquisition process while allowing the nuclear weapons states the time needed to negotiate a nuclear disarmament treaty among themselves.

What has happened in practice over the course of more than forty years is to expose the NPT as a sham, at least from a Westphalian perspective. In effect, a geopolitically administered regime of hard power politics overrode the NPT, especially in two respects: first, the obligation to seek elimination of the weapons by way of disarmament was ignored by the nuclear weapons states, and secondly, a second mind game was devised called "arms control" that pretended to be taking steps on the path to nuclear disarmament, but was in reality a means of doing the opposite — stabilizing the nuclear weapons status quo, perhaps at lower quantitative levels, but definitely without moving toward the elimination of the weaponry. Arms control measures were agreed upon from time to time to avoid expensive and risky extensions of the rivalry between nuclear weapons states, and to satisfy the public relations dimensions of the insistence by nuclear weapons states that their governments were sincerely seeking a world without nuclear weaponry. Arms control measures, while possibly reducing risks of nuclear war, should never have been treated as fulfilling the treaty obligation of the nuclear weapons states to work diligently toward the elimination of the weaponry altogether.

Beyond this, the geopolitical management of the NPT was selective, discriminatory, and coercive. Some non-nuclear weapon states were allowed to stay outside the treaty framework, and even their stealth acquisition of the weaponry was overlooked, while others were not only subject to the inspection provisions of the NPT but could become targets of military intervention if suspected or even just accused of seeking to acquire nuclear weapons of their own. India, Pakistan, Israel, and North Korea each jumped the barriers of prohibition with minimum backlash. The most prominent example of enforcing nonproliferation was the 2003 aggression against Iraq based on mistaken and misleading pretenses, possibly knowingly so – that Iraq was secretly acting to acquire the weaponry and already possessed stockpiles of chemical and biological weapons. As Iraq was previously classified by the U.S. government as a member of the "axis of evil" it became an obvious candidate for counter-proliferation in the form of military aggression. Subsequently, a similar beating of war drums against Iran, another member of the axis of evil, threatened war to disrupt an alleged Iranian quest for the bomb. This represents a further confirmation that the NPT is a legal regime that is enforced beyond the bounds of the treaty or of international law whenever it serves the geopolitical interests of the United States, or as in this instance, its regional partner, Israel. So this pattern of unequal enforcement, either being excessive in some cases and non-existent in others, illustrates this double-edged nature of international law under current conditions of world order, which constitutes the global governance framework. Namely the legal text prescribes a set of conditions that follows from Westphalian diplomacy based on sovereign equality and the geopolitical regime governing nuclear weaponry is driven by inconsistent considerations of affinity and hostility toward particular countries, with resulting patterns of selective and discriminatory enforcement and non-enforcement.[14]

Another telling example is connected with international criminal accountability of political leaders with respect to the laws of war and the obligation to refrain from the commission of crimes against humanity. This idea of individual criminal accountability was initiated as a practical matter after World War II when German and Japanese leaders were held criminally accountable in elaborate trials held at Nuremberg and Tokyo.[15] These legal proceedings have been appropriately criticized as "victors justice," even though those accused were given fair trials and available evidence demonstrated that the charges of crimes under international law were well enough documented to validate conviction and punishment. The deficiency was not a matter of convicting the innocent, but rather a failure to indict and prosecute those among the victors who were also guilty.

If the idea of criminal accountability is to be treated as part of the legal order, there should be no impunity for the victors in a war, including in a "just war." In relation to World War II, the atomic bombs dropped on Hiroshima and Nagasaki were certainly one of the most shocking atrocities of World War II, and yet because committed by the victorious powers there was no impulse whatsoever to question the legality of the use of such weapons, much less a willingness to consider criminal action against those that authorized the bombs to be dropped on Japanese cities crowded with civilians at a stage in the conflict when diplomacy could have ended the war.

In his final statement to the court at Nuremberg the American prosecutor, Justice Robert Jackson, made what I've called the Nuremberg promise, that those who sat in judgment of the German (and in separate proceedings, the Japanese leaders) would in the future be subject to those same principles, that same framework, as applied to the Nazi defendants, or otherwise this trial would lack legitimacy. The German philosopher Karl Jaspers, in his *The Question of German Guilt*, makes this argument even more cogently and comprehensively than Justice Jackson. Jaspers very persuasively sets forth his acceptance of the idea that German leaders were properly punished because they were truly responsible for engaging in criminal conduct.[16] And global rule of law really depends on holding those who act for the state accountable, but if this accountability is not based on the logic of equality then it lacks legitimacy as acceptable law.

The integrity of law depends on treating equals equally, and so whenever equals are treated unequally there arises a realization that the process of exacting justice as defined by international criminal law is subordinated to the self-serving geopolitical realities of the situation. We have no problem thinking about leaders like Saddam Hussein or Slobodan Milosevic as properly subject to this framework of international criminal accountability. But when it comes to imposing criminal responsibility on Tony Blair or George W. Bush for waging an aggressive war in Iraq or for the authorizing of torture in the war on terror we realize that even paragons of liberal legality refuse to question this departure from the probity of law. The ideas of treating equals equally is kept out of our collective consciousness as we are accustomed to dealing with these issues of fundamental justice with deference to hierarchy and discrimination, through a prism distorted by what Harold Lasswell called "the nationalization of truth." The Jackson/Jaspers conditional acceptance of victors' justice in the World War II context was coupled with the insistence that the approach taken at Nuremberg must be later validated by a genuine legal regime of accountability that did treat equals equally. In effect, the one-sidedness of the Nuremberg approach needed to be erased by a credible willingness of the World War II victors to submit their own behavior to similar standards of accountability in the future. To posit such an expectation was an acknowledgement of the problem of legitimacy posed by victors' justice. It was also a naive exercise in wishful thinking about the prospects for overcoming such impunity in the future. This display of wishful thinking reflected a failure to realize that the operation of geopolitics set and continues to set firm limits on the application of international criminal law to those who manage hard power in world politics.

In 1945, and ever since, there never existed a basis for an expectation that victors in a major war would allow themselves or their allies to be criminally prosecuted, especially in an international venue in relation to the war policies. It is true that some battlefield war crimes were prosecuted even if committed by the winning side, although infrequently and with mild punishments inflicted as compared to what was done to the losers. In the aftermath of the Bush presidency, there was some murmuring that the Obama administration would at least examine whether grounds existed for national criminal prosecutions of the perpetrators of torture and other abuses, but it never got very far. Those who controlled the policy space agreed that any effort to hold the Bush leadership accountable for relying on torture in addressing terrorist suspects or other alleged violations of international law would be extremely divisive within the United States, even to the point of making governance problematic.

A third issue area where the geopolitical dimension of global governance evokes great suspicion from the perspective of international law relates to international uses of force for allegedly humanitarian purposes. It is illustrated by the legal debate surrounding the issue of humanitarian intervention, which can be illustrated by reference to the UN-backed NATO intervention in Libya during 2011. The United Nations Security Council at the time reluctantly authorized a no-fly zone that was argued, probably correctly, to be urgently required to protect the people of the city of Benghazi from an imminent massacre conducted by the Qaddafi regime.[17] This humanitarian undertaking was quickly transformed into a sustained effort to change the outcome of an internal civil war, which appeared to be the intention of the intervenors all along, but was never acknowledged during the UN debate or authorized in the vote approving of a limited humanitarian mission. Such a manipulation of international law and UN diplomacy was not only an abandonment of the rule of law by a mission but also a maneuver that greatly exceeded the scope of the UN mandate. This failure to abide by the terms of what the UN Security Council authorized undermines confidence in the capacity of the UN to impose agreed limits on the use of force. It also erodes trust in whether those proposing a humanitarian undertaking are disclosing the full range of their motivations and goals.

There are other issues raised as well. First of all, the UN is exposed as unable to protect its constitutional integrity by its failure to challenge such a blatant disregard of a limited mandate to use force with UN blessings. The same disregard also went unchallenged in the operational autonomy exercised by the American-led coalition in the first Gulf War of 1991. More seriously, perhaps, is the degree to which such expanded uses of force challenges in a specific instance the dynamics of self-determination as the basis for post-colonial governance within sovereign states. After all, the right of self-determination is set forth in a common Article 1 in both human rights Covenants, and deemed inalienable.

This broader reliance on intervention also is one more instance of a generally dysfunctional effort to achieve hard power resolutions of conflicts as a means of controlling political outcomes. Over and over again reliance on hard power since the end of World War II has proved a failure, either producing an adverse outcome to that supported by the intervention or intensifying civil strife at great human cost. The Afghanistan War, which began over ten years ago, is a prototypical example of a situation in which the imposition of military power yields chaos and resistance, and is likely to end up with political results that deviate sharply from Washington's hopes and expectations in 2002 when the war was initiated. Properly understood this declining agency of military superiority is an encouraging underlying historical development that has been almost completely suppressed and unacknowledged by political realism. As a result the effort to restore the policy relevance of the interventionist option for diplomacy is an ongoing effort of the Beltway crowd of Washington think tank experts and policy wonks.[18] Realism continues to provide the operative code for shaping the foreign policy of geopolitical actors, especially the United States and Israel despite the costly failure rate and the heavy human costs imposed by such war making.

REFRAMING THE SEARCH FOR
POLICY IN A GLOBALIZING WORLD

My essential argument is that we need a revised horizoning to underpin global governance if it is to be effective and more in line with broadly shared ethical values and ecological limits. A shift in emphasis away from what might be called "scientific" knowledge, that is reliance on empirical observation, data, history that can be useful for understanding the past, coupled with a greater reliance on "normative knowledge": the resources of the political, moral, cultural and spiritual imagination, which need to be historically and culturally interpreted and applied. It also follows from Stephen Gill's observations in his *Global Crises and the Crisis of Global Leadership* concerning the persistence of an Orientalist epistemology that continues to control Western thought despite the collapse of the colonial structure.[19] For constructive results, it is essential that this kind of normative knowledge be informed by de-Westernized outlooks and perspectives. The rise of the non-West is changing the geopolitical landscape, and will increasingly influence approaches to how conflict and policy should be addressed and resolved. Already China and Russia, and to a lesser extent Brazil and India, are challenging the U.S. disposition to use military force under UN auspices, and such opposition is likely to increase in the future.

Such a civilizational expansion of inclusion in the geopolitical hierarchy contains promise for the future quality of world order. This promise would be expressed by bringing the operative meaning of basic legal norms, procedures, and institutions, into greater harmony with ideas of global justice, especially in relation to the use of force and the regulatory governance of the world economy. Non-Western opposition to American militarism is likely to encourage much more fidelity to the logic of equality as the foundation of law and legitimacy, as well as to view with greater respect the constraints on the use of force written into the UN Charter and confirmed by the International Court of Justice.

It remains an open question as to whether it will become politically opportune to raise anew issues that are deeply embedded in the existing legal frameworks, constitutional frameworks which to some extent creates the illusion that the logic of equality really controls international behavior rather than the geopolitical logic of inequality. For instance the UN Charter prohibits violent geopolitics by restricting permissible uses of force to self-defense or to enforcement undertakings expressly authorized by the Security Council. Recourse to non-defensive force is categorically prohibited in Article 2(4) of the UN Charter, an authoritative treaty. But this narrowing of discretion to rely on force in world politics has been completely ignored by the practice of violent geopolitics.

Reverting to the earlier critique of realist foreign policy it is reasonable to conclude that in important respects the horizon of desire was earlier influential in drafting the UN Charter as an authoritative legal text that was supposed to guide states in the future. It is a matter of bringing the dormant to life in a behavioral sense, reinforced increasingly by considerations derived from horizons of necessity. The language set forth in the Preamble to the Charter announces that the main purpose of the UN was to save succeeding generations from the scourge of war. The UN was established in the aftermath of a highly destructive war as a war prevention system and in its inception was not seen as an organization that would play a major role in mandating military intervention designed to impose political solutions on conflicts internal to sovereign states. In fact it seemed substantially precluded from doing so by Article 2(7), which prohibited the UN from intervening in the internal affairs of member states unless there was a direct bearing on international peace and security. The UN Charter offers one important illustration of the degree to which horizons of desire are already present in the constitutional framing of world order. This offers a potentiality for realizing this logic of equality and reciprocity, which is both an essential aspect of international law, and the basis for the pursuit of global justice in what remains a state-centric world.

But the situation is not so clear. The UN Charter sends mixed signals by walking a constitutional tightrope between affirming the equality of states and accommodating the hierarchical claims of geopolitics. A geopolitical dimension in the clearest form imaginable legalizes inequality through conferring a right of veto upon the five permanent members of the Security Council. It should be obvious that from the perspective of law and legitimacy the veto provides an all-purpose exemption from the duty to obey the Charter, as well as gives permanent members an instrument that can block any action whatsoever by the Security Council. This veto power represents an extraordinary form of deference to hard power thinking and the logic of hierarchy that lie at the core of political realism. The veto also abandons even the pretense that these five victorious countries of World War II should be subject to the same rules as the rest of the international community. This accommodation of geopolitics was deliberately built into the Charter by the architects of the post-World War II arrangements. It was part of a wider effort to learn from the mistakes made by the League of Nations. It was believed in 1945 by American leaders and others that it had been a huge error in 1918 not to acknowledge formally the managerial role played by major states, which was why several of the most powerful countries (including the United States) were either unwilling to join or quick to withdraw from the League when their positions opposed the policies of a major state. In this regard, the veto was a means of enticing and sustaining membership, and it worked, as all major states joined and have remained members of the UN.

Another context where horizons of desire are already present in an authoritative legal form is in Articles 25 and 28 of the Universal Declaration of Human Rights, a clear illustration of what Baxi in his chapter discusses under the rubric of "sentimental popular reason." Article 25 promises every human being a standard of living adequate to meet basic human needs, including housing, education, social security, disability, and old age. This is a radical promise given the extent of impoverishment throughout the world and taking account of the wide disparities of circumstance that existed at the time the Universal Declaration was agreed upon. At the same time the Universal Declaration is an authoritative text that, although initially in the form of a mere "declaration," is more recently widely viewed by human rights specialists as expressive of customary international law. Article 28 is even more ambitious because it says that it is itself a human right to have an international order that is adequate for the realization for all other human rights. Such a normative promise implicitly passes judgment on the existing hierarchical, exploitative form of world order that then existed and has evolved without lessening its features inconsistent with the normative promise of providing a framework hospitable to the fulfillment of human rights in general. Article 28 reminds us that within this commitment to a just world order is a promise, if it were to be actualized, of an existentially just society. Of course, Article 28 has remained through the years no more than a dormant, often forgotten, potentiality, that is not seen by those acting within horizons of feasibility, and probably not, even from those critical voices invoking horizons of necessity. We need to ask ourselves and others what set of circumstances would make such a dormant set of circumstances assume a behavioral role as catalyst for dramatic global reform.

CONCLUDING CONJECTURES

I think three tentative conclusions emerge from thinking about law and legitimacy as it pertains to the future of global governance:

1. An affirmation of the centrality of normative knowledge and a corresponding downgrading of the reliability of what is customarily regarded to be scientific knowledge. With such an understanding a growing dependence on Baxi's extension of reason to encompass sentimental popular reason and insurgent reason, and their challenge to the authority of public reason as generally understood.[20]
2. A recognition of the gradual ascendancy of soft or normative power, that is, based on cultural values, ethical norms, and the guidelines of law, as the principal agent of historical change. Additionally, an appreciation of the narrowing efficacy of hard power as the source of either stability or change.

3. A shift away from West-centric set of priorities and orienta-
    tions in the conduct of world politics both in the pathways of
    traditional diplomacy and in such sites of policy formation as
    the UN, regional arrangements, and private sector initiatives.

Against this background I would propose the further observation
that this projected ascendancy and positive potentiality of soft
power is utterly dependent on popular mobilization. It will not
occur, at least at early stages, through the efforts of the managerial and leadership classes who are wedded by habit and interests
to the status quo. The soft power range of options offers a much
more hopeful alternative than relying on the enlightened behavior
of governments or actors and other political and economic elites.[21]
Governmental actors and their private sector allies remain, in my
view, helplessly addicted to hard power solutions.

This addiction is expressed by the continuing over-invest-
ment in military options and as with any addict the psychological
dynamics of denial preclude confronting the record of failure
and disappointment. As a result these elites keep repeating the
same type of political failure, although each iteration has distinguishing features of context. The United States, for instance,
learned nothing of its defeat it suffered in Vietnam, nothing
except to disguise that defeat and try to repeat the experience but
corrected by tweaking doctrine, changing tactics, and introducing
new battlefield weaponry. There is no doubt that hard power was
efficient and effective in the colonizing wars of the nineteenth
century, but has lost its edge since the middle of the twentieth due
to the mobilization of nationalist resistance that neutralizes the
impacts of military superiority.

There exists a new confidence in the capacity of people to
shape their future. And it has taken two principal forms. The first

form is what I call "legitimacy wars" and really derives from the Gandhian understanding that an innovative reliance on nonviolent popular militancy can often prevail over oppressive political conditions, but only after a difficult and often prolonged struggle. This understanding laid the foundation of the anti-apartheid campaign of the 1980s and early 1990s that was waged on a symbolic global battlefield through tactics of boycott, divestment, and sanctions that did what was seen through the prism of feasibility as a political impossibility. That is, achieving a mainly nonviolent *political* transformation of the South African racist regime was a stunning precedent for soft power ascendancy.[22]

Similar tactics are now being increasingly relied upon by the worldwide Palestinian Solidarity movement. This Palestinian campaign symbolically views the entire world as a battleground and emphasizes the legitimacy of Palestinian aspirations and the illegitimacy of Israeli policies obstructing the attainment of Palestinian rights. The principal instruments of Palestinian soft power, additional to the resistance and steadfastness of Palestinians, have been the boycott, divestment and sanctions movement, which is growing impressively on a global scale. Another tactic has been the formation of "freedom flotillas" (civil society convoys of unarmed small ships) that seek to deliver humanitarian assistance to the long blockaded people of Gaza, as well as expose the unlawfulness and immorality of the blockade that has lasted for more than five years. Such an initiative is attempting to relieve people from a condition of unlawful collective punishment that neither the interstate system nor the UN is willing or able to do. In other words, the nonviolent energy underneath these "legitimacy wars" is filling a normative vacuum created by the failure of states and international institutions to implement the most fundamental rights of people. And to say that the people of Libya should be protected and that the people of Gaza should be ignored is to succumb to a geopolitical calculus of value that is corrosive of any search for global justice.

The other phenomenon that I think offers us a genuine foundation for hope is what has been called the "Arab Spring," this series of upheavals that are continuing to unfold in various ways throughout the Arab world and beyond, although with admittedly troublesome backlash aspects. Even the youth protests in Spain and Madrid, as well as the Occupy Movement, are spillovers from the Arab Spring. *Time* magazine, interestingly, even if misleadingly, selected Wael Ghonim the Egyptian Google executive, as the most influential person in the world of 2011. This is probably a misperception as to how the Egyptian uprising was shaped, which was self-consciously leaderless, but it is a perceptive recognition of the emergence of soft power ascendancy in this historical period. Mohammed Bouazizi, the young vegetable vendor who fatally set himself on fire in a small interior Tunisian city represents another less conscious aspect of soft power. His act of personal desperation turned out to be the match that lit the revolutionary flames that swept across the region, presumably because his bold gesture catalyzed the dormant desperation of many others. It is clear that despite the unfinished and uncertain character of the outcome of these events, remarkable and irreversible achievements have taken place. While visiting Egypt shortly after Mubarak's fall in 2011, a consistent line of responses from people who had participated as activists in the uprising, and who otherwise had very diverse views, was a sense of surprise. None thought that they would ever live to witness a robust and effective challenge from the Egyptian people to the regime that would manage actually to get rid of the hated Mubarak leadership. Such an outcome was seen as something beyond their capacity to imagine until after it happened, and maybe while it was happening. Now it must be acknowledged, the effects of counter-revolution seem determinative of Egypt's near term future.

Let me end this chapter with three generalizations. First of all that we are living in a period of great turmoil and contradiction, that makes any kind of predictive future particularly untrustworthy and even makes interpretations of the present radically uncertain, precisely because they are incapable of anticipating the implausible which is likely to be very prominent in shaping the future. Secondly, we are also living in a period of severe danger and high risk because governmental forces and the global economic order confine their gaze to horizons of short-term feasibility despite the global scale and longer time span of validated dangers. Entrenched elites, in the spirit of neoliberal globalization-from-above, confine their ambitions to caretaker and facilitative roles: the maintenance of unjust, wasteful and unsustainable structures of hierarchy, inequality, and exploitation. And thirdly, and in a sense dialectically, we are living in a period of great excitement and hope that derives from the decline of hard power, the recovery of confidence in people-driven, nonviolent forms of political mobilization and an emergent ambitious popular subjectivity, and the preliminary envisioning of a just world order based on a logic of human dignity, legal equality, and overall legitimacy. These goals presuppose a strong engagement with horizons of necessity and desire, and provide our best ground for hope about the future, but depend on a double affirmation: affirming what I call the "politics of impossibility," because public space seems frighteningly dominated by "crackpot realism" and various expressions of desperation that avoid rather than respond to real world challenges.

What I am insisting upon as necessary and desirable is treated as utopian, and even dystopian, by the guardians of the domains of feasibility, that is, as fanciful and unattainable. I counter by advocating the politics of impossibility, which admits that if feasibility is the criterion of action, our civilizational and biological destiny as a species is darkening. Embracing the impossible as necessary and desirable depends on an ethical and spiritual commitment to activate the potential of long-term legitimacy when undertaking the reshaping of global governance. It seems right from this perspective to end with some inspiring words from the most renowned spiritual figure in the Western religious counter-tradition, namely St. Francis: "start by doing what's necessary, then what's possible and suddenly you are doing the impossible."

6

RESPONDING TO
THE GLOBAL CRISIS

LIVING TOGETHER ON THE PLANET

Jacques Derrida in an essay resonant with implications asks the central question as to "how we might live together well on this planet."[1] He notes that the global circumstance establishes an unavoidable condition of living together, whether justly or unjustly, peacefully or belligerently, prudently or imprudently. It is a matter of historical interpretation how human societies have lived together in the past, even when not in direct contact. The developments in transportation, communications, and organization over the course of the last few centuries have altered our sense for better and worse of what it means, and might mean, to live together. I think it is not controversial to conclude that the human species has never managed to live together well, although certainly some periods are clearly worse than others. Whether humans have the capacity to live together well even in small communities is certainly an open question, with a skeptical response seeming to follow from any comprehensive look at past history.[2]

The utopian tradition has tried to supply visions of how the collective life of the species might be enhanced, offering an imaginative response to the Derrida challenge. The most abiding vision of utopia is based on the establishment of relatively small communities that establish their own ethos of harmony with each other and with nature, usually based on principles of equality, modesty of lifestyle, and nonviolence.[3] Such a mode of planetary living together is paradoxically based on living apart from larger collectivities that dominate modern society as a result of continuing urbanization. It also seeks to establish models of self-sufficiency that have minimal reliance on external resources and are thus far less vulnerable to outside pressures brought about by scarcities. Their autonomy insulates such communities from demands associated with an overarching commitment to the wellbeing and harmony of the species as a whole.

There is a second tradition of utopian political thought that is convinced that living together tolerably well presumes, perhaps necessitates, political unification generally taking the form of world government. This outlook rests on the belief that current political divisions, accompanied by the reality of autonomous sovereign states, generates conflict and warfare.[4] This understanding of the global situation has led some to believe that the fundamental obstacle to living together well arises from this governmental deficit that can be addressed by establishing stronger global institutions underpinned by a constitutional arrangement and capable of upholding international law, especially on matters of peace and security.[5]

A third tradition of utopian thought emphasized the aftermath of colonialism as creating a new development agenda that would address issues of poverty and global inequality, especially emphasizing the emergence of non-Western societies and the establishment of a more cosmopolitan and egalitarian ethos and praxis of world order.[6]

In the modern period, these utopian strivings have never achieved the status of a political project. The dominant tradition of theorizing has been beholden to the persistence of a state-centric world order in which hopes are pinned on moderation, cooperation for mutual benefit, countervailing or balanced power, and above all, prudent self-restraint on the part of the main power-wielders.[7] A cruder version of such perspectives is associated with the fatalistic traditions of political realism that views war and its prevention as the main drivers of history in a human setting in which individuals and states pursue their self-interest by rational means, but without heeding the constraining impacts of law and morality.[8] The best that human society can do according to these fatalistic realists is to build a fragile form of sustainable world order that provides security for the dominant states on the basis of a mixture of fear, threat, and more recently, surveillance. This kind of living together is very much the narrative of the present, and reflects the effects and character of technological innovation on the organization of war and peace, especially digitization.

More than two centuries ago Immanual Kant authored an essay entitled "Perpetual Peace," in which he envisioned a world of states that did find a way to reconcile the persistence of states as the fundamental form of political community with the vision of a warless world. His "democratic peace" theory was based on the spread of republican democracy, reinforced by demilitarization, the binding ties of commerce, and a cosmopolitan spirit of hospitality toward strangers.[9] As Michael Doyle has influentially argued, democracies seem disposed not to wage war against other democracies, although they are quite often disposed to engage in aggression against non-democratic adversaries. The appeal of this Kantian path is that it neither requires reliance on an all-powerful world state nor makes the existence of a peaceful world dependent upon the prior establishment of humane governance within territorial communities.

Some argue, and I would situate myself among them, that the advent of nuclear weaponry, exposed an apocalyptic facet of the intolerability of current modes of living together in a world dominated by sovereign states.[10] Even before nuclear weaponry, the destructiveness of warfare made many question whether the war system of security was any longer morally tolerable. What nuclear weaponry did was to raise the more fundamental question of whether such a state-centric system and larger civilizational wholes were sustainable, besides being intolerable.[11]

This question is posed more pointedly by the prospects of catastrophic climate change arising from the buildup over time of greenhouse gasses in the earth's atmosphere.[12] In both instances, there exists an option of renouncing nuclear weaponry and regulating emissions associated with industrial activities, but despite the recognition of the gravity of the threats to the human future, the political will required to make these adjustments is absent. If this is so, a space traveler from elsewhere in the universe may someday write an epitaph for the species: "unable to live together any longer" or simply, "the disastrous effects of living together badly." I am not prepared to accept such a discouraging reading of the future, and do maintain that human society can learn to manage its problems tolerably and sustainably, but only if certain politically difficult adjustments can be made. These aspirations fall somewhat short of Derrida's ambitious framing of the question, but not as much as it might appear. It will not be possible to achieve a world without nuclear weapons and massive poverty or to address climate change responsibly without finding alternate ways of living together individually and collectively other than those that are associated with modernity, Western consumerism, and the linkage of security and war. In effect, to respond effectively to horizons of necessity that constitute the crux of the deepening global crisis will depend on developing from almost zero a serious political responsiveness to horizons of desire. In this understanding, horizons of feasibility (politics as the art of the possible) will need to be declared irrelevant or worse, a smoke-screen that subordinates the severity of the challenges to habitual modes of operation. Only a politics of impossibility premised on necessity and desire can offer hope for living together well enough to overcome the intolerable aspects of the present and the well-evidenced prospects of an unsustainable future.

In effect, then, the question of living together well becomes a normative inquiry as well as an empirical one.[13] We can no longer be confident of living together at all unless we can learn to live together better, even if not well. This is a new defining feature of the human condition in the early twenty-first century, and has never existed before, at least in modern times where only fragments of the whole were faced with survival threats.[14] Such threats dwell in a domain of uncertainty as to their magnitude and probability, and efforts at quantification are misleading, and tend to be unreliable.[15] What will count most is whether a credible reframing of political life can find effective ways to reduce risks of catastrophic disruption from human causes without producing a regressive backlash.

That is, it is no longer adequate for scholars and policymakers to explain how the state-centric or Westphalian System operates in its current historical phase, including providing some recommendations to enhance peace, stability, and justice.[16] What is needed now is the development of a set of structural and normative changes that cannot be brought about without a paradigm shift that is an expression of what might be best understood as a *postmodern global imaginary*. This postmodern imaginary would exhibit a reorienting of political consciousness to take much fuller account of the wellbeing of the *whole* (the world) as well as remaining attentive to the viewpoints of the *parts* (sovereign states). The modern imaginary is dominated by the goals and values of those who represent sovereign states, which is expressed in foreign policy by the privileging of national interests and transnational capital efficiency, as well as by extremely weak mechanisms for promoting collective goods.[17] This modern imaginary has its *horizontal* dimension premised on the juridical equality of states in interaction with the *vertical* dimension resting on the geopolitical inequality of states.

RECONFIGURING THE GLOBAL IMAGINARY: A POSTMODERN PARADIGM

As suggested, the study and practice of world politics as perceived by the modern state-centric paradigm is increasingly dysfunctional from the perspective of long-term sustainability.[18] On this basis, the current crisis in global policymaking and problem solving is essentially insoluble. To begin the process of thought outside this anachronistic realist box requires the "as if" postulation of an alternative paradigm more reflective of globalizing developments, especially sustainability and equity challenges.

From empirical to normative cognitive mapping

The political understanding of the world continues to be mainly shaped by the modern paradigm that is derived from the anarchical premises of state-centrism. There were two versions: the dominant notion of sovereign territorial states as exclusively constitutive of world order for the indefinite future; the secondary idea that although states remained the most significant source of order and power, there was a slow evolution taking place toward a more complex reality in which civilizations, regions, and international institutions played a growing role in accommodating complexity, interdependence, and fragility of the contemporary world and are assisted or opposed by the increasing role and leverage of transnational criminal organizations, extremist movements, and civil society organization.

The insufficiency of this modern paradigm is associated with its underestimation of the scope and depth of global scale challenges, and with the related inability of the modern paradigm to generate solutions that are responsive to personal and collective goals of sustainability, stability, spirituality, and equity.[19] Positing an alternative postmodern paradigm then is defined by reference to filling this gap between what "is" and what "is needed," which is essentially a capability to shape and implement policies that serve the common and most enduring interests and desires of humanity. Without such a capability the challenges posed by the possession of nuclear weaponry, climate change, world economy, massive poverty, and others cannot be met. This is, then, a *normative* assessment that the mechanisms presently operative within a state-centric world order will fail unless supplemented in coming decades by a more geo-centric world order.

From borders to limits

The modern paradigm that continues to shape our thought and policy on global issues perceives problems and challenges through a state-centric optic that is preoccupied with bounded territorial space. The rather simple ordering logic associated with this optic is that the territorial sovereign is exclusively autonomous within its borders, and that in those settings that are not territorial – oceans and outer space – there is complete freedom to use limited only by the duty to respect the freedom of others. There are two assumptions that are built into this modern allocation of formal authority to govern. The first is that what the state does territorially will not cause serious harm elsewhere, and therefore its governance policies are not subject to any international restrictions on its freedom of action other than those to which it has given consent. The second is that the claims to act in the global commons can all be accommodated, that a condition of abundance ("enough for all") exists. Reducing this conception of world order to its essential properties implied unlimited authority within states, unlimited freedom outside states.

Borders were the defining reality of the old paradigm. Of course, there were complications that made the total picture less clear: the inequality of states, discretionary warfare, polar regions, 200-mile exclusive economic zones. And yet the maps that imaged political reality and were inscribed in political consciousness, and given expression in the rules and principles of international law, reflected this fundamental picture of a world of borders separating sovereign territorial entities. Border management sought control over entry and exit, and citizenship and nationalist ideologies generated bonds between governments and people within these territorial enclosures.

From the middle of the last century this kind of fragmentation of the earth became increasingly problematic in multiple respects. Perhaps, most dramatically, it is possible to anchor the argument in two cataclysmic happenings: the Holocaust brought about by the savagery of Nazi genocide; the atomic bombings of Japanese cities at the end of World War II. What these happenings demonstrated was the unacceptability of relying on the logic of state-centricism, and the need for some unconditional outer *limits*. In response, gestures were made to acknowledge this perception. The Universal Declaration of Human Rights implied the view, although without enforcement prospects, that the internal governance of states was subject to specified limits, and if these were exceeded, then respect for sovereignty was at risk. Similarly, proposals for nuclear disarmament were premised on the need to rid the world of such destructive weaponry, and if not, to put severe limits on the right to use even if the security of the state was at stake.[20]

With the advent of globalization, the rise of mega-terrorism, and climate change concerns, this emphasis on limits, and the claims of a borderless world have greatly increased in relevance. It is my assessment that it has become appropriate to contend that only an optic that can comprehend the global interest and the human interest is compatible with sustainability and any hope for achieving a world order that is more peaceful and just. Such a position implies a paradigm shift in prevailing political consciousness that is urgently needed, yet not at all likely to exert enough influence to reshape behavior for the foreseeable future. This gap between what is needed and what is likely is disguised by denial, extremism, and various forms of escapism, and so the peoples of the world are exposed to intensifying risks of expanding magnitudes.

Such a pessimistic conclusion is supported by the continued vitality of state-centric decision-making in relation to global policy. As a result, the limit conditions that should be providing the guidelines for sustainable and acceptable behavior are consistently ignored. Statist logic continues to prevail whether it is a matter of regulating the activities of the global marketplace, prohibiting reliance on nuclear weapons for state security, restricting carbon emissions, or preventing genocidal behavior. The dominant states are particularly myopic, having been long accustomed to pursuing their interests without any systemic constraints. And this statist logic, with the instruments at the disposal of governments, acknowledges the problems rhetorically but is at a loss to find viable solutions. Instead, what is done is to test limits in ways that pose devastating dangers for the future, including drone technology, cyberwarfare, neoliberal global economics, fracking for natural gas and deep sea drilling for oil in fragile eco-systems, genetically modified foods, population growth, and per capita and aggregate economic growth. These "fixes" are based on the practices and worldview of states, as enhanced by technological innovation and guided by materialist ambitions, and despite their poor results and the shrill warnings surrounding continued reliance, are unlikely to be superseded anytime soon by any concerted attempt to base global policy on the human interest.[21]

From citizen to global citizen to citizen pilgrim

The paradigm shift must also engage individuals and reshape the societal ethos. At present, the typical citizen is socialized by reference to a nationalist ideology, which aligns a citizen's perspective with a national interest perspective on global policy issues. Such an orientation creates a political climate in which governmental actors, especially in democratic societies, need to act to minimize burdens and maximize benefits for its national human community in all international transactions. This embedded code of conduct is reinforced by the ideals of patriotism, the primacy of national security, and the criminalization of treason.

These behavioral features, which are deeply embedded in the state-centric structure, are to an extent challenged by assertions of "global citizenship." To be sure, global citizenship can have many points of reference, but the commonality among these, is a sense of belonging to the world as much as belonging to the nation and state. It is possible to imagine, although not easy to conceive of it happening, enfranchising the people of the world to cast votes in American elections as an appropriate recognition of the extent that what happens in the United States impacts on societies throughout the world.

The notion of global citizenship is consistent with a *spatial* conception of world order, but it is less responsive to a global setting in which limit conditions are situated in the future, making *time* a crucial component of an adaptive consciousness.

For this reason I have advocated in recent years that the most constructive way to situate citizenship in our historic moment is by reference to the idea of "citizen pilgrim."[22] The intended emphasis is placed on a journey, as in a pilgrimage, to a future situation that overcomes the torments of the present and its threatening impending realities. A citizen pilgrim is conscious of the dimension of time, and also of globalized space, in exhibiting her dedication to overcoming the multifaceted challenges of the early twenty-first century by reliance on the human interest.

From part to whole

Implicit in this whole argument about a paradigm shift is the centrality of grasping what it means for the future of world politics to be able to assert and demonstrate in many contexts for the first time in human history that "the whole is greater than the sum of its parts." For the modern period an identifying feature of the system was to acknowledge that "the sum of the parts was far greater than the whole," and for most purposes there was no meaningful content for any claim suggesting the primacy of the global or the human in achieving a problem-solving solution. As already argued, the frustrating failures to shape satisfactory solutions for a series of global problems is due to a continuing dependence on state-centric mechanisms. That is, the problem-solving and policy-forming frameworks are dominated by states, and their calculations of national advantage and priorities. In certain settings, these frameworks can produce outcomes consistent with the human interests as when states bargain or compromise to achieve mutual interests. Where the perceptions of interest and the situation of actors are uneven or contradictory, then there is no path to reach an agreement.

In some settings, corporate and financial perceptions are guided by the globalization of market forces, and these can influence to a significant degree the outlook of governmental actors. It would seem that the global economy is administered in accord with the global economic interests of the private sector in promoting the efficiency of capital. Even if this were true, and there are many deviations due to the play of economic forces and the varying susceptibility to such influences by governments, the results are far from serving the human interest in either long-term sustainability or short-term equity and human security.

To make the paradigm shift operative behaviorally will require expanding the mandate and capabilities of global institutions. It will also require detaching these institutions from their current subordination to geopolitical forces associated with the vertical dimensions of state-centricism.

The UN System can perhaps be modified in structure and operating procedures to allow this transition from an organization serving the interests of sovereign states to one that serves the human interests by adopting the outlook of the whole. Among the concrete steps that would advance these goals are the following: the establishment of a popularly elected global parliament charged with advising on the human interest;[23] a global source of revenue from some transnational activity, such as international air travel or luxury goods duty; a global peace force tasked with responses to natural disasters and impending or unfolding humanitarian catastrophes that is trained to pursue nonviolent methods of conflict management and resolution. The idea behind this package of illustrative moves is intended to show what might be involved in making the global center strong enough to serve the human interest, and overcome the continuing obstacles arising from both the horizontal and vertical dimensions of state-centricism.

From "realism" to "global realism"

This proposed reorientation of perspective presupposes an altered understanding of political reality. The persisting attachment to "realism" is premised on the agency of hard power capabilities in relation to security and statist perspectives with regard to policy formation with due recognition of the inequality of states in exerting influence. The realism that is being advocated here insists on the relevance of a series of converging forces that can only be dealt with effectively by imposing global limits, thereby impinging on the territorial autonomy of sovereign states. In one sense, the reorientation does not entail an abandonment of sovereignty but a robust doctrine of globally responsible sovereignty. What this is meant to suggest is the will and capacity of political actors to favor the human interest in global policy-making arenas. Such realism to be acceptable must substantially replace coercive threats and tactics with ones that rely on persuasion and agreement, but also give the power of decision to global procedures and institutions that can operate without the approval of specific states.

Whether to claim the banner of realism for this new outlook is itself an issue to be addressed. On the one side, the relationships between a world of states, of borders, and spatial allocations, is so linked to the realist interpretation of world order that it is necessary to challenge its validity from a twenty-first-century perspective, and put forward a new set of ideas as explanatory and prescriptive.

On the other side, such ends may be better achieved by abandoning the rhetoric of state-centric world order altogether, and adopting a new label for what is being proposed. One partial adjustment might be to adopt a terminology of "global realism."

RESPONDING TO THE GLOBAL CRISIS

The evidence as to trends and prospects point to the existence of a multidimensional crisis of limits that cannot be resolved by the instruments and worldview associated with state-centric world order. At the same time, there is no basis for supposing that a transition to a more globally centered world order consistent with values associated with democratic pluralism, human rights, and social justice can be embraced as a political project at this time. Rational analysis and argument is no match for entrenched social forces and ingrained political habits. In this respect, without a cultural revolution of global scope there seems to be little basis for believing that the crisis can be overcome in an acceptable manner.

Beyond state-centrism: a negative scenario

A few years ago it seemed plausible to envision a partial transformation of state-centric world order by the emergence of the United States as an essentially non-territorial global state, with alliances and military bases spread around the world, with the commons dominated by navies in every ocean and space fully militarized. This global domination project, reinforced by the 9/11 attacks and the neo-conservative ideology that shaped foreign policy during the presidency of George W. Bush, aimed to achieve centralized control over security, including energy resources. This kind of concentration of global policymaking seemed dysutopic as it both overrode rights of self-determination and imposed a homogenizing neoliberal version of democratic governance throughout the world. In this sense, it would be unlikely that this imperial centering of authority would be sensitive to the challenges posed by the possession of nuclear weapons or the problems associated with global warming, but would on the contrary retain such weaponry and favor economic policies that would promote growth regardless of environmental harm and societal inequities.[24]

This reliance on a globalist approach to problem-solving arising from the role played by a global state seems *conceptually* to make the situation worse. It also seems empirically to be a fading prospect as the stagnant condition of the world economy combined with the inability of the United States to turn its military superiority into political outcomes in a series of wars weakens its will and capacity to achieve the requisite degree of control.[25] At the same time, the increased claim to fight its enemies on a globalized battlefield with the use of drone technology, cyberwar tactics underscored the obsolescence of state-centric conflict based on dividing zones of war and peace by reference to borders. In this respect, late modernity retains the state-centric features of the Westphalian Era that prevent a functional and equitable response to global challenges while exhibiting a post modern approach to warfare that postulates a borderless world, and acts accordingly. It is also expressed by encouraging flows of money and capital with minimal regulation by states, while restraining unwanted flows of people through the erection of walls and procedures of exclusions, converting rich states into enlarged "gated communities," and electronically monitoring borders to prevent and punish unlawful entry.

In other words, there are evident strains on the horizontal and legitimating forms of state-centric world order, while the emergence of a new radicalism with respect to vertical and legitimately dubious forms of state-centric geopolitics displays the inability and unwillingness of dominant states to operate within the playbook developed over the centuries by international law. This interface between the statist past and the increasingly globalist future is replete with contradictions and defies a pre-set ordering logic. Such a pattern strongly suggests treating the realities confronting the peoples of the world as taking place during a time of historic transition with respect to world order.

DANGERS AND OPPORTUNITIES IN A PERIOD OF TRANSITION

Horizons of feasibility[26]

These horizons of feasibility are connected with what appears to be attainable given political constraints. It is the domain of normal politics, and tends to guide politicians confronted with policy options, and is synonymous in addressing global issues with perspectives associated with realism. There is a margin of disagreement among leaders as to what constitutes the outermost horizon of feasibility and the location of this horizon shifts in times of stress, as after wars.[27] On occasion, miscalculations about the constraints produces surprises. For instance, it was supposed that a more robust response to climate change threats could be fashioned under UN auspices than has proved so far to be the case, while the establishment of an International Criminal Court seemed well beyond the reach of normal politics. There are explanations for each exception, especially after the fact. The frequency of unanticipated developments in international political life suggests the weakness of the predictive capacities of social science.

The hypothesis of this chapter is that horizons of feasibility are trapped within and conditioned by a state-centric paradigm, which as has been contended, lacks the capability to respond to the global crisis in an effective and equitable manner. In effect, an operating logic based on the interaction of sovereign states is not capable of protecting the human interest in a period of intensifying globalization, not only in relation to the economy and security, but also with respect to culture and identity.

Horizons of necessity

Even more so than is the case with feasibility, the precise location of horizons of necessity are impossible to pinpoint. Because we are dealing with likely futures, and we lack strong predictive capabilities, future projections are conjectural and likely mistaken either by underestimating or overestimating the magnitude of supposed risks. At the same time, when trends point to what a consensus of scientists identify as dangerous and harmful or when weaponry is relied upon that is capable of inflicting catastrophic damage, prudent action would strongly encourage sharply reducing such risks by all available means. What our experience in the last several decades suggests is that normal politics is not capable of reducing these risks in a manner that conforms to either an understanding of prudence or in response to such values as the avoidance of indiscriminate killing or sensitivity to the rights of future generations.

In effect, horizons of necessity cannot be accommodated by normal politics constrained by horizons of feasibility. This gap between feasibility and necessity suggests the challenges and frustrations that have been so evident in recent decades. Can this gap be closed in acceptable ways? We have dismissed as unacceptable the project of global domination by a single state, which in one sense was a realist response to the global crisis. But other ways exist to ignore or pretend to close the gap that seem to deepen the crisis rather than overcome it.

Horizons of extremism

As the public is confronted by the gap between feasibility and necessity, it will often become receptive to viewpoints that deny the magnitudes of the alleged risks or offer irrelevant ways of responding. For instance, the rise of religious authority in relation to the environment that advances the position that all that happens on earth is a matter of God's will, and there is no use for humans to try to alter this divine supervision of earthly experience. Or the world will be able to deal with such pressures as the limited reserves of fossil fuels exert by extracting natural gas and shale oil and gas from deep under the earth's surface through reliance on dangerous technological innovations. The vulnerabilities of such techniques were suggested by the BP Deep Horizon oil rig explosion in 2010 and the Fukushima reactor meltdown in 2011. The pressures to access energies both to meet consumer demand and maximize corporate profits leads to reassurances that future disasters can be avoided by making sure that technological approaches are handled more cautiously. But can we really entrust the human future to such reassurances, whether from religious or corporate sources? It seems extremely foolish and self-destructive to do so, but if we are limited to normal politics it is quite likely that religious and technological extremism will diminish even what could be achieved by acting within horizons of feasibility. It would seem that only horizons of desire have any prospect of overcoming the global crisis in ways that are effective, equitable, and of sufficient magnitude.

Horizons of desire

The gap between feasibility and necessity with respect to the protection and promotion of human interests cannot be closed by normal politics. Beyond this, it is unacceptable to close this gap by way of political unification under the auspices of a single state claiming to provide global governance for the system of states as a whole. And it seems undesirable at this stage of political evolution, and given the current degree of inequality that exists in the world, to establish a world government by a compact among states; such an outcome might become desirable if it was a result of a bottom-up democratizing process throughout all regions of the world and gave maximum expression to principles and goals of subsidiarity. The European Union's experience serves as a cautionary model, despite the acknowledgement that the main impetus from its founding was top down. The lingering financial crisis in Europe can be interpreted in many ways, including the vulnerability to crisis of international institutions when economic integration is far more advanced than political integration. In such circumstances, it is hardly surprising that when the economic order shows strains, governments are inclined to act on the basis of national interests even if the damage to other participants is serious and to regional interests may be devastating. The acute tensions between Greece and the European Union along with its most important members during 2014–15 is illustrative of how statist structures and neoliberal institutions and ideological dominance continue to control European policymaking despite the claims of regional community.

At the same time, enduring the gap increases the risks of catastrophic harm in the near future, and neglects the opportunities for enhancing the quality of life for many people throughout the world. One can think of desire by reference to the Millennium

Development Goals or the provision of electricity to the 1.5 billion persons now without reliable access. Or it is relevant to posit desire in relation to such policy issues as climate change, nuclear disarmament, and economic stabilization.

What then can be currently discerned on the horizons of desire? There are several hopeful lines of development that can only be set forth in a most superficial way here. Perhaps, most in keeping with the advocacy line being adopted, is the emergence of a global democracy movement that is enlisting grassroots support throughout the world, and was first noticed and appreciated in 2011. Whether it can persist, and grow, remains to be seen, but it does exhibit sensitivity to the human interest, including the establishment of humane forms of global governance. There is a Manifesto for Global Democracy that has been endorsed by a growing number of intellectuals and activists from around the world.[28] There are more specific transnational movements in the spheres of environment, human rights, gender equality, and peace that are animated by their attachment to the human interest and their great affinity with likeminded persons regardless of their nationality.

A second promising direction of development is by way of regionalism. If this kind of post-Westphalian world order is to become globally significant it will be important for the EU to solve its problems, including rectifying the mismatch between economic and political integration that currently exists.[29] There are significant moves toward regional cooperation and policymaking in Latin America, Africa, and Asia. Whether these advance to the point of transcending national interests without regional interests serving as a mere self-regarding replacement, and no real embodiment of human interests takes place, remains to be seen. The EU has generally acted more responsibly in relation to climate change negotiations than have most national governments, but there is as yet no evidence of a major substantive shift in political identity resulting from regionalization.

Religion is a great unknown. Each world religion contains universalizing elements that would encourage promotion of the human interest. Also, religions fit within a borderless world rather naturally, especially considering the many diasporas that have intermingled peoples of differing religious and civilizational backgrounds. The existence of religiously and ethnically defined states (Iran, Israel) is inconsistent with the loosening of ties between sovereign states and political identities.

Another significant unknown is connected with the impact of the emerging geopolitical actors constituting a more multi-polar world: China, India, Brazil, Russia, and Turkey, and possibly others.[30] These countries have risen to prominence primarily through their success in trade and investment that raised the per capita living standards of their populations, political stability, and soft power diplomacy. It may be that this softer style of geopolitics, while not attuned directly to the human interest, may provide a more sensitive recognition of the need for *limits*, which in turn could prompt more readiness to achieve cooperative and longer-term adaptation to the various kinds of scarcity that are threatening to intensify conflict and erode sustainability unless addressed from a global perspective.

CONCLUSION

The framing of world order by reference to a global crisis associated with a troublesome and highly dangerous transition from state-centric borders to globally allocated limits is a fundamental challenge that human society has never before faced on such a grand scale. Past challenges have led to the collapse and disappearance of particular civilizations, and more recently to the phenomenon of "failed states," but the reverberations of failure were confined in space, and not threatening to the system itself. These past issues also involved not living successfully in relation to the play of natural forces, some manageable, others not, while the present crisis is mainly a product of anthropocene activities: carbon emissions, population growth, nuclear weapons and nuclear energy, resource depletion.

Altering these activities in accordance with the imperatives of horizons of desire, or to meet the requirements of horizons of necessity, cannot be achieved by normal politics. In this central respect the future of humanity depends on the emergence of a populist form of global democracy that manages to encapsulate an ecumenical spirituality, which from the vantage point of the present seems to be counting on a politics of impossibility.[31] But impossibility can happen, black swans make their presence felt in countless ways throughout the world. Recent historical ruptures were not within the active political imagination of those who were credentialed experts on world politics: the fall of the Berlin Wall and the collapse of the Soviet Union; the mostly peaceful transformation of racist South Africa into a multiracial constitutional democracy; the pro-democracy Arab uprisings of 2011; the Occupy Movement. In this respect, closing the gap between feasibility and necessity seems impossible, but as is contended here, this does not mean it cannot happen.

7

TOWARD A GLOBAL IMAGINARY

A LEMMING MOMENT?

Mark Mazower ends his synoptic book devoted to Western approaches to global governance with the following mystifying words: "The idea of governing the world is becoming yesterday's dream."[1] What Mazower appears to mean is that grand alternatives to the Westphalian framework of world order, whether based on political integration, global law, supranationalism at the regional level, or functionalist visions of a networked world were at one time political projects of practical interest but have one by one been put aside after reaching some kind of dead end of disillusionment. As a result, such ambitious ideas of post-Westphalian global governance with sufficient integration for central guidance now have only "historical" relevance as examples of "yesterday's dream."

There is a counterintuitive dimension of this skeptical conclusion as never before has the need for structural, ideological, and substantive drastic modifications of the Westphalia framework seemed more needed if human security, ecological stability, human rights, and political viability are used as optics of appraisal. Reverting to Mazower's metaphor, yesterday's dream has become today's necessity, yet depressingly, he is rather convincing in his pessimistic assessment of present horizons of expectation for several reasons, especially if "the world" is conflated with "the

West": post-Cold War disillusionment with any proposals that are perceived to be utopian; a dramatic weakening of American leadership in identifying and upholding global public goods as compared to the period following World War II; overall decline of West-centric civilizational authority and self-confidence, combined with a corresponding rise to geopolitical prominence of non-Western political actors and non-state extremist political movements. These factors are reinforced by such situational developments as the prolonged world economic recession, the financial crisis and loss of confidence in the European Union, and the ironic post-Marxist materialist worldview that subordinates politics to economics in the policy priorities of democratic electorates.

Such skepticism is further reinforced by recent experience in a number of critical institutional arenas: the failure to reform the composition of the UN Security Council despite widespread agreement that the geopolitical landscape has shifted significantly since the Organization was established in 1945; the failure to make credible follow-up to Barack Obama's 2009 vision of a world without nuclear weapons, and the absence of any sustained political mobilization of support for such a prospect in civil society; and the disappointments associated with the results of annual climate change negotiations at the global level that seem incapable of translating warnings about the effects of global warming as overwhelmingly endorsed by climate scientists into an appropriate regulatory framework responsive to the challenge. These illustrations are abetted by more concrete disappointments including the failure of the UN to establish some kind of emergency peace force to address humanitarian and natural catastrophes and the refusal of the International Criminal Court (ICC) to consider allegations of criminality that involve the behavior of major state actors, especially the United States. The ICC is probably the most "utopian" undertaking since World War II at least in its presumed claim to impose standards of criminal accountability upon those who act on behalf of sovereign states, but during its first decade of operations it has deferred to the geopolitical constraints of a state-centric world, what I describe as the vertical dimension of Westphalian world order reflecting the inequality of states. This deference has been shown in a number of ways: by the refusal of the main states to become parties, by the unwillingness of the ICC or UN to challenge the impunity of those who act on behalf of these states, and by the UN inability to carry out the recommendations of the Goldstone Report, which addressed a clear instance of flagrant violations of international criminal law arising from Israel's Operation Cast Lead 2008–09 attack on Gaza.

I would like to put this discouraging picture in a framework delimited by the interaction of three horizons of expectation that I hope brings some clarity into my inquiry relating to this workshop:

1. Politics of feasibility (HF): politics as the art of the possible, what constitutes a political project with attainable goals.
2. Politics of necessity (HN): what is needed to reach certain goals that constitute urgent global public goods (e.g. nuclear disarmament; regulation of greenhouse gas emissions; poverty eradication).
3. politics of desire (HD): what would both close the gaps between feasibility and necessity, and also accord with widely endorsed human values (e.g. combining nuclear disarmament with moves toward general and complete disarmament; climate justice as an integral element in regulating GHG (greenhouse gasses) emissions and working more widely toward interactive harmony with nature; an effective

combination of providing all persons with basic needs in a manner that accords with affirming their individual dignity by providing "decent work" as a universal human right.

It is my overall argument that the gaps between HF and HN are unsustainable, although assessments of the specific timing and forms of collapse remain speculative, contested, and hidden from view, and are essentially indeterminate. It is my view that these gaps can only be closed via HD, which by means of a conceptual maneuver is situated outside of the domain of normal politics. For reasons of convenience, I label this domain as extraordinary politics, that is, politics as the art of the impossible. Further, reverting to history, the extraordinary happens in relation to many unanticipated jumps in the domain of political behavior (e.g. the end of the Cold War and the implosion of the Soviet Union; the generally peaceful transformation of apartheid South Africa into a constitutional democracy; the Arab Awakening). Such a pattern, theorized by Charles Jenks as "the jumping universe" and Talib as "the black swan" phenomenon, suggests that what seems impossible happens consistently throughout history.[2] It also should be understood that as a result of intrusions of the unanticipated, drastic regressions also occur, including catastrophic developments (e.g. the rise of Naziism, followed by the Holocaust; the successful harnessing of the atom and the evolution of nuclear weapons; the linkage between greenhouse gas emissions and global warming).

From this perspective, in the face of such perceived gaps between feasibility and necessity on matters of collective survival, it is also likely that extremist movements with bizarre solutions to global challenges will attract significant followings. Such "solutions" include divine intervention or apocalyptic design, paranoid politics that blames the danger on some fraction of humanity such as a rival religion or ethnicity. This tendency for society to be attracted to such pathological extremes seems to be what Gramsci had in mind when he warned of the appearance of "morbid symptoms" during periods of fundamental societal transition. The embrace of technogeopolitics during a period when the limits of planetary carrying capacity are being tested makes ours a time of unprecedented danger. The rise of fundamentalist religion and politics is to be expected under such conditions, making it particularly important for those dedicated to HD as conceived within broad humanist and cosmopolitan traditions of rationality to articulate and promote their understanding of how best to close the gaps between HF and HN. Such articulations must liberate reason from its Enlightenment moorings by enlargements of two kinds: incorporating the wisdom and ethics of the East and by encouraging what Upendra Baxi refers to as "insurgent reason."[3]

EXPLAINING THE GAPS

It is acknowledged that what justifies the label of "necessity" is a matter of interpretation and judgment. In this chapter, I am associating necessity positively with the improvement of the human condition as measured by widely accepted human rights standards and negatively by the goal of avoiding catastrophic damage to human wellbeing, most dramatically in relation to threats mounted against the survival of the human species and its world civilizations, as well as the avoidance and mitigation of humanitarian and natural catastrophes, respect for the carrying capacity of the earth. As far as "desire" is concerned, it is related to supplementing what is necessary with what is desirable. The desirable can be understood in relation to the promotion of health, security, empathy, and happiness or satisfaction as ends to be sought beyond the domain of mere necessity. While necessity might require constraints on aggregate economic growth that impose heavy burdens on individuals and society, desire can move in different directions by promoting fairness in the distribution of the benefits of economic growth or through education that moves toward substituting a love of nature for the gratifications provided by consumerism.

For several centuries the Westphalian framework as the foundation of world order achieved tolerable results, at least for the countries comprising the West, including exhibiting a capacity for cooperation among sovereign states and a flexibility with regard to the participation of independent states.

Among the notable achievements in these regards was the management of the global commons in a manner that accommodated diverse interests, the establishment of international institutions and procedures to facilitate cooperation among states, and the expansion of membership to accommodate the collapse of European colonialism. Of course, such a plural order was problematic if viewed from various historical standpoints in relation to horizons of desire. War, exploitation, and oppression persisted, and notions of territorial sovereignty shield states and their leaders from accountability in the event of severe violations of standards of natural justice. Even here Westphalian adaptation was evident in the development of international criminal law, including the establishment in 2002 of the International Criminal Court, war crimes tribunals, and the overall rise of international human rights in the course of the last sixty years. These undoubted achievements are diminished to a significant extent by the realization that double standards create a very uneven and geopolitically tainted record of compliance and enforcement. Impunity for the powerful, accountability for the weak exhibits this morally and legally stratified application of norms purporting to establish universal standards of behavior.

Arguably widening the gaps between horizons of feasibility and horizons of necessity occurred on the battlefields of World War I, and especially World War II, with the dramatization of this gap associated with the use of atomic bombs against Japanese cities in 1945. In theory, such a gap could be closed by reaching a verified and implemented agreement to destroy existing nuclear weapons arsenals and an accompanying pledge never to develop or possess such weapons in the future. Despite giving lip service to such a goal, a credible commitment along these lines has never existed. Instead what has taken place is the spread of these weapons to a series of leading states combined with a nonproliferation treaty that has produced a legal regime based on a two-tiered world. The treaty provisions seeks to avoid such an impression by obliging the nuclear weapons states to pursue nuclear disarmament in good faith and to share technology helpful for nuclear energy with non-nuclear weapons states. But after more than fifty years it is evident that the regime was an oligarchy among nuclear weapons states, as well as exhibiting non-compliance with the disarmament provision contained in Article VI of the NPT.[4] Given the apocalyptic scale of the risks, reliance on this structure is reckless in the extreme;[5] for an effort to overcome the gap see the trenchant analysis and proposal set forth by Daniel Deudney.[6]

An ironic feature of this evasion of the challenge of necessity in relation to nuclear weapons is to make the United States and its allies self-appointed managers of the nonproliferation regime. Such a geopolitical role, a thinly disguised implementation of the vertical side of the Westphalian logic, has eroded the legal effort to criminalize non-defensive international warfare by creating a new pretext for aggressive war. The Iraq War of 2003 was undertaken allegedly to address the prospect of an Iraqi nuclear weapons program and the continual threats directed at Iran are based on its alleged quest for nuclear weaponry. The double standards in this setting are particularly blatant as the diplomacy directed at Iran omits any mention of Israel's nuclear weapons arsenal. In effect, Westphalian efforts to address the gap between feasibility and necessity have so far avoided catastrophic consequences, but without removing unsustainable risks and inappropriate double standards over time.

There are several mutually reinforcing explanations for why this gap cannot be closed by the problem-solving mechanisms and cooperative arrangements normally effectively relied upon within the Westphalian framework. This can be best illustrated by reference to four fundamental features of the current phase of Westphalian world order, and by two aggravating situational considerations. The absence of strong central decision-making mechanisms diminishes capacity to address challenges that can best be met by giving primacy to the realization of *global interests* and the production of *global public goods*. The state-centric structure of world order is organized on the basis of the promotion of *national interests* with global public goods an incidental consideration. Robert Johansen made an important academic and normative contribution thirty years ago by encouraging American foreign policy to be shaped by an enlightened reconciliation between national and global or human interests.[7] I prefer "global interest" to "human interest" to avoid an impression of anthropocentrism, and a recognition that other aspects of global reality deserve protection, and not just for the sake of human enhancement or pleasure. In this regard, the failure to arrange for nuclear disarmament and for the control of greenhouse gas emissions is illustrative of definite and critical global challenges that are acknowledged, but not addressed. To deal adequately with such global challenges requires a major reform of present structures and processes comprising global governance with a sufficient capability to promote effectively those global interests that are visible on horizons of necessity. Such reforms can also help fulfill aspirations associated with horizons of desire (e.g. prohibition of nuclear energy facilities; GHG emissions reductions in accord with agreed criteria of climate justice).

To some extent, over the course of the Westphalian Era, less demanding global interests have been promoted effectively either because they overlapped with the national interests of major states or due to hegemonic leadership that includes some sense of responsibility for protecting global interests. There are many examples: public order of the oceans; protection of Antarctica; control of ozone depletion; avoidance of conflict in outer space and moon; international humanitarian law. The failure in relation to nuclear weapons and climate change can be partly explained because in both settings national interests did not overlap sufficiently with global interests, and hegemonic leadership was not inclined sufficiently toward producing a consensus. In these two substantive contexts the issues raised touch on the core concerns of the nation state: security by means of hard power as measured by destructive capabilities and economic growth and profitability of capital. In both instances, entrenched bureaucratic and private sector resistance to achieving global interests was a further complicating factor.

A recognition that Westphalian structures of authority are preoccupied with *borders* in the sense of defining and defending territorial limits, while the policy agenda of the twenty-first century is above all concerned with *limits* (people, growth, GHG emissions, shared use of the global commons, ecological risks – deep sea oil drilling, fracking, financial instruments; globalization; internet guidelines). The Westphalian approach is premised on sovereignty over enclosed territory and shared use in global commons, with formal autonomy the basic condition within states and freedom and reciprocity the fundamental means relied upon to arrange beneficial use outside of states. This allocation of regulatory logics works reasonably well for short-term behavior, and has been abetted by numerous networks dedicated to promoting cooperative behavior among states and non-states, but it is not well adapted to address non-territorial concerns or to deal with severe pressures on various aspects of the global commons. When dealing with limits rather than borders, time as well as space becomes a crucial element in devising and implementing an effective and humane approach.[8] The leadership of sovereign states are preoccupied with very short time cycles, and are not receptive to curtailing security or economic growth if the alleged harm is situated in the future or if the locus of harm is remote from the territorial community. For instance, global warming is unevenly distributed in such a way that the areas where the temperature rise has been greatest and most damaging is far removed from the areas of greatest per capita and aggregate GHG emissions.

A preoccupation with limits, for instance, with deference to carrying capacity of the earth, is not congenial with either the structure or ideology of current world order thinking with its nationalist and territorial dispositions.

The United States, which to an extent is a *global state* in addition to being a territorial entity due to its force projection on a global scale (network of hundreds of foreign bases; navies in every ocean; military dominance of space; CIA penetration and surveillance; special forces operations in foreign countries;

globalization of capital and finance) lacks the leadership orientation at the present time to address these challenges associated with
limits. This lack contrasts with its historic success in restoring
security and prosperity to a world of borders in the period after
World War II. The point being argued is that this relative incapacity of the United States to exert benevolent leadership is partly
conceptual (unaccustomed to think in relation to "the world" as
distinct from countries *in the* world) and partly situational (the
substitution of neoliberal for Keynesian economics; the polarization of domestic politics, and the rise of ultra-nationalist and
chauvinistic political forces, e.g. in relation to gun control).

The exclusion of non-state civil society (CS) actors from
policy forming arenas accentuates these shortcomings of Westphalian world order in the setting of the early twenty-first century.
These CS actors, especially those organized on a transnational
basis, have a natural inclination and strong motivation to reflect
commitments to global interests and global public good. Their
orientation is shaped by ideas of the *human interest* as transcending
the national interest, and an informal commitment to the reality of
"world citizenship" and of "global civil society."[9] In this respect,
the aggregate of CS actors function as, in effect, "the conscience
of humanity" in relation to global policy, despite acknowledging
divisions and tensions. The most evident expression of this CS
role has been in the context of global policy conferences on such
themes as poverty, climate change, human rights, population:
governments operate strictly within constraints set by calculations of national interest, while CS actors are mostly inclined to
shape their outlooks by reference to their perceptions of global
interests. Illustrative substantive contexts include the movements
and campaigns that built support for the Anti-Personnel Land-
mines Treaty and the establishment of the International Criminal

Court, both initiatives undertaken in the face of geopolitical resistance at various stages. To date, the institutions of world order, including the UN, have given lip service to the relevance of global civil society, but have not been willing to alter membership and participation rules and procedures to accommodate the spectacular quantitative and qualitative development of this CS dimension of world order. Similarly, proposals to move in more inclusive and democratizing directions, for instance by establishing a global peoples parliament, has not met with a positive response from within the UN and elsewhere.[10]

The rearticulation of territoriality as the defining feature of the Westphalian conception of world order. The multiple impacts of globalization include drone and cyber warfare and mega-data surveillance, space satellites, nuclear radiation, global media, transnational crime, and transnational political violence on diluting sovereign authority over territorial space. In effect, the last half-century has witnessed an extraordinarily robust trend toward the *de-territorializing* of world order. This trend is evident in the fundamental reconfiguration of conflict, which replicates the shift from conflict between territorial entities, and the present period in which the central conflict ("The Long War") is between a non-territorial network of political extremists and their affiliates and a global state that projects its hard power to the far corners of the planet.[11] To act to uphold the authority of territorial states in relation to unwanted flows of information and people, *re-territorializing* counter-moves have been made such as blacklisting and blocking internet sites and building walls along borders to prevent illegal crossings by immigrants and migrants.

In an opposite direction is the encroachment of territorial claims on spheres of activity previously classified as belonging to "the global commons." The extension of coastal claims of states, for security and resource reasons, from three- to twelve-mile territorial limits, complemented by the establishment of exclusive economic zones of 200 miles, and by continental shelf claims of the same extent, or further depending on geological configurations. These enhancements of territoriality reflect the growing importance of living and non-living resources of the seas, including the energy reserves situated beneath the continental shelf. Such a pattern has given rise to a dramatic increase in maritime disputes, including several involving overlapping claims to uninhabited islands islets whose value is associated with off-shore marine and material resources.

In effect, the cosmopolitan perspectives that are dominant in the CS archipelago of actors, operate in zones of advocacy that bridge both the gaps between HF and HN, as well as between HN and HD, demanding what is deemed necessary while positing what is desirable. Whether their influence and impact can be enhanced in the years ahead may well determine the degree to which the global/human interest outlook gains traction.

MODIFYING EXPECTATIONS

The above analysis unavoidably leaves readers with a rather gloomy set of expectations. Perhaps, the most disheartening feature is the weak commitment to civilizational and species survival in the face of unacceptable risks associated with weaponry of mass destruction and projections of disastrous levels of average global temperature rise. Short term, narrowly conceived special interests and traditional national security ambitions have so far decisively trumped the wisdom of prudence. At the same time, as distinct from pre-modern civilizational challenges, as depicted by Jared Diamond, the contemporary challenges are primarily a result of human activities, and in principle can be altered by human intervention. It is for this reason that sage observers have described this period as "the anthropocene age," underscoring human agency.

The structural, ideological, and situational context seems to work against timely adjustments to horizons of necessity, much less attentiveness to horizons of desire. The rational mind can only cope with such prospects by denial, escapism, or indulging some kind of bizarre reading of human destiny: various views of end times. Yet we know that human experience cannot be fully explained or confined without taking account of radical uncertainty and hidden forces. When Tolstoy asks why historians always get the history of the future wrong, he contends that their gaze is limited to the surface of things, while change is a product of forces that erupt from below the surface. These eruptions cannot be predicted, but their occurrence can be made more likely by working on behalf of a future that we believe to be necessary and desirable, and a refusal to be relegated to passivity by a dysfunctional understanding of what is feasible. We have to hope that the gradual heating of the global crucible will lead the mythical frog to jump to safety before it is scalded to death.

In this sense, defying conventional wisdom and rational assessment about the future is an indispensable precondition for constructive thought and action with respect to prospects for what I have previously described as "humane global governance."[12] Such an outlook also reflects the spirit underlying the slogan of the World Social Forum: "Another World is Possible," which contradicts the TINA (there is no alternative) prescription on behalf of neoliberalism so influentially inflected by Margaret Thatcher. More broadly, such a path follows the admonition offered by David Graeber to overcome the anti-utopian cultural disposition that followed from the false labeling of Nazism and Stalinism as "utopian."[13]

The utopian quest can be articulated in rather different ways. The strongest conventional view of promoting a positive world order transition from a Westphalian plural world order is to perceive world government in some form as necessary to manage the disarmament process and thereby overcome the menace of catastrophic war. It is also posited as desirable because it enables a concentration of energy and resources on productive activities. Over the course of time, and with faith in the power of human rationality, the project of establishing a world government is conceived of as feasible because long-term trends suggest centralization of authority and political integration, as well as a fundamental human drive toward unity.[14] A modification of this vision that falls short of addressing the deficiencies of the present arrangements of power and authority, contends that the world is already the beneficiary of a benevolent world government in the form of the American role in providing stability and supplying the ingredients of humane governance.[15]

The best arguments for world government in either the federalist form of Clark/Sohn or the quasi-imperial form of Mandelbaum is premised on the analysis of necessity. Such a position also supposes that through the intervention of reason in the federalist case and leadership role of the United States in the Mandelbaum approach, the gap associated with feasibility can be or is being overcome. In my terminology such a utopian project is dysutopian, and should be rejected from the perspectives of horizons of desire. It is dysutopian on several grounds: a tendency to freeze the existing structures of inequity and to create a rigid hierarchy of power, privilege, status; an ensured dynamic of resistance on the part of those sovereign entities and popular forces that fear the authoritarianism and the likelihood that a globally centralized governmental structure would overcome opposition by relying on oppressive means, which would undoubtedly include high levels of surveillance and reliance on drones to patrol the world.

To a degree the Mandelbaum model is descriptive of the manner in which global security is currently managed, which is by the United States as the sole global state acting alone and in concert with its Western allies, leaving states to exercise self-government so long as they accept the basic discipline of neoliberal globalization.[16] Such embodiments of world government are rejected for two principal reasons: non-responsiveness to the agenda of global interests as set forth above; inconsistent with values associated with global justice, and embodied in the overlapping zones of agreement contained in the Universal Declaration of Human Rights, and the two covenants. A more tolerable variant of world government scenarios for the future is the idea of regionalization as a halfway house. This perspective looked more promising a few years ago before the European Union hit major bumps in the road to establishing a regional federation that could serve as a model for other regions.[17]

These post-Westphalian conceptions are essentially top-down conceptions, both in their origins in the minds of thinkers and strategists, and in their image of historical agency, which relies on the persuasive effects of reason and self-interest, including a collective will to survive. Another orientation is bottom-up, democratic in conception and agency, a result of movement for "governance-from-below," a confidence in local empowerment and its global potentialities ("act locally, think globally"). Graeber offers the following prescription for those he calls "radical intellectuals": "to look to those who are creating viable alternatives, try to figure out what be the larger implications of what they are (already) doing, and then offer those ideas back, not as prescriptions but as contributions, possibilities – as gifts". The attractiveness of such an approach relates to the assurance that the transformation will challenge existing hierarchies, and will exert its influence by the weight of popular demands.[18] The shape of the Arab upheavals in 2011 exhibited this orientation toward political action on a national scale, challenging existing governance structures without offering an alternative ideology or even program, and avoiding any impression of vanguardism, that is, a small elite guiding the masses. Such a "new" politics inspired the worldwide Occupy Movement. Two years later the results are disappointing. The Arab upheavals have not led to more humane national governance, have produced massive collective violence, and the Occupy Movement displayed no capacity to sustain itself.

In reaction, I would favor some combination of elements as providing the foundation for an approach to humane and responsive challenges of global governance in the twenty-first century. The nature of the global interest requires stronger central institutions of authority to handle such concerns as weaponry of mass destruction and climate change. At the same time, worries about further entrenching injustices and anti-democratic modes of collective administration, suggest the importance of having changes in global governance come about as responsive to pressures from below, democratizing in process and result. What will give rise to such a movement cannot be currently discerned. This is a period of waiting, and hopefully not for the sort of large-scale catastrophe that would effectively discredit the existing structure and ideology of world order. A period of waiting should not be seen as a period of inactivity. Local struggles for justice and for ecologically sustainable means to provide food, water, clean air to particular communities can be considered a form of world order pedagogy. Also, broader issues ranging from identification with the symbolic struggle of the Palestinian people against the last remnant of colonialism to the grassroots advocacy of nuclear disarmament can help shape the climate of public opinion to enlarge the political options of governmental leaders. In effect, there is no blueprint for humane global governance, but there are attitudes, actions, and aspirations that can set the stage in such a way as to heighten the chance that historical opportunities as presented will be acted upon in positive ways.

Perhaps, this recommended engagement with present/future can be best expressed enigmatically: "it shouldn't be such a task to live in the present conscious of *futureness*."[19] Or more prosaically, that we cannot close the gaps between feasibility and necessity in humane and sustainable ways without activating the normative imagination that is synonymous with "horizons of desire."

8

FRAMING AN INQUIRY: STRONG SOCIETIES/ WEAK STATES

INTRODUCTORY PERSPECTIVES

There are a great variety of state/society relationships in the world, and also a bewildering array of spatial and temporal contexts that shade our perceptions of strengths and weaknesses. This array reflects such basic conditions as geography, weather, resources, size, population density, stage of development, technological setting, continuity and quality of leadership, ideology, education, religion, culture, and many more. Acknowledging this context dependence injects a cautionary note into any reliance on analytic and ahistoric approaches to guide inquiry into that intriguing category of political entities that can be described as being "strong societies" embedded in "weak states."

Conceptually, it seems also important to question whether "societies" should be automatically considered coterminous with "states." Do some states have multiple societies within their borders? For instance, minorities predominantly resident in a particular region within a state (Kurds in Iraq or Turkey, Pashtuns in Afghanistan, and Catalans or Basques in Spain) seem to exist in a distinct "society" even if enjoying the nationality associated with the state, such as engaging in international travel using a national passport and casting votes in national elections. Societal decentralization often takes the form of a federated state structure or the establishment of political entities that are neither federal units nor outside the domain of territorial sovereignty. Such societies within states can be strong in the sense of being culturally autonomous and politically semi-autonomous, often retaining their own language, culture, traditions, institutions, and grievances. If their relations to the dominant state are hostile, these societal formations can be thought of as "captive nations."

If such societies claim rights of self-determination, which is an inalienable right of all "peoples," then there is posed an international law issue of some magnitude. Supposedly, it is not valid to assert a right of self-determination in the full sense of secession if it would fragment a sovereign state enjoying diplomatic status. At the same time, if the secessionist project is successful in creating a separate existence acknowledged as such by other states and the UN, then a new state comes into existence (Bosnia, Slovenia, and Croatia). It is difficult to generalize about this relationship between society and state because so many variations exist, both with regard to the nature of the state/society relationship and what kinds of strength and weakness are being considered.

Another preliminary observation that complicates, in a different manner, such an interpretative exercise, is the historical experience of the non-West in the period since 1945. Two important intersecting and contradictory phenomenon can be discerned. First, the colonial experience carried with it a nationalist message that was given a certain global salience when proclaimed by Woodrow Wilson after the First World War as "the right of self-determination," which was intended by Wilson to apply narrowly to the peoples living in what had been the Ottoman Empire, and was not meant to challenge the legitimacy of the European colonial empires. Whatever Wilson's intentions, this limited innovation in political identity was quickly universalized by Vladimir Lenin and others to apply to the entire colonial world. There is a charming anecdote that Ho Chi Minh, who was in Paris working as a pastry chef during the Versailles peace talks, was so impressed by the relevance of the ideal of self-determination to the future of Vietnam that he petitioned Wilson asking if he might study at Princeton, the university that Wilson had headed before he became president of the U.S.

My Hegelian point is that articulating this ideal as related to the nationalist evolution of the European states induced in diverse ways the strengthening of many societies vis-a-vis the colonial states, making such state structures less able to maintain internal law and order than had been the case earlier, superimposing a national societal layer of domestic unity without distinguishing in some instances the societal identity of one or more ethnic or religious sub-state societies.

Nationalist resistance temporarily created a strong society vis-a-vis the colonial state, but in the post-independence worlds of Asia and Africa both the state and society often seemed weak.

The contradictory observation is that the colonial state, in particular, relied on many instruments to weaken society, including disempowering the indigenous population from having the capacity to govern.

As a result, when independence came, the postcolonial state was weak with respect to competencies needed for good governance, lacking the educational and bureaucratic base to administer society in an effective and humane manner. The intentionally disempowered postcolonial state was also often challenged by the postcolonial society that had been deliberately weakened by the colonial experience, either through a divide-and-rule mentality or by way of enforced civilizational assimilation.

This emphasis on overall context and the importance of the colonial backdrop for many states and societies conditions inquiry, and might be clarified by reliance on case studies of varying transitions from colonial to postcolonial status. Joel Migdal develops a series of case studies of this transition process, but within analytic framing of state/society relations.[1] It would also be illuminating to compare civilizational experiences of state/society interaction around strong society/weak state hypotheses. I will venture one such impressionistic comparison – the soft revolutions in East Europe during the late 1980s and the so-called Arab Spring that commenced at the start of 2011. In both settings, the governments lacked political legitimacy, and securitized state/society relations so as to maintain order in the face of an alienated and hostile population. These East European societies had greater experience with political independence and possessed political cultures that conceived of themselves as part of the West, and sought the benefits of post-Enlightenment modernity. Such a background translated into relative strength in the form of societies which were capable of replacing the satellite regimes that had governed subject to Soviet hegemonic guidelines with constitutional democracies that did not have the burden of severe polarization, although there were certainly diverse views about the construction of the post-Communist state.

In contrast, the countries in the Middle East and North Africa (MENA) region lacked a deep experience of modernity, and even those non-Arab countries at the edge of the region that self-consciously embraced the Western path – that is, Turkey and Iran – did so in the face of a deep Islamic culture among the masses that resisted the adoption of the Western path, and experienced strong indigenous cultural revivals and also divisive forms of polarization. What is exhibited throughout MENA is a different type of strong society that reverts to traditional cultural ways and religious belief, which in turn generates counterrevolutionary movement tendencies that restore a coercive state apparatus imposing its will on a dissatisfied and subjugated citizenry.

The Egyptian experience since 2011 is paradigmatic, and because it is the central and most populous state in the region, its narrative deserves special attention. Three phases can be distinguished: (1) the largely nonviolent challenge to the corrupt authoritarianism of Hosni Mubarak's rule; (2) an experimental period of inclusive democracy that included parliamentary and presidential elections, as well as a constitutional referendum, elections that brought the Muslim Brotherhood to power and confirmed the democratic weakness of Egyptian urban liberal elites; and (3) an orchestrated crisis of legitimacy directed at the elected government of Mohamed Morsi culminating in a popularly backed military coup against the political leadership followed by a bloody crackdown on all opposition, but especially the Muslim Brotherhood, whose status changed overnight from governing party to criminalized terrorist organization.

A new constitution was drafted, new elections held, and General Abdel Fattah el-Sisi, the coup leader, became president. In effect, the strong Egyptian state of the Mubarak era based on its capabilities to establish order was reconstituted, partly by popular demand in view of widespread disappointment with the democratic interlude between January 2011 and June 2013. The experience of overthrowing two governments based on the mobilization of discontent has undoubtedly changed state/society relations in significant ways, making it more difficult for the state to dominate society and creating in society a sense of having the right and capacity to hold the state accountable. In this regard, the state/society interaction in Egypt, and throughout the Arab world, has altered the weak/strong assessment in unpredictable ways.

Does this Egyptian story reveal to us a strong or weak state? A strong or weak society? This is the puzzle. I would contend that the state is weak if it needs to keep order by a reliance on fear-mongering by an apparatus of state terror and police brutality. Contrariwide, a society is strong if it sets effective limits on the powers of consensual government and exhibits a will and capability to mount credible resistance if these unwritten limits are overstepped.

CONCEPTUAL CLARIFICATION

An initial conceptual issue is to clarify what is meant by "strong" and "weak" from both state and societal perspectives, as well as nationally and internationally. A conventional idea of a "strong" state is the possession of a preponderance of hard power resources sufficient to address effectively the full range of internal and external challenges to political order and territorial integrity of a sovereign state. That is, this conception of the strong state, with an ideological lineage associated with political realism, is essentially based on being an effective state.

Authoritarian states that sustain stability provide good examples, for instance, Mubarak's Egypt or Joseph Stalin's Soviet Union. Another idea of a strong state is an emphasis on a capacity to meet such challenges with minimum reliance on hard power, depending more fundamentally on soft power by way of respect for law, consent from the citizenry to govern via free elections, and creative diplomacy to establish everyday order and national security at acceptable levels. That is, such a strong state is viewed by the preponderance of people under its control and internationally as a legitimate state. This status is exemplified by states that qualify both as constitutional democracies and are not facing serious threats of insurrectionary violence or external attack.

The European idea of nation state was essentially generated as a state-building strategy that sought to overcome the medieval heritage of identity as local and based on religious affiliation. Nationalism filled the void, and created a political entity consisting of a state that represented a society internationally as well as governing it internally within fixed boundaries. To create an effective state presupposed a corresponding loyalty, identity, and coherence, which was achieved by a secular ideology of nationalism divorced from religion, ethnicity, and local affinities. This idea of the nation state was essentially a fiction as minorities often felt that the state was dominated by either a given ethnicity or religious orientation, and that claims of national unity were designed to obscure patterns of domination. When the state is successful in generating the loyalty and identification of people resident within its boundaries, then the actuality of a nation state has been achieved, giving strength to the state that can mobilize its citizens for a variety of actions ranging from sacrifices in wartime to the celebration of national holidays.

From the time of Niccolo Machiavelli to the present, it has been understood by leading political thinkers that it is better to rely on the respect of the governed than to impose order by inducing fear. Governing on the basis of consent and respect is self-perpetuating, while governing on the basis of state terror and force gives rise to oppositional plots and can lead to insurrection. At the same time, making all generalizations unreliable in specific instances, the primary public demands are associated with sustaining order so that there is security in everyday life and the economy functions to provide the population with what is needed for subsistence. There is a proverb popular in the Arab world that expresses this expectation: "people would rather endure 100 years of tyranny than a single year of chaos." With this outlook, maintaining order is the defining attribute of what is perceived to be a strong state.

With regard to "strong" societies, the emphasis would be upon zones of autonomy in which local forces provide human security and order, or upon a capacity to resist external intervention from above or without on the basis of non-accountable local and ethnic leadership and nationalist patterns of loyalty that distinguish between loyalty to the state and loyalty to the nation or nations, or to a particular community. The anticolonial wars of the prior century as occurred in Indonesia, Indochina, and Algeria are illustrative of societies making a transition from "weak" (easily dominated by external actors) to "strong" (capable of restoring nationhood and territorial sovereignty in the face of exploitative foreign ruling elites), that is, of becoming a sustainable nation state. The warlord or militia state is one in which nationalist sentiments on the scale of the state is only operative in relation to external enemies, and when such a threat subsides, then decentralized societal and ethnic patterns of governance and deep cultural traditions generate tolerable levels of localized order most of the time.[2]

Weak states/strong societies are most vividly characterized by situations of conflict and resistance where the nation is the site of struggle for controlling the future of the country, and the state is either an antagonist or marginalized. Some of these issues have been explored by Mary Kaldor in her depiction of the distinctiveness of "new wars," although not with this state/society distinction in mind.[3] What is evident is that the weak state cannot deal with such security threats as insurrectionary violence, civil strife, drug cartels, transnational crime, and external intervention, nor can the weak society. The strong society, however, has impressive soft power capabilities based on nationalist sentiments and perseverance that can often outlast the hard power dominance of intervening forces collaborating with a weak state. As the Afghan proverb expresses this inverted balance of forces: "you have the watches, we have the time." In effect, the governmental center of authority is weak, and easily displaced by a hard power regime-changing intervention, which occurred in Afghanistan (2002) and Iraq (2003), but the society was unconquerable, and thus strong. The dimension of time can offset deficiencies in weaponry and combat capabilities.[4] The indigenous society has the psycho-political edge in such conflicts because of its nationalist resistance to foreign rule that became unconditional, but this was not manifest until the last half of the twentieth century and only then exhibited a willingness to persevere against the militarily superior foreign adversary, accepting huge sacrifices to achieve its goals. In contrast, the intervening side, calculating on the basis of hard power expectations, tends to have a conditional commitment to its goals, losing the will to persist if the costs exceed certain levels, becoming disillusioned with such undertakings as casualties rise and prospects for success diminish.

The American response to the September 11, 2001 attacks by way of overseas warfare illustrate the resilience and resolve of strong societies that became the scene of such regime-changing interventions. George W. Bush epitomized a failure to distinguish between regime change involving the governing elite in a state and exerting control over the society when he spoke about the early battlefield success after the March 2003 invasion of Iraq beneath the banner "mission accomplished." Yes, the mission of overthrowing the regime of Saddam Hussein was accomplished, but the real purpose of the attack was to create a new stable Western-oriented state/society nexus that would serve both strategic and neoliberal interests not only in Iraq, but also in the region.

The Vietnam War may be a primary instance of soft power resistance prevailing on the basis of determined nationalist resistance despite extreme hard power inferiority. What followed the societal victory in Vietnam, however, was the imposition of a coercive version of a strong state, sustaining security by coercive means. In effect, in anticolonial contexts the countries of Indochina displayed extraordinary strength, first against the French colonial rule and then against their American successor, but when it came to postcolonial realities, these societies seemed weak in relation to authoritarian and corrupt states. In effect, strength and weakness of societies and states are partly historically determined, with non-Western societies weak before the spread of the ethos of nationalism and the rise of indigenous confidence in the ability to challenge colonial structures of domination. For some participants, including Jawaharlal Nehru, a transformative event was the defeat of Russia by Japan in the 1905 Russo-Japanese War that was interpreted as an Asian country triumphing over a European adversary, and thus indicating a shifting power balance between West and East.

GLOBAL SETTING

As argued, the historical, ideological, and geopolitical context is always relevant to an interpretation of the weak state/strong society phenomenon. During the Cold War, geopolitical discipline empowered the political leadership in many otherwise weak states, enabling coercive governments to inhibit insurrectionary violence due to the help of outside forces.

Often geopolitical rivalry can produce a surge of societal strength, as during the Iranian Revolution when the Iranian people briefly united to overthrow the Shah's regime, but quickly regressed in the face of oppressive policies of the new Islamic leadership, which seemed to craft an Islamic or theocratic version of a strong state that has proved capable of handling both external challenges (e.g., Iraq, 1980) and internal dissent.

The September 11 attacks have created new forms of geopolitical discipline and the rise of transnational insurrectionary violence that exerts unprecedented pressure on state-centric conceptions of world order. The advent of drone warfare and global surveillance networks, as well as the countervailing capabilities of extremist political movements able to inflict major harm on major states, suggests a new international reality where almost no states are "strong" in the sense of being able to avoid perceptions of acute vulnerability, as well as uphold their security on their own, and no societies are "strong" in the sense of being able to mount resistance to authoritarian centralization or deal with mega-terrorist tendencies that are either transnational or in their midst.

INTERNATIONAL LAW, UNITED NATIONS AUTHORITY

The Westphalian assumptions embedded in the United Nations Charter were altered, if not subverted to a significant extent, by the geopolitical concessions associated with a grant of veto power to the winners in the Second World War. The organized international community has not been able to make states and societies secure in relation to the war system, but the state is seen as generally weaker than society. It was possible, for instance, in Afghanistan and Iraq to achieve regime change by the application of hard power superiority, but neither legitimacy for the new political order nor minimal societal order. That is, Afghan and Iraqi societies have been more difficult to subdue and administer as compared to the identities and orientation of state structures, which could be transformed so far as leadership is concerned, but not made effective or legitimate. In the nineteenth century, this distinction between state and society seemed less relevant.

Military intervention and gunboat diplomacy was impressively effective and efficient so far as resources were concerned, relying on superior European military technology to change governmental structures of authority and subdue whatever societal resistance was encountered, which was often far more than minimal but rarely able to repel the colonialists and their domestic collaborators.

The European conquest of the Western Hemisphere is paradigmatic for the colonizing era, with small numbers of armed European colonial soldiers and settlers taking over entire continents without any deference to the claims of indigenous populations. What has changed in the late twentieth and twenty-first centuries? Three prominent features may be noted. First, the rise of nationalist consciousness; second, greater confidence in resistance capabilities, especially the value of indigenous perseverance; and third, the spread of small arms and the development of guerrilla tactics designed to address the realities of asymmetric warfare from the perspective of the side lacking modern military technologies. The failure of military intervention in this period is stunning given the extent of hard power disparities and the extent of innovative weaponry and tactics. It has created a growing awareness of this dimension of strong societies, and has given rise to a reluctance to rely on military intervention to gain overseas political and economic objectives except for operations that do not require an extensive or sustained ground presence (drones, cyber attacks, air strikes and missiles, and special forces thrusts).

MODERNITY AND DEVELOPMENT

The strong and legitimate state is able to pursue modernity and development while providing the society with some realization of social justice and developmental progress. Gross inequality, persisting massive poverty and unemployment, and corruption undermine the claims of the state as entitled to the acquiescence of the populace, and increase incentives for recourse to insurrectionary challenges and the invocation of tradition as an expression of societal strength. This interaction was evident in the first phase of the Arab Spring, but the weakness of Arab societies exhibited the reemergence of a coercive state in a second phase that relies almost exclusively on hard power violence and state terror to sustain order, and sacrifices all claims to legitimacy except the populist priority of order as compared to democratic chaos. It is possible that an authoritarian state achieves various degrees of developmental success, including the improvement of the material conditions of life for the great majority of inhabitants as was true for the dictatorial regimes in Libya and Iraq. Arguably China has had the most spectacular version of a mixed normative record that has combined harsh authoritarianism with extraordinary materialist progress in a strong state/weak society interaction, especially in the aftermath of the Tiananmen Square events of 1989.

In the Arab world, Syria and Egypt represent different enactments of what takes place if and when strong and corrupted states are challenged by mobilized societal forces. It would appear that since 2011 Syria has become the scene of a regional and global proxy war, suggesting the limits of analyzing states as autonomous units constituting world order. Interregional and intraregional forces can weaken a strong state or strengthen a weak society, and vice versa. What would have ensued in Syria if there had been no covert efforts by outside actors to shift the balance for and against the state cannot be known. The outcome, for now in Egypt, in comparison, seems to reflect relatively the interaction of autonomous domestic forces initially organized against the Mubarak regime, which, after an interlude of democratic exploration, refocused their opposition on the Muslim Brotherhood and its political leadership under Mohamed Morsi, and which eventually came to exhibit the hegemonic ambitions of the armed forces for restored authoritarianism and crony capitalism. At this stage, the only conclusion that can be reached is that the Arab countries have strong states and weak societies, at least with regard to the political dimensions of state/society internal relations. The opposite is true for external relations, with the state trading weak international capabilities and foreign policy independence for the reinforcement of its internal control of society.

The post-intervention strife and chaos in Libya and Iraq, and the unresolved state/society strife in Yemen are illustrative of patterns in which state and society neutralized one another. Each appear weak in relation to either security or developmental goals, although Libya and Iraq have the benefit of rich oil deposits and Yemen is particularly stressed by the absence of resources and water scarcity and interventionary neighbors. In this respect, Libya and Iraq have the economic potential to achieve balance and strength, but whether it has the political potential to realize human rights is very much in doubt, given the societal tensions of an ethnic and regional nature. Because Yemen is without much economic potential, it would seem that only the restoration of some version of an authoritarian state could impose societal order and bring the proxy sectarian dimensions of the conflict between Iran and Saudi Arabia under control.

Whether there will be a third phase of the Arab Spring remains uncertain. There is no doubt that the peoples of these countries have the experience of rising up to impose their will on the political process, a subjectivity that did not exist before the upheavals of 2011.[5] Arguably, as well, the second rising of the Egyptian people in 2013 that collapsed and criminalized the elected Morsi regime can either be interpreted as expressive of the new strength of Egyptian society or as the pushback of the pre-2011 established statist order that involved an alliance between the armed forces and secular urban and capitalist elites, and at this point seems to reflect a collaboration based on the convergence of interests.

The future will make clear whether Egyptian society now has a veto over the governing process or is once more reduced to passivity. Tunisia, with its strong labor unions and vibrant nongovernmental organizations, seems to provide the best example in the region of a new balance between state and society that rests on constitutional compromise. It has so far contained, but not without considerable disruption, the tensions between Islamic and secular affinities, but exhibits in far less drastic form than Egypt, the resilience of the old elites that flourished in the dictatorial periods of rule under Bourguiba and Ben Ali.

TIME AND SPACE

The ideas of strong and weak, state and society, assume the centrality of territorial boundaries in determining political balances. Such hermetic imagery is challenged by the pervasive significance of transnational actors and networks, explored by

Anne-Marie Slaughter, and by more overarching ideas of global governance.[6] More radical than this contemporary complexity of spatial relations is the growing realization that political legitimacy depends on addressing problems associated with protecting the carrying capacity of the planet as a whole, for example in relation to climate change, demographic stability, and limits on per capita consumption. This focus on time, the future, as a dimension of governance suggests that all states and most societies are "weak" in their realism about approaching limits, perhaps fatally so. In this regard, the best hope for the future is a transnational civil society movement that strengthens some societies with regard to an awareness of the dangers posed by these threats, and creates a climate of opinion and action that influences the policy responses of states in the direction of responsible behavior, especially with respect to global challenges ranging from climate change to mass migration.

In effect, the transnationalism of a globalizing world makes all states and societies vulnerable to a wide spectrum of forces that they cannot hope to control. The anti-immigration politics in more affluent states are pushing toward reinforcing the autonomy of political communities, reinforcing political fragmentation at the expense of an emergent biopolitical species unity. The interactivity of capital flows and business activity are suggesting the diminishing relevance of national boundaries and identities. Thus, in addition to the strength and weakness of states and societies, it is important to consider these variables in the setting of regions and civilizations.

CONCLUSION

The altered global setting and the changing patterns of conflict destabilize any settled meaning of "strong" and "weak" in the context of state/society relations. It may help to think of "strong" in post-realist terms as mainly established by legitimacy criteria that incorporate capabilities criteria, but that also give weight to normative considerations of human rights, democratic electoral procedures, non-corruption, good governance, and rule of law. In relation to society, "strong" may be better comprehended as capacity and will to resist abuse from above and intervention from without; that is, a combination of normative expectations of equity and efficiency and nationhood, as well as an ability to learn from past mistakes and to take account of future needs relating to climate, energy, food, and water. For instance, in countries where the Muslim Brotherhood has had the greatest popular strength it is partly a consequence of providing social services and security to impoverished neighborhoods ignored by governmental authorities, and thereby confirming the failures of the state to protect the people under its sovereign control from the hardships of poverty, crime, and corruption, or the depredations of ethnic and religious communal tensions. In short, the widespread failures of states to overcome challenges of human insecurity in their midst.

Stated another way, the strong state is able to uphold the political independence and territorial integrity of the country, and to promote development in a manner that is efficient and equitable, while managing national control of modes of operation and distribution of benefits. The strong society is able and willing to exert pressure on the governing process so that human security is being achieved by stages, development proceeds on an equitable basis, local and women's empowerment exists, and red lines that should not be crossed by accountable leaders are clearly set forth and generally respected.

9

DISRUPTIVE LEGACIES OF WORLD WAR I

IDENTITY POLITICS A CENTURY LATER

I admit to surprise that a place as distant from Europe as New Zealand would have had such a strong interest in World War I until I looked a bit deeper into its relationship to that war, to the British Empire, and to the country's prevailing sense of imperial duty and overseas loyalty to the West at that time. Discovering that more than 100,000 New Zealanders participated in the Great War as either soldiers or nurses in a population of just over a million exhibited the exceptionally strong bonds then existing between the people and government of New Zealand and Great Britain, a national monarchy at the center of a vast global empire that still was widely accepted as the mother country, exercising control over its foreign dominions that were no longer treated as colonies but were not yet completely independent sovereign states. Such an appreciation of the bond is further strengthened by the realization that of those New Zealanders who went to war 16,697 died and another 41,317 were wounded, resulting in an astounding casualty rate of 58 percent, which was considerably higher than either Canada or Australia, or Britain itself. In view of such losses it is to be expected that Auckland would build an imposing war memorial museum honoring the memory of those who fought in World War I.

New Zealand also participated in World War II in a similar spirit of Commonwealth solidarity despite the formal loosening of the imperial ties as a result of the 1931 Statute of Westminster. It may have been relevant that the Pacific dimension of the war seemed less distant. The prospect of a Japanese victory certainly worried the people of New Zealand and undoubtedly appeared dangerous to the national security of New Zealand. Unlike the First World War, the second posed a kind of direct and immediate threat to both New Zealand and Australia by challenging the balance of power in the entire Pacific region. This security dimension validated New Zealand's involvement in World War II from a realist perspective of state interests, reinforcing the still strong psychological identification of interests, values, and traditions as between the two countries.

I wonder what New Zealand would do if Britain become engaged in a future major war. It raises questions of whether a generally shared political culture, sentimental memories, and current identity has moved away from what might be called "the settler post-colonial stage" to an outlook weighing national interests more in the manner of a normal sovereign state. This sense of "normalcy" is descriptive of the typical approach of sovereign states confronting the momentous choice of assessing its security interests in wartime situations. It is a deep challenge for democratic societies, especially when account is taken of the fact that any individual engagement in non-defensive wars is a call upon citizens to risk their life and limb on behalf of the nation, and sometimes might seem to many a remote, and even dubious, political cause.

I cannot help but wonder whether New Zealand continues to possess this mentality of unquestioning solidarity and deference that in the past has so automatically linked its national destiny with that of Britain considering differences in national consciousness, a more diverse ethnic demography, a more assertive indigenous influence, and altered threat perception in the early twenty-first century. It is also relevant to take note of the changed status of war in international law as a result of New Zealand's membership in the United Nations and the prohibition on recourse to force except under strictly limited conditions of self-defense contained in the UN Charter. Or is there a divided consciousness present in the country between conservatives who continue to give great weight to the empire rechristened and downsized as "the Commonwealth" several decades ago and more liberal or progressively minded New Zealanders who think either more nationally or even may be beginning to view themselves as global citizens, and possibly consider national security issues from more ethnically oriented perspectives detached from the past so intertwined with the United Kingdom.

It occurs to me as a non-Kiwi outsider that a comparison of national identity in 1914 and 2014 must be quite illuminating in relation to such issues of shifts in prevailing national identity as would a similar comparison be for my country where the shift from isolationism to globalism has been so dramatic, and in many respects, disastrous, especially in recent history. It seems also that one enduring impact of the Cold War has been to move both Australia and New Zealand a bit further from Britain and closer to America, mainly resulting from the increased dependence on American military prowess should New Zealand's security ever become directly threatened. Such a tactical realignment was reinforced by Britain's dramatic strategic decline as a world power, dramatized by the humiliating fall of Singapore in 1942 to Japan and the 1956 failure to protect the Suez Canal in the face of the challenge posed by Nasser's Egypt. The rise of China has also had a heavy influence on the recalculation of New Zealand's foreign policy alignments.

The sentimental bond to Britain remains strong, of course, but has not been tested in a serious way since the Cold War, although New Zealand's participation in Asian wars to contain Communist expansion seemed to join the past of empire with the present of geopolitics and hegemony.

I think also of the orientation of American foreign policy that continues to give some weight to Anglo-American traditions of solidarity that developed over the course of the last century, but mainly withholds any involvement in war outside of alliance commitments on the basis of self-interested realist calculations of the concrete national interest engaged combined with strategic factors associated with geopolitical ambition. It should be remembered that unlike New Zealand, in the world of 1914, the United States had to overcome its break with Britain in its war of independence as well as its strong traditional stance of noninvolvement in European wars. The U.S. did not enter the war until towards the end of 1917 and then when provoked, in part, by unrestricted German submarine warfare, as well as being disturbed by the ideological consequences of a possible German victory. Of course, in this cross-Atlantic relationship, it has for decades become Britain that subordinated its autonomy as a sovereign state to what became in Britain an unpopular willingness to follow wherever the United States leads, as in the disastrous Iraq War (2003) during which the British Prime Minister, Tony Blair, was often derided as "Bush's poodle." It is also relevant to recall that in 2013, the House of Commons refused to back Prime Minister Cameron's call to join with the United States in carrying out air strikes in Syria in response to an alleged deadly use of chemical weapons by the Assad regime;

as we know, when Britain withdrew and Russia negotiated the removal of chemical weapons stocks from Syria, the United States also controversially decided against launching any attack. Not long ago Washington was annoyed by the call of the British Parliament to recognize Palestinian statehood suggesting that the poodle can get free of its leash from time to time. I raise these preliminary questions mainly in the spirit of inquiry, seeking a better understanding as to how those living in this country now view their past history in relation to the imperatives national and human security in the present global context.

In my visit to the country more than thirty years ago, I became involved in the then controversial policy of disallowing American naval vessels suspected of carrying nuclear weapons to make use of NZ ports, and recall the debate at the time. The U.S. Government takes the position that it refuses to either confirm or deny the presence of nuclear weapons on its naval vessels. The debate at the time centered on the interplay of benefits and detriments to NZ as a member of ANZUS, the Pacific alliance that was part of an American-led global network of Cold War regional treaty frameworks. It also raised questions for some about the legal and moral status of nuclear weapons under international law. It is worth contemplating whether in this century alliance geopolitics and regional trade and investment relations have gradually come to overwhelm the more ethnically and historically valued multi-state frameworks of the Commonwealth. Now that New Zealand has been recently elected to the UN Security Council, which is itself a notable achievement for a small state in a hotly contested competition, might not the stage be set for a move toward a more cosmopolitan worldview to take hold here in the country? Such a posture would be widely appreciated in other parts of the world, especially if New Zealand began to act as a global voice of conscience that was as concerned with promoting the *human* interest as it is with protecting its *national* interest.

LEARNING FROM THE FIRST WORLD WAR

I do not pretend to possess a deep historical knowledge of the complexities surrounding the peace diplomacy that unfolded at Versailles after World War I and in the following years. The focus of this chapter is upon the legacies of the First World War rather than making any attempt to discuss how we now remember these momentous events of a century ago. I came to appreciate that the enduring reverberations of World War I tell us far more about present trials and tribulations in world politics than most of us realize. I was particularly struck in this regard by a passage in Hannah Arendt's great book *The Origins of Totalitarianism*: "The days before and the days after the first World War are separated not like the end of an old and beginning of a new period, but like the day before and the day after an explosion. Yet this figure of speech is as inaccurate as are all others, because the quiet which settles down after a catastrophe has never come to pass. The first explosion set off a chain reaction in which we have been caught ever since and which nobody seems able to stop. The first World War exploded the European comity of nations beyond repair, something which no other war had ever done."[1] This is an extraordinary statement that seems an exaggeration when we first listen to such grandiose claims, but as I will try to show, this assessment remains essentially accurate more than fifty years after Arendt's book was published. For most of us the impacts of World War I are still obscure, and few have effectively connected the dots between then and now. There are historians of the period that tell us lots about the play of forces in Europe a century ago, and there are abundant pundits who tell us how to understand the present reality. What is in short supply are those who connect the past with the present in ways that illuminate what has gone wrong and what might be done about it.

So much has changed in the world that such a distant war is mainly regarded as one more historical occasion buried in the realities of its time. In my view such a perception should be corrected. If we look back a hundred years we get a better understanding of the terrifying turmoil now going on in the Middle East, that it can and should be traced back to some prevalent attitudes and fundamentally wrong decisions made in the peace diplomacy that followed the war. The severity and pervasiveness of this turmoil cannot be properly understood or addressed without exploring its World War I roots.

There is one misleading dimension of Arendt's words, the implied Euro-centric character of world order as an enduring reality. In important respects, Europe since losing its colonies after World War II has become marginalized as a major participant in shaping world history. This assertion is not meant to deny that Europe was clearly responsible for setting in motion the events that shook the foundations that existed a hundred years ago, and then and now pose obstacles and create opportunities in the search for peace, justice, and even stability. Such global developments as the world hegemonic role of the United States, the rise of China, neoliberal globalization, the emergence of the BRICS makes any contemporary projection of a Euro-centric world as simplistic and misleading. Despite this caveat it remains crucially relevant to grasp, even if belatedly, the 1914 reverberations that persist. Achieving a better understanding of these reverberations may help to make our world a bit more secure, more just, and less prone to violence.

With this purpose in mind, I will consider four policy clusters or impacts that owe their origins and unfolding to the disruptive impacts of World War I. In part, these developments arose because of various efforts to vindicate the immense suffering, sacrifice, and sense of loss resulting from the war. There existed a strong incentive to convince a skeptical public that the war produced positive results and that lessons could be learned to avoid breakdowns of order in European and world politics. Both idealists and realists strained to make the peoples of Europe and their overseas allies feel that the sacrifices made in the war were justified partly by being translated into positive features associated with the onset of peace and a post-conflict international setting. For some governments this mainly involved the benefits attributed to the spoils of victory measured by extending the colonial reach to strategically valuable and resource-rich countries. For others, a pattern also present following the Second World War, but revealingly not after the Cold War, the strong interest associated with building a future world order that would discourage, if not prevent, the recurrence of major wars in the future. The United States was particularly identified with this effort to establish institutions and procedures that would discourage and delegitimize recourse to war. Against this general background it is possible to examine these four policy clusters that exhibit some general characteristics of the legacies of World War I in the world order of today.

1

The recognition that World War I and its aftermath had profoundly dislocating effects on societal coherence and political authority throughout Europe. The war is widely believed to be responsible for unleashing polarizing social forces on left and right both dedicated to overturning the established order. This surge of radicalism took opposed political directions with the left promoting revolutionary change from below and the right favoring totalitarian rule from above for the sake of order. These strong political demands exhibited the extreme and complex alienation of contending social classes in several of the countries that had experienced the intense traumas of the war. What eventuated from this ferment was a lethal mixture of domestic and international ideological orientations associated with a variety of fascist and communist political movements, their most dramatic manifestations being the Russian Revolution and the rise in Germany of National Socialism. The messianic militarism of fascism (and Japanese imperialism) led to violent confrontations with the liberal democracies and with Soviet communism that reached their first climax with the outbreak of World War II, and their second with the Cold War. This rise of extremisms created as its dialectical legacy a political resolve by the victors, aside from the Soviet Union, to do their best to avoid embittering the defeated nations as occurred in the aftermath of World War I. The main Western powers went further by making strong efforts to restore these devastated countries to economic and political normalcy as soon as possible. In this regard the occupations of Germany and Japan, absorbing the lessons associated with some of the mistakes made in the aftermath of World War I exerted their influence in such a way as to nurture political moderation and hostility toward extremism in the defeated countries as well as to avoid any political backlash against punitive measures directed at the defeated countries. Attuned to the cultural sensitivities of these defeated countries encouraged such initiatives as retaining the emperor system in Japan. One strategic idea, absent a hundred years ago, was the importance attached to treating the enemies of yesterday as the new friends of today, and the allies of tomorrow. Such a process was only partly what was learned from the mistakes of the past. It was also responsive to the conflict patterns taking shape after 1945 that brought the West under American leadership into a rivalry with the East under Soviet leadership.

Western postwar diplomacy of 1945 was influenced both by the World War I mistake of imposing a punitive peace on Germany and the realization that the wartime alliance against Fascism would not be viable in peacetime. In the second phase of the struggle of moderate governments against political extremism, this time taking the form of the long Cold War, whose conduct managed to avoid the catastrophic threat of a third world war that would likely have been fought with nuclear weapons. With the collapse of Communism and the disintegration of the Communist bloc in Eastern Europe after 1989, and the accompanying triumph of Liberalism, there occurred in the West a short-lived exultant mood of triumphalism captured by Francis Fukuyama's striking image of "the end of history."[2] Such a West-centric Hegelian interpretation of the outcome of the Cold War acquired some added plausibility when China's drive toward modernization under Deng Chau Ping brought this gigantic country into the neoliberal world order, which the once leftist Brazilian leader, Fernando Henrique Cardozo, acknowledged to be "the only game in town." That is, the victory over Communism was understood as facilitating a globalized world economy that was guided by a market-driven ideology that has been identified as "neoliberal" or the policies flowing from what came to be called "the Washington Consensus."[3]

Leaving aside the anti-Western extremisms that came to the surface in the Islamic Revolution in Iran, a cost of this complacent celebration of Western secular liberalism was to foster an intolerant attitude toward visionary politics, whether of a radical or utopian variety. The politically influential classes endorsed the belief that only incremental change is constructive and feasible, and that any greater political or moral ambition necessarily plunges society, if not the world, into a descending spiral that inevitably produces terrorism and extremism. This reading of history goes back to the French Revolution as well as forward to an account of the Soviet experience, referencing Nazism along the way. Over-learning and distorting this superficial lesson of the First World War is very disempowering in the present global setting where it is only "a necessary utopianism" that might meet the challenges of nuclear weapons and climate change.[4]

Unlike the rise of extremisms in the aftermath of World War I there was no comparable experience after World II. This is undoubtedly partly a reflection of the reality that a large proportion of the public in the occupied countries felt that their extremist leaders had brought destruction upon the country by the embrace of morally unacceptable and politically imprudent policies. It also partly resulted from the success of the United States as the prime victor quickly recasting itself in the role of principal protector against the unfinished agenda of defeating expansionist extremism. On the basis of such a feeling the Soviet Union after World War II was quickly seen to be a surviving extremism with values and goals that were antithetical to Western liberal individualism, a reality supposedly confirmed by the Soviet moves to exert permanent control over Eastern Europe. Left European intellectuals themselves later turned against the excesses of Stalinism, a collection of essays by prominent personalities, and published under the intriguing title, *The God that Failed*.[5]

In an important respect, the Cold War can be viewed as the final stage of a continuous global war being waged by moderates and capitalists against socialists and extremists, or liberals against totalitarians, that began with the assassination of Archduke Ferdinand in Sarajevo and ended seventy-five years later with the collapse of the Berlin Wall.

2

A second, somewhat ambiguous reverberation from the First World War were ideas about imposing some kind of accountability for violations of international law by those acting in the name of the state. The seemingly progressive idea was that there needed to be a law that overrode sovereign claims of being only accountable internally, especially in the context of aggressive war.

The impulse was confused and controversial from the outset as the insistence on accountability became intertwined with the eagerness of the winner to demonstrate that it deserved to win. In its initial expression, which seemed dubious given the origins and character of the First World War, was the idea that losers in a major war should be held collectively responsible for causing the damage and suffering and that, correspondingly, the behavior of the winners should not be scrutinized. The victorious governments should be at liberty to determine the punishment to be imposed. In the Versailles arrangements this took the form of requiring Germany to pay significant reparations to offset the damage its war machine had caused the victorious allies and to accept strict limitations on the form of military capabilities that it would be allowed to develop and possess in the future. Such a punitive peace as embodied in the Versailles Peace Treaty definitely accelerated the German descent into a struggle between extremisms, and created a national mentality of defiance, humiliation and wounded pride. Such a German reaction seemed understandable as it was difficult to draw a sharp moral line between the military behavior of victors and vanquished other than by reference to the way the conflict was finally resolved on the battlefield, which seemed quite detached from questions of moral and legal responsibility for the war and its conduct. As a result, Germans felt bitterly betrayed by an emergent political order that seemed to reject that principle of comity among sovereign states that Arendt referred to, which had in the European setting treated losing states in war as no more morally reprehensible or politically dangerous than the winner.

Yet this idea that there was a moral and legal dimension to warfare that must be factored into post-war arrangements survived to live another day. It surfaced in the war crimes trials held in Germany and Japan after the Second World War, most spectacularly in the prosecution of the surviving leaders of the two countries in the much studied Nuremberg and Tokyo trials, which were precursors to the establishment of the International Criminal Court. The Nuremberg approach was generally vindicated by the consensus view that the Nazi experience was such an unprecedented assault on European values and civilizational pretensions, first by so overtly launching a major aggressive war that produced tens of millions of deaths and then by the commission of numerous atrocities in its course, especially genocide against Jews and other minorities. The Tokyo trials were far more controversial as the onset of the Pacific theater of warfare was as prompted by the deliberate encirclement and squeezing of the Japanese economy as it was by the surprise attack in 1941 on Pearl Harbor. This moral and political ambiguity is heightened as soon as one takes into consideration the failure to impose any accountability on the victors for the use of atomic bombs against Hiroshima and Nagasaki or for the fire-bombing of Tokyo. The cry of "victors' justice," the title of a book by the historian Richard

Minear, seemed understandable, if not altogether justifiable.[6] In the German case the American prosecutor, Robert Jackson, tried to soften the one-sided approach toward individual criminal responsibility taken after World War II by declaring a Nuremberg Promise, namely that in all future wars those governments sitting in judgment in relation to the Germans would submit themselves to the same discipline of international criminal law. This Nuremberg Promise was broken by each of the victors, none of whom have ever accepted the application of a procedure of criminal accountability being applied to themselves, and have opted out to the extent possible from ever being subject to the authority of the International Criminal Court. The United States and Europe continue to make a political use of international criminal law by supporting the prosecutions of their recent enemies, including Slobadan Milosevic, Saddam Hussein, and Muammar Qaddafi, and finance the ICC in its focus upon the criminal wrongdoing of sub-Saharan African leaders while granting de facto impunity to the West.

In effect, the idea of criminality associated with war could have taken either of two forms, as an emergent branch of the rule of law that would apply the same standard of accountability and judgment to the victors as to the vanquished or it could accept the double standards of imposing accountability on the defeated and granting impunity to the victor. Robert Frost's poem, "The Road Not Taken," expresses such a choice in more personal and universalistic language:

> *Two roads diverged in a wood,*
> *And I took the one less traveled by,*
> *And that has made all the difference.*

Unlike the poet, the statesmen of the world have chosen the more traveled road of political realism and geopolitics, which had long been accustomed to the amoral dualism of one law for the strong, another for the weak. This realist ethos was concisely set forth long ago by Thucydides in the Melian Dialogue in his History of the Peloponesian Wars: "The strong do what they will, the weak what they must." What World War I initiated was a moral/legal translation of this political tendency that liberals viewed as a step forward, conservatives generally regarded as a risky departure from realism, and progressives viewed as a hypocritical and misleading effort to seize the high moral and legal ground.

The impulse was partially revived after World War II, but individualized by way of war crimes trials thus abandoning the war-provoking collective guilt attributions of World War I. These had consisted of imposing onerous burdens on a defeated country at the very time when its population was struggling with the urgencies of survival in the ravaged conditions of post-war realities. It is regrettable that this idea of a punitive peace was revived in dealing with Iraq after the Gulf War of 1991 as if the lesson of World War I's self-destructive breach of comity was irrelevant when dealing with the global South that never had enjoyed the benefits of comity. And even the relative success of the restorative approach taken after World War II was ignored in the vindictive approach toward Iraq, eventuating in the disastrous Iraq War with its totally failed occupation policy, now understood as partly responsible for the horrifying emergence of ISIS out of the ashes of the Iraqi armed forces purged of its Sunni leadership and officer corps.

3

The horrors of warfare that caused millions of casualties and destroyed economies in the period 1914–1918, gave rise to a vibrant peace movement, and to the willingness of the peoples of Europe to look with favor toward a fundamental revision of world order based on the institutionalization of peace and security at a global level as well as moves against arms dealers ("merchants of death"). The establishment of the League of Nations was the most visible result, but hampered from its outset by the sovereignty oriented statesmen who dominated diplomacy, as well as by an American leadership that was ambivalent about giving up America's traditional non-involvement in European conflicts and its related posture of isolationism based on the insulating presence of oceans on either coast as the foundations of security. Of course, there was more to the American position as it combined this non-interference in Europe with a determination to resist European interference anywhere in the Western Hemisphere. The enunciation of the Monroe Doctrine in 1823 gave tangible expression to this two-sided American diplomacy that incorporated contradictory principles.

After every major war in Europe there have been attempts to learn from the experience and avoid the recurrence of such a traumatizing and dislocating experience that had given rise to such massive suffering. This tendency was evident in every major post-war instance of diplomacy since the birth of the modern European state system in 1648 via the Peace of Westphalia. In part this was a reaction to the tendency of political leaders to fail to anticipate the true costs and harmful societal impacts of war, whatever its outcome, inducing a concerted effort to insulate Europe from future mistakes of the same kind.

The Thirty Years War led to the Westphalian framework based on territorial sovereignty in 1648, later reinforced by legally acknowledging the right of the sovereign to determine the religion of the state. The Napoleonic Wars led to the Concert of Europe in 1815, which attempted to create collective mechanisms for resolving disputes by diplomatic negotiation rather than war and through a consensus as to the nature of legitimate government that a pledge to act collectively against the sort of revolutionary challenges that had been posed by Napoleon. World War I produced the League of Nations and World II the UN, the Bretton Woods institutions, and encouraged the establishment of collective mechanism for mutual cooperation that evolved into the European Union.

In contrast, the Cold War produced nothing at all, perhaps demonstrating that since it was never really a war, there were no mistakes to be overcome. In retrospect this seems like a tragic failure of leadership in the West, particularly the United States, to use the atmosphere of relief and liberation after the fall of the Berlin Wall to achieve nuclear disarmament and a stronger UN. What was revealed by this lack of political innovation was a geopolitical complacency and a preoccupation with taking advantage of the globalization of the world economy in line with the economistic priorities of neoliberal capitalism. The political leadership in the United States, and the West generally, lacked imagination and the public lacked motivation. There may be a species destiny contained in this regressive learning curve, especially as the case for global reform has grown stronger as a result of the integrative impacts of technology and economic behavior, and due to the global scale challenge of climate change. At present, the world system seems gridlocked with respect to structure. It is incapable of meeting any formidable global challenges to human wellbeing except during that brief window of opportunity that is opened in the immediate aftermath of a major hot war, and then mainly with adjustments that do not undermine the established hierarchy of power and privilege.

We notice that despite widespread scientific and public agreement on the dangers posed by nuclear weaponry and climate change, the problem-solving mechanisms available in the world have not been responsive, and show no signs of being able to surmount the peaceful obstacles posed by vested bureaucratic and private sector interests. We must ask ourselves whether it would require yet another war of global proportions to shake off this disabling lethargy that is literally endangering the very survival of the human species. And given the weaponry with which such a war would likely be fought, and its dire environmental impact, whether the human race confronts the unprecedented dilemma of being unable to act effectively without a war and likely being so devastated that if even such a catastrophic war occurred there would be no capacity to act reconstructively.

Returning to our focus on the legacies of World War I it is certainly appropriate to note that for the first time in history the impetus to form a global institutional mechanism with the overriding mission of preventing future wars entered the mainstream, at least rhetorically. The extraordinary suffering, devastation, and societal dislocation of a long war that accomplished very little politically or ethically that could be called positive led to social demands to ensure that less destructive means of achieving international peace and security could be developed. As well, the missionary vision of Woodrow Wilson that called for organizing the peace in durable ways captured the imagination of the European public in ways that helped make the establishment of the League of Nations seem to many a realistic project. The concrete implementation of such a vision was obstructed by the thinly disguised colonial ambitions of Britain and France, abetted by the secret machinations of diplomats and also by the Bolshevik Revolution in Russia that threatened the European established order to such an extent that a counter revolutionary intervention was organized to reverse the outcome. Globalist impulses were also captive to American ambivalence that could not decide whether to abandon the tradition of avoiding entangling alliances, especially centered in Europe, and assert itself internationally as a global leader in peacetime as well as during large wars. The U.S. failure to join the League was certainly a blow to the hopes of those who believed that peace and security could only be preserved in the future by establishing alternatives to balance of power geopolitics, and was a deficiency corrected after World War II, but with the debilitating concession of a veto to the victorious powers who were self-anointed as the peace enforcers, except against each other, which meant that the step forward from the view of participation was nullified by the step backward in relation to political effectiveness. Overall, neither the League nor the UN faced directly the need to constrain state sovereignty and geopolitical impunity if the true objective was to build a sustainable architecture of peace.

Mark Mazower in his perceptive book *Governing the World* confirms the view that the birth of the League was "abrupt" and that war served as its "midwife."[7] For Mazower, who does not discuss the prior contributions of post-war statecraft to global reform, poses as the central question for those planning the peace after World War I, how to explain the birth of a new political idea. He considers the critical question to be why the dominance of statist views of world order seemed to give way with so little opposition to the sort of internationalism embodied in the League concept. He wants to know "why, in other words, some of the most powerful states in the world threw their weight behind the construction of a permanent peacetime world security organization and built the League of Nations" [117]. Perhaps, as

Mazower doesn't consider, the embracing of the League project was facilitated by the realization that such a feeble form of institutionalization was nothing more than window dressing for the pre-existing state-centric world order that would neither inhibit colonialist diplomacy nor confuse or distract realist political leaders from the persisting agency of hard power geopolitics as the foundation of world order and disorder.

In the background were ideological issues that pointed in both directions. The League as established was at once perceived as a threat to sovereignty oriented nationalists and by most internationalists as far too weak in authority and structure to carry out its mission of preserving the peace. It was clear that if a strong state emerged with a serious set of grievances about the status quo together with the means and will to mount a challenge by force of arms the League structure would be paralyzed or complicit. As we all know, both Germany and Italy in Europe and Japan in Asia did emerge with a revisionist agenda to be implemented by force that could only be dissuaded by countervailing power, which underscored what was already known, that the League was useless if a challenge to world order required the deterrence or defeat of major aggressor states. The most convincing demonstration of this impotence was posed by the rise of European Fascism, especially as it manifested itself in the Nazi rise to power in Germany.

4

The least commonly acknowledged legacy was the degree to which the "peace" concluded after the First World War contributed over the decades to "war," strife, chaos, and authoritarian rule in the Middle East. This outcome resulted from the unwillingness of the European colonial powers to abide by their promise made during the war to grant independence to the Arab peoples as soon as peace was established in exchange for tangible Arab support of the Allied war effort by rising up and fighting against the Ottoman Empire. The Arabs fulfilled their part of the bargain, but Britain and France did not. Through secret diplomacy, highlighted by the Sykes-Picot Agreement of 1916, these European colonial powers cynically plotted behind the scenes to achieve a division of Ottoman lands between themselves without regard either to their earlier commitment to the Arabs or to the dynamics of ethnic self-determination as envisioned by Woodrow Wilson.

This diplomatic process based on colonial ambition, and little else, was responsible for the emergence of a series of particularly artificial states with borders drawn to reflect the strategic priorities of Britain and France relating to the location of oil and protection of trade routes, especially upholding the navigational security in the Suez Canal. This approach to the Middle East has been responsible for successive waves of instability and suppression of minorities, as well as perceptions of illegitimacy by those affected, generating intense conflict and a disregard for contrived political boundaries.

Among the most anguishing legacies of the First World War is the current acute turmoil that afflicts almost the entire Middle East. Of course there are many intervening developments during the past hundred years that are relevant to explain the specific patterns of conflict that are present in the region. Nevertheless, as the perceptive regional expert, Mohammed Ayoob argues, it is the colonialist aftermath of the collapse of the Ottoman Empire that constitutes "the primary factor" in accounting for "the mayhem and anarchy" in the region.[8] Ayoob is critical of those who are content to attribute these regional torments to Islamic radicalism and sectarian tensions between Sunni and Shi'ia believers. He believes that this substitution of proximate for the more illuminating root causes leads to a faulty understanding of the underlying situation and what must be done about it.

An earlier line of explanation associated with Bernard Lewis attributed the problems of the region to Islamic cultural resistance to a transition to Western style modernity. Of course, the importance of Middle Eastern oil to keep the world stable is a central part of the regional drama, and linked closely to such other concerns as American interventions in the region, preoccupation with the spread of radical Islam, the avoidance of the spread of nuclear weapons, and the destabilizing Israeli claims to uphold its security by periodic aggression and disproportionate reliance on force. In one way or another each of these issues can be traced back to the difficulties associated with the collapse of Ottoman rule as the occasion for the arrangements put in place after World War I.

The diplomacy of World War I was rather confusing and contradictory when it came to the Middle East. As mentioned, particularly Britain encouraged Arab leaders to revolt against Ottoman rule, promising postwar independence in the form of a regional Arab state. At the same time Woodrow Wilson was advocating a quite different approach, proposing the establishment of a series of successor states to the Ottoman control of the region based on the principle of nationality as the means to realize his overriding goal, the self-determination of peoples. In opposition to this the British and French were secretly plotting to divide up the region without regard to such considerations, but rather to satisfy their overriding interest in gaining control over territories that contained oil and satisfied certain strategic interests. The British were preoccupied with safeguarding the Suez Canal, staking claims for countries nearby including Jordan and Palestine, while the French wanted to be near the old Silk road to facilitate trade with Asia by overland routes, and were eager to create a distinct Christian state that would satisfy Maronite aspirations that led to the establishment of Lebanon.

However, there were also some relevant anti-colonial influences at work in the Versailles peace negotiations associated with American influence, yielding a compromise taking the form of the mandates system. This upheld the British/French ideas about post-Ottoman territorial delimitations, but instead of agreeing to colonial title, these two governments were given unrestricted administrative control over these territories as "a sacred trust of civilization" that included a vague commitment to grant independence at a future time. Without the impact of World War II on the colonial system it is doubtful that political independence would have been achieved without greater struggles against British and French tutelary administrative regimes throughout the region.

As Ayoob persuasively points out, the legacy of these arrangements was the creation of a series of artificial states that experienced great difficulty in governing effectively. Ayoob identifies what followed as "state failures" that have generated the extremism and sectarianism that continues to afflict the region, not the reverse. It seems correct that when sovereign states are not natural political communities severe inner tension and instability inevitably results. The denial to the Kurds of a state of their own has created very disruptive issues of minority and self-determination challenges to state legitimacy that constitute one dimension of persisting problems in Iraq, Syria, with spillovers to Turkey and Iran. What has recently become evident is the capacity of non-state actors to "outgovern" and even militarily defeat the formal governance institutions of the state. This extraordinary development has been recently acknowledged in relation to the extensive areas under the undeniably harsh and brutal control of ISIS, and also in Afghanistan where from the perspective of human security of the people, the Taliban is doing a better job of meeting the daily health and security needs in Afghanistan than the heavily subsidized government in Kabul.[9]

This radical form of state failure has given well-organized and dedicated Islamic civil society actors a political base that includes a reputation for getting things done without corruption, and contrasts with governmental practice that is perceived as being both corrupt and incompetent.

The other source of fundamental tension and controversy in the region is associated with the Israel–Palestine conflict. This encounter also emanated from a colonial gesture during the final stages of World War I. In 1917 Lord Balfour made an initially secret commitment to the Zionist Movement that Britain would look with favor at the establishment of a Jewish homeland in historic Palestine. In keeping with the spirit of the time, the population of Palestine was never consulted, although Arabs were an overwhelming majority and severe conflict between Jewish migrants and indigenous Arabs resulted with no satisfactory outcome in sight.

Understandably many Arab scholars are outraged by this colonialist intrusion on the political development of the Middle East. Walid Khalidi, the noted Arabist, called the Balfour Declaration "the single most destructive document in the twentieth century." This may be hyperbole, but there is no doubt that the unresolved Palestinian quest for self-determination has caused several regional wars, as well as inflicted on the Palestinian people both a catastrophic dispossession in 1948, the *nakba*, and a brutal land grabbing occupation in the West Bank, East Jerusalem, and Gaza that has continued since 1967. The Israeli state has increasingly assumed an apartheid structure of civil/military administration over the fragmented Palestinian people. The United States has assumed the role earlier played by Britain in protecting Israel's interests in what has been a hostile environment, ignoring Israel's frequent violation of international law and elemental morality, and above all, its unwillingness to cooperate in reaching an agreement with Palestinian people based on equality of rights as the foundation for a sustainable and just peace.

CONCLUSION

For several reasons it seems correct to view World War I as the biggest rupture in global history since the French Revolution, and more revolutionary in its impact than subsequent major wars. Perhaps, most notable is the degree to which World War I exhibited interconnections between mobilizing the resources and enthusiasm of national societies for engaging in war and the decline of the capacity to rely on diplomatic compromises to bring wars to an end in a manner that minimizes the suffering experienced and the dislocation caused to affected populations. As Raymond Aron expresses this idea, "it was peculiarly difficult to end by negotiation in the traditional way a war that had become a war of peoples and of ideas."[10] The public had to be induced to believe in the war, which encouraged inflated claims that issues in contention were of fundamental importance or that the enemy was pursuing evil ends by criminal means. This heightened polarization of international disputes and conflict captures part of what Arendt meant by pronouncing the end of European comity.

In line with such an observation is the elaborate commentary of Gabriel Kolko set forth in his important study, *Century of War*.[11] Kolko insisted that the World War I initiated a process of war making in which the leaders and citizens anticipated and planned for a short war, and instead experienced a long and far more destructive, alienating, and costly war than they had been led to believe. In its course this kind of war causes vast human suffering that creates a wide range of serious societal dislocations. Kolko writes about both the specific deforming impacts of this particular conflict and its exertion of influence over the character of subsequent major wars. He writes, "it is so desperately imperative that we escape from the present uneven yet steady descent along the path of war on which the mankind has been locked since 1914."[12] He is highly critical of political leaders for their "ignorance that has cost humanity a price in suffering beyond any measure." In effect, World War I initiated a modern tendency for what Kolko calls "the consummate irresponsibility" of leaders who are "playing with the lives of anonymous people who are sent off to die" without any appreciation of or concern about the societal costs that will be incurred.[13]

We in America remember the anger aroused caused by the Bush presidency promising that the Iraq War would be a cakewalk in which the American occupiers would be welcomed as liberators. It was an arduous decade-long campaign that ended in political failure, substantial withdrawal of any combat presence, and there was no welcome for the occupying American and British forces in Iraq despite widespread opposition in the country to the autocratic regime of Saddam Hussein.

In effect, the kind of war making that occurred in World War I and took new technological forms in World War II is a virus that continues to lie dormant in the body politic. It is exhibited by the refusal to seek the abolition of nuclear weaponry or the globalizing of the rule of law, and by the insistence that our side in every war is essentially innocent and good and our adversary is evil, even barbaric.

The current global war on terror is inscribed in public consciousness in accordance with the kind of moralizing self-assurance that guided the peacemakers at Versailles almost a century ago. Unfortunately, the imperative lesson as to the dysfunctionality of war has not yet been learned by either the leaders of the most important sovereign states or their publics. The only useful thing that has been learned about war is the importance of exercising caution in the nuclear age whenever a crisis in international relations occurs. We must pause and ask ourselves what seems to be a decisive moral and political question, which may also be an ultimate survival question: "is caution enough?" And if not, "What must be done?" We certainly do not want people coming together one hundred years hence to lament the persistence of war as the defining feature of world history.

10

THE 4+ LOGICS OF GLOBAL ORDER

It is highly misleading to describe "world order" as consisting exclusively of sovereign territorial states. This misimpression is further encouraged by the structure of the United Nations, whose members are states, and only states.

The UN was established in 1945 in the aftermath of World War II, reflecting a West-centric orientation that emerged at the time, quickly morphing into the Cold War rivalry between the two states that were geopolitically dominant and ideologically antagonistic: the United States and Soviet Union.

Even in the UN, however, this surface allegiance to statism is misleading. The geopolitical dimension was highlighted in the UN Charter by conferring a veto power on five winners in the recently concluded war, which amounted to the grant of a right of exception with respect to international law. And then there are the semi-sovereign states that are accorded full membership in the UN although not possessing the traditional attributes of effective control over territory, including daily administration of governmental functions. Palestine is an example of what might be called "a virtual state," its statehood being affirmed in various diplomatic and institutional contexts, including being legitimated by the UN in 2012, but its daily actuality as a political entity ruled by Israel is anything but sovereign. Or consider the island groups in the Pacific that have been admitted to the UN. For instance, the Republic of the Marshall Islands is a full member of the UN, although its UN grant of independence included a compact of free association with the United States in which the U.S. assumes responsibilities for the defense of the islands in exchange for the maintenance of a missile-testing facility on Kwajalein Atol. Under these conditions one finds it hardly surprising that these semi-sovereign entities vote sheepishly with the United States on such issues of no national concern as the former annual maintenance of sanctions on Cuba or insulating Israel from UN criticism. And reaching back it is worth remembering the Soviet bloc consisting of Eastern Europe that without exception voted within the UN in support of their Russian masters, and could hardly be perceived as politically independent in the manner that is supposed to identify the essence of sovereignty. In effect, there are many gradations of effective sovereignty that are encompassed by the UN operating conception of statehood, which are manipulated by political maneuvering and shaped by the realities of governance.

Additionally, there are differences in hard and soft power that make the interactions among states within the UN exhibit more inequality than is suggested by this still prevailing Westphalian juridical myth of the equality among sovereign states. Some states contribute far more to the UN budget than others, and their views carry more weight; others are richer, bigger, more informed about some issues, are better at lobbying for support, and some play above their diplomatic weight by clever political maneuvers. And there are several kinds of non-states active behind the scenes that exert varying degrees of influence depending on the subject matter.

Global policy is mainly shaped outside the UN by a bewildering array of formal and informal actors that participate in a variety of ways in international life. The world economy is substantially controlled by business-oriented alignments such as the World Economic Forum that meets annually in Davos, Switzerland, or the gatherings of economically powerful states grouped together as the G-7, later becoming the G-8, and more recently the G-20 to accommodate shifts in trade and investment patterns, and give recognition to such new alignments as the BRICs.

As such, the shorthand designation of world order by reference to the 1648 Treaties of Westphalia that brought the Thirty Years War to an end serves as a convenient starting point for understanding the way authority and power are deployed in the world. Yet it must be supplemented by the recognition that the Westphalian state-centric framework has evolved through the years. Beyond this, it is not sufficient to rely on a statist logic to explain the main patterns of behavior that constitute world politics in the twenty-first century, which reflect the agendas of political extremist groups and transnational corporations and banks, as much as they do states. In fact, national governments are often subordinated to and instrumentalized by individuals and groups promoting the interests of business and finance.

STATIST LOGIC

Despite these qualifications, states do remain the main political actor on the global stage, and the principal agent of diplomacy. The doctrinal ideas of territorial sovereignty and border control continue to provide the basic organizing principles for the conduct of normal transnational relations. It is further important to realize that most political leaders and their chief advisors are "realists" who purport to act on the basis of maximizing national interests and accompanying values even when they are in actuality serving the interests of transnational capital to the detriment of their own citizenry.

The boundaries of the state shape the outer limits of political community for most persons living on the planet, but some states contain within their borders one or more specific ethnicity that deems itself a distinct people and nation, which if it perceives itself as the target of discrimination or even a victim of submerged identity, may come to regard itself as "a captive nation" that seeks a separate political existence that ensures the preservation of cultural memory, national pride, and freedom from discriminatory patterns of governance. In this sense, the "nation" represented by such a phrase as "the national interest" may be profoundly misleading if understood to refer to the interests of an entire population within international borders rather than that of the dominant ethnicity or religion. Throughout the world there are many internationally unrepresented peoples seeking to form their own state in accordance with the right of self-determination, which if carried to extremes, threatens the unity of almost all sovereign states.

Sometimes, this process is a forcible one as with the establishment of Kosovo with the help of NATO in 1999, sometimes it is a consensual separation, as with the establishment of Slovakia. Democratic states may offer restive minorities the opportunity to secede by referendum as in the recent case of Scotland, but some forms of secession are forcibly resisted as was the case with American Civil War or more recently, the PKK efforts to establish in eastern Turkey a separate state of Kurdistan, as well as Spain's treatment of the main separatist movement of the Basque people as essentially a terrorist organization.

Many individuals depend on citizenship to avoid the acute vulnerability of "statelessness," which is a status without rights or protection, and underscoring the continuing primacy of states in the life of most people regardless of globalization, whether consciously realized or not. The plight of economic migrants and refugees fleeing combat zones and environmental black holes suggests the humanitarian ordeal experienced by many people who are not securely connected to a state that is capable of providing the fundamental ingredients of sustainable life circumstances, much less human security. Refugees may be citizens with rights in the country they escaped from, but generally find themselves victimized anew by the country within which they are seeking sanctuary. Some governments adopt humane and generous approaches to refugees and stateless persons, but it is voluntary, sovereignty-driven, and the affected individuals are not the recipient of effective rights even if "human rights" are conceptually based on being human, and not on the basis of citizenship or nationality.

GEOPOLITICAL LOGIC

As statist logic is premised on equality before the law and in formal diplomatic relations, geopolitical logic is premised on inequality and the right of exception with respect to that portion of international law concerning issues of war and peace, and what is called "national security," or more broadly, "vital interests." While statism is descriptive of the horizontal dimension of world order within the Westphalian framework, geopolitics constitutes the vertical dimension that has been present ever since the modern structure of world order emerged in Europe in the mid-seventeenth century. Various empires exhibited the formalization of this vertical dimension as did European colonialism and American gunboat diplomacy, which at its height until World

War I, dominated much of the world. The anti-colonial movements of the last half of the twentieth century produced many newly independent sovereign states, universalizing the horizontal development of world politics, and shifting the political balance away from the West.

In the post-colonial global setting of the early twenty-first century the vertical dimension of world order is disguised to some degree because it was weakened and discredited in the past hundred years. These disguises make reference to certain normative justifications for the imposition of political will by the strong on the weak. Among the most prominent of these legal and moral arguments favoring otherwise prohibited uses of force are "self-defense," "humanitarian intervention," "responsibility to protect" or "R2P," and "nonproliferation." In each situation, depending on the facts the rationalization may be more or less plausible as a cover for a strategically motivated geopolitical maneuver. It seemed somewhat plausible to liberate Kosovo from Serbia in 1999, given the imminent threat of ethnic cleansing in the aftermath of the Srebrenica atrocity, but it was also clearly motivated by a parallel set of interests associated with maintaining NATO as a useful instrument of coercion in a post-Cold War setting. Kosovo created an opportunity for such a demonstration conveniently coinciding with the fiftieth anniversary of the alliance. Similarly, it seemed reasonable in 2011 to intervene in Libya to prevent a civilian massacre by Qaddafi forces in the city of Benghazi, although it was undoubtedly also true that the high quality of Libyan oil fields added a strategic incentive to the humanitarian impulse to protect threatened Libyan civilians. In contrast, without oil, the atrocities taking place in Syria contributed to a much weaker expression of international concern, although multiple reasons for this weakness also exist. Each of these situations is complex and distinctive, opening the way for contradictory interpretations as to the humanitarian effects of action and non-action, as well as the assessment of the relevance of the strategic interests at stake.

The geopolitical logic trumps statist logic in relation to international uses of force, and helps explain the marginalization of international law and the UN in the war/peace context, especially when tracking the behavior of the P5 (that is, the five permanent members of the Security Council). The constraints that are operative with respect to geopolitics derive from considerations of cost/benefit analysis, pressures exerted by group politics, prudential concerns about nuclear weaponry and avoiding casualties to its military personnel, and the sporadic anti-war restraints of public opinion (especially in liberal democracies). In the recent American-led coalition created as a response to threats posed by ISIS ("Islamic State of Iraq & Syria," also known by other names), President Obama did not even bother to justify recourse to force by reference to either international law or the UN, and seemed concerned only that he had a legal basis, which meant Congressional authorization within the American constitutional framework to act as he did. Revealingly, as well, much of the domestic controversy focused on what kind of specificity is necessary to authorize recourse to warlike behavior undertaken by the president in his role as commander-in-chief. Is it necessary to renew participation by Congress in each separate instance rather than rely on some general grant of authority? The tenor of this debate confirmed the impression that acting contrary to international law and without a UN mandate for recourse to non-defensive force is not very relevant in geopolitical contexts, and this is so even for a political leader such as Barack Obama who is a winner of the Nobel Peace Prize and seems sincerely to seek the alignment of American foreign policy with adherence to international law.

COSMOPOLITAN LOGIC

Partly as a result of economic globalization and partly due to the impact of global challenges associated with nuclear weapons and climate change, the migrant crisis in Europe, there is an emerging appreciation that neither statism nor geopolitics can protect overall human wellbeing and survival aspects of what might best be called the human or global interest. Despite decades of aspirational language, there seems to be no prospect in the immediate future of freeing humanity from the looming threat of nuclear catastrophe. The challenge of the weaponry has been geopolitically degraded in the form of creating a nonproliferation regime that distorts priorities by conceiving of the main danger of the weaponry as deriving from countries that do not have nuclear weapons rather than those that do. The 2003 aggressive war undertaken by the United States and the United Kingdom against Iraq was mainly rationalized as a counter-proliferation undertaking, epitomizing the subordination of cosmopolitan interests in getting rid of nuclear weapons (and other weapons of mass destruction) to the geopolitics of managing their control and dissemination.

A similar dynamic is present in relation to climate change, and the failed effort to contain the emission of greenhouse gasses, especially carbon dioxide. The UN mechanisms for lawmaking treaties have been unable to agree upon an obligatory framework that takes account of the scientific consensus on the need for strict regulation of the buildup of carbon in the atmosphere, and the resultant harmful effects of global warming. As a result the situation worsens, and irresponsibly the growing risk of harm from global warming and the burdens of adaptation are shifted to the future.

A further dynamic exhibiting these tensions involves the influx of unwanted asylum seekers and illegal immigrants whose search for sanctuary is an expression of state failure generating personal desperation. People fled their homeland only under the most dire of circumstances, especially when their journey is beset by known dangers of death and torment.

Without the formation of a political community of global scope it is unlikely that cosmopolitan logic will have any significant impact on behavior that reflects strong national interests and geopolitical priorities. The preconditions for such a development do not seem present as nationalist ideologies and the unevenness of material circumstances and civilizational identities continues to ensure the dominance of statism and geopolitics despite dysfunctional implications for the future of the human species. This persistence raises some deep questions about whether there exists a sufficient *species will to survive*. Until the advent of the Anthropocene Age such an imperative did not exist. Survival threats when they occurred were of limited scope, directed at particular societies or civilizations, that is, posing sub-species threats, but not endangering the species itself. What distinguishes the Anthropocene is the impact of *human activities* on the fundamental balances that have allowed life and social development to proceed for the species as a whole.

There have been past cases where cosmopolitan concerns have been addressed because competing logics were *not* seriously engaged: public order of the oceans, prohibition of ozone-depleting technologies, ecological preservation of Antarctica. Until the atomic attacks on Japanese cities in the closing days of World War II the cosmopolitan horizons of human activity were treated as matters of idealistic and spiritual concerns, but not relevant to issues of bio-political persistence. Even Woodrow Wilson's dream that the League of Nations would cause the institution of war to fade away was never taken seriously by the political leaders of the day, especially in Europe, who well understood that their privileged position of vertical control (that is, colonial system and accompanying exploitation) rested on an atmosphere of permanent war to ensure that "the natives" would not mount a challenge, and when they did, the military prowess of the rulers would rely on disproportionate force to restore their abusive pattern of control.

CIVIL SOCIETY LOGIC

The perspectives and activities of civil society occupy a broad and diverse spectrum of concerns, and contain elements of the other three logics that together compose world order, but not uniformly. Civil society activism is motivated by a range of concerns, some visionary, others reactionary. The progressively oriented normative motivations of transnational civil society actors have established an existential constituency disposed toward the realization of human and global interests. These actors have been active in relation to the promotion of human rights, environmental protection, nuclear disarmament, and climate change. That is, these civil society perspectives often merge in these venues with cosmopolitan perspectives, and present unified critical responses to statism and geopolitics. The counter-conferences at global policy events under UN auspices illustrate such encounters, and are likely to intensify as the awareness of global crises grow and the experience of the seriousness of such unmet global challenges as climate change, nuclear weaponry, and migratory flows increase.

In a larger historical sense, the question before all of us is whether civil society can become an agent of historical transformation in relation to cosmopolitan logic, thereby joining thought with action. Only such a reconstituted political imagination has any chance of producing policy and behavioral adjustments that make the human future a brighter prospect than now appears to be the case.

Hope to balance despair depends on our according *unrealistic* confidence in the capacity of progressive civil society movements to achieve transformative results, what I have described in the past as "the realism of a politics of impossibility' or 'a necessary utopianism." Nothing less seems responsive to the magnitude of the civilizational challenges already negatively impacting on human wellbeing. I have little doubt that those "realists" we rely upon as dutiful, taxpaying citizens are leading us down a path heading toward doomsday. It is time we shifted our allegiances and energies to the citizen pilgrims among us who are pointing us toward a humane and sustainable future for life on planet earth. In so directing our energies for transformation we need to be aware that the challenge is not just a matter of supporting humane and sensible *policies*, it is also a question of *structure* that allows problems to be addressed from global and human perspectives, thereby superseding national, religious, civilizational, and ethnic perspectives.

11

QUESTIONING PERPETUAL WAR IN AN ERA OF DRONE WARFARE

It might have been expected that President Obama chose to portray his second term approach to counter-terrorism at the National Defense University in 2013.[1] The choice of venue was itself a strong assurance that nothing would be said or done on that occasion that challenges in any fundamental way the global projection of American military power, and its associated conception of the security needs of the world's first "global state."[2] Obama's skillfully phrased speech was about refining technique in foreign policy, achieving greater efficiency in killing, critically interrogating the post-9/11 war mentality, while at the same time extolling the self-mystifying glories of American exceptionalism.[3]

That is, only the United States, and perhaps Israel and NATO, possessed an entitlement to use force at times and places of the actor's choosing without consulting the UN, respecting the constraints of international law, and heeding the admonition in the Declaration of Independence to show "a decent respect for the opinions of mankind." Such exceptionalism, especially as enacted by recourse to aggressive wars, invites resistance, polarizes political struggle, weakens the United Nations, and defeats any hope that stability will be achieved by the gradual realization of global justice rather than through the crude tactics of hard power diplomacy and militarism.[4]

There were several points of light in the otherwise dark sky of the Obama foreign policy firmament at the time.[5] Perhaps, the most promising aspect of Obama's presentation was its carefully hedged call for reexamining the still prevailing response to the 9/11 attacks as "perpetual war." From the outset this cautious, yet welcome, questioning represented an ironic inversion of Kant's prescriptions for perpetual peace. In Obama's words, "a perpetual war – through drones or troop deployments – will prove self-defeating and alter our country in troubling ways." Depending on how we read world history since 1939, it can be understood as an era of perpetual war with a brief intermission after World War II and between the end of the Cold War and the 9/11 attacks. Certainly, during the course of this period the United States has been continuously mobilized to engage simultaneously in two major regional wars on a moment's notice. This posture of a continuous readiness for war has definitely militarized state/society relations in the country.[6] There was nothing in Obama's speech to draw attention to the perils posed by such a militarized state, having achieved global military dominance, and creating a domestic "miliary-industrial complex" that would make even Dwight Eisenhower tremble with fear.[7]

Obama also critically questioned the character of the 2001 unlimited mandate to use force overseas without including any requirement of a specific prior procedure to obtain Congressional approval in Authorization to Use Military Force Act (AUMF). In Obama's words, "Our systematic effort to dismantle terrorist organizations must continue, but all wars, must end. That's what history advises. That's what our democracy demands." At the same time, Obama avoided directly challenging this AUMF legislation enacted to give the government precisely the legal authority to use force anywhere and at any time to wage war against supposed terrorist adversaries and their governmental guardians, and without delays associated with gaining in each instance authority from Congress to act. Such broad authority can be validly used even where there is no terrorist threat, as was the case for Iraq when it was invaded in 2003. Ten years later Obama was asking Congress "to determine how we can continue to fight terrorists without keeping America on a perpetual war-time footing." He then declared that what is needed is "to refine, and ultimately repeal, the AUMF mandate." Whenever politicians qualify a recommendation with the word "ultimately," I know almost for sure that an end game is unlikely, and is probably not even desired.

What Obama made evident is that although he had the right instincts with respect to renouncing "the war on terror," his political will to support the recommended course of action was far too weak to produce action, or maybe even to generate a needed debate on security for the country and the world, given the less feverish atmosphere and altered realities of mid-2013. Obama seemed comfortable framing counter-terrorist security policy as war so long as it is moving toward an understanding that war on terror will become more limited in scope at some future point, and that at least it has become possible to announce an intention to decide that the war on terror is over, and that incidents of terrorism should be hereafter handled as criminal acts, which is what happens in the rest of the world – Obama certainly took a step back from the fire, but failed to make any effort to put out the fire itself.[8]

To be sure there was in the speech many rhetorical flourishes that were probably designed to please liberal critics of drone warfare and Guantanamo. Such rhetoric invited a comparison with the far more bellicose and imperial language relied upon by George W. Bush, but Obama's approach was in a form that was sufficiently nationalistic to appease the right-wing jackals that give him little, or no, slack. Obama voiced his commitments to fight the extremists wherever they are found, while abiding by law, living up to ethical standards, and upholding the Constitution. He contended that his presidency "has worked vigorously to establish a framework that governs our use of force against terrorists – insisting upon clear guidelines, oversight and accountability that is now codified in Presidential Policy Guidance that I signed yesterday," a boast bound to raise more than a few skeptical eyebrows. Obama also did acknowledge that "this new technology raises profound questions – about who is targeted, and why; about civilian casualties, and the risk of creating new enemies; about the legality of such strikes under U.S. and international law; about accountability and morality." At the same time, this welcome willingness to suggest the need for some comprehensive rethinking was confusing, hedged by claims that all that has been done up to now has worked and that the drone war, despite a few mistakes, has at all stages been consistent with the international laws of war, the Constitution, and international morality.[9] It is notable that Obama refers to "profound questions" that deserve to be asked and answered, but craftily refrains from answering them himself, just as he was rather polite to Medea Benjamin, when she interrupted his talk from the floor with a direct challenge to use his authority as Commander-in Chief to close Guantanamo, which he responded to by saying that she deserved an attentive audience, although he was in substantial disagreement with what she was proposing, but without saying why and how. In assessing Obama's performance, I am reminded of the early downplaying among Soviet dissenters of Mikhail Gorbachev's claims to be a radical reformer: "He is giving us *glasnost* (freer speech) without *perestroika* (substantive and structural change), but he promised us both." In effect, when a policy is fundamentally at odds with law and morality *glasnost* is never enough.

Nevertheless, Obama was reacting to a tsunami of recent global criticism that amounted to an admission that the conduct of drone warfare and the maintenance of Guantanamo, for better or worse, had gravely damaged America's diplomatic reputation, generating acute resentment around the world, and quite likely was spawning the very extremism that drones are supposed to quell. The Obama presidency is attempting to step back from this precipice of disconnect without falling into an ambush staged by his detractors at home. As several Beltway pundits have pointed out the speech was long on vague generalities, short on policy specifics. It called in several ways for a more "disciplined" approach to the war on terror, yet at the same time claiming at some length that what has been done during the Obama years was "effective" and "legal," climaxed by the covert operation in Afghanistan that executed Osama bin Laden. In effect, the speech was acknowledging that the projection of American force around the world had become problematic, but could be fixed without making any very major shifts in behavior or objectives. Such a proposed tweaking of policy hardly qualifies as "profound" even if fully enacted, which is quite unlikely.

The speech was notably short even on those specifics that had been anticipated by those who ventured their expert opinion as to what to expect. For instance, it was expected that the controversial "signature strikes" whereby combat-age males have been targeted and killed if they are seen congregating in an area of a foreign country habitually inhabited by suspected terrorists, even if there is no concrete evidence of their relationship to political violence and extremism. Obama never even mentioned signature strikes.

Nor did he refer to the supposed likelihood of an announcement of returning the CIA to its primary role as a spy and intelligence gathering agency rather than as acting in a variety of paramilitary roles, although the drone policies relating to authorization and accountability will continue to be shrouded in secrecy and deniability at long as major responsibility for the use of drones remains headquartered at Langley. Of course, the purported significance of such a reassignment of responsibility for the drones may be part of the liberal hype. It seems unrealistic to expect a great breakthrough in transparency and control just because the Pentagon rather than the CIA would be presiding over the attacks. It could be illuminating to ask Chelsea Manning and Julian Assange what they thought about transparency at the Pentagon.

But there is much more at stake than was discussed in the lengthy speech. In trying to make the case that drone warfare is less invasive, resulting in fewer civilian casualties, Obama never even alluded to the severe degree to which drones terrorize any society exposed to their habitual use. Drone warfare, this supposedly miraculous counter-terrorism weapons system, is in its enactment a novel form of intense state terror that is enraging public opinion against the United States around the world, and not only at the places subject to attack, although especially there. A Yemeni citizen, Farea al-Muslimi told the U.S. Senate in recent hearings, about the attitudes toward drones in his home village, "when they think of America, they think of the fear they feel at the drones over their heads." In Pakistan, American drones have had a disastrously negative impact on public attitudes toward Islamabad's relationship with the United States, evoking acute and widespread grassroots hostility throughout this key Asian country. Even in Afghanistan, where the political violence shows no signs of abating, the former American handpicked leader,

Hamid Karzai, is now saying that the prospects for Afghan stability and peace would be enhanced by the departure of American-led NATO forces. This is a rather astounding about face for a leader so long dependent on Washington largess and human sacrifice, and should have induced Obama to raise some of those more profound questions about the viability and inherent morality of the continued U.S. insistence on projecting its military power to the far reaches of the globe. For whose benefit? At what costs? With what effects?

There is another line of prudential concern that was nowhere to be found in this less unconditional embrace of drones, which although deglamorized to some degree, remains an embrace. Some seventy countries currently possess drones, although not all of these have acquired attack drones, but the day is not far off when drones will be part of the military establishment of every self-respecting sovereign state, and then what? Obama spoke about the right of the United States to kill or capture suspected "terrorists" wherever they may be in the world if deemed by the government to be an imminent threat to American security interests and not amenable to capture. But is there not a de facto golden rule governing international relations: "what you claim the right to do to others, you authorize them to do." Of course, this is often modified by invoking the geopolitical bronze super-rule that is operative, at least in relations to most of the non-West: "we can do to you whatever we wish or feel the need to do, and yet there is no precedent created that can be invoked by others." American exceptionalism has long parted company with the central idea that international law is dependent for its effectiveness on the logic of reciprocity: namely, that what X does to Y, Y can do to X, or for that matter to Z, but with the technology of drones emergent, we may soon come to regret resting our claim on such a one-sided anti-law prerogative. A hegemonic approach to international law has been relied upon in relation to nuclear weapons, with a somewhat similar pronouncement by Obama in 2009 to work ultimately toward a world without such weapons. Four years later the meager effort to realize such a vision should be a cautionary indication that the future military application of drones is unlikely to be restricted so long as the United States finds their role useful, and given this prospect, a borderless future for violent conflict throughout the world should give Pentagon planners many a sleepless night.

There is another feature of the Obama approach that bears scrutiny. The discipline and care associated with his plea for a more restrictive approach to counter-terrorism is basically entrusted to the suspect subjectivities of governmental good faith in Washington. At least, the Wikileaks disclosures should have taught the citizenry that secrecy at high levels of public sector policymaking is intended to place controversial behavior of government beyond public scrutiny and democratic accountability. Obama is asking the American people to put their trust in the judgment and values of bureaucrats in Washington so as to ensure that democracy can be restored in the country, and a better balance struck between security and the freedoms of the citizenry. Perhaps, while waving the banner of national security, you can fool most of the people most of the time, but hopefully there are limits to such bromides from on high despite a compliant media.

In most respects, the song that Obama sang at the National Defense University does not live up to the melody. Obama refrained from taking what would have been the most natural and welcome step: belatedly putting the genie of war back in its box, and finally rejecting this dysfunctional blending of war and crime. After all, the deaths and displacements of the wars waged in Afghanistan and Iraq were major failures from the perspective of counter-terrorism, and one would think that such an adjustment was overdue. The root error committed immediately after 9/11 was to move the fight against al-Qaeda from the discourse of crime to the framework of war without any kind of thoughtful rationale. In the traumatic atmosphere that prevailed after the attack, this rushed transition to war partially done under the influence of neocon grand strategy that was actively seeking a global writ to intervene well before the attacks occurred, especially in the Middle East. The Bush entourage made no secret of its search for a pretext to take advantage of what was then called "the unipolar moment," a phrase no longer in fashion. It needs to be remembered that back before 9/11 the Democrats were being chided for their wimpish foreign policy during the 1990s that wasted a rare opportunity to create the sort of global security infrastructure that was needed to realize and protect the full potential of neoliberal globalization, which included a preoccupation with ensuring that the oil reserves of the Gulf remained accessible to the West. Although the United States has been chastened by its military setbacks in recent wars, its underlying grand strategy has not been repudiated or revised, and even now with so much at stake politically and militarily, there are strong pressures mounting to intervene militarily in Syria and to launch yet another aggressive war, this time against Iran.

If effect, we the peoples of the world, can take some slight comfort in the cautionary approach evident in the Obama tilt away from the hazards of "perpetual war," but until the more fundamental aspects of the American global role and ambitions, and its related militarism become the crux of the debate, we and others should not rest easy!

12

CHANGING THE POLITICAL CLIMATE: ONE INDIVIDUAL AT A TIME

"After the final no there comes a yes
And on that yes the future of the world depends."
(Wallace Stevens, "The Well Dressed Man with a Beard,"
Selected Poems (New York: Vintage, ed. H. Stevens, 1972: 190)

POINTS OF DEPARTURE

The most daunting challenge of adapting to the realities of the Anthropocene era is achieving a soft transition (that is, without major warfare, economic collapse, global environmental crisis) from state-centric world order to a geo-centric reconfiguring of political community that enables the emergence of effective and humane global governance. The dominant existing framework for transnational and global political action is still largely entrapped in old habits of thought and action wedded to the primacy of the territorial sovereign state and myopic time horizons that are too short to shape adequate responses to profound emergent challenges to the human future.[1]

Empowering state actors and educating publics to be more humanly and globally oriented and far-sighted in their pursuits would generate hopes for a brighter future.[2] Such empowerment depends on a widespread reorientation of individual identities toward a new model of citizen, called here "citizen pilgrim," whose principal affinities are with the species and its natural surroundings rather than to any specific state, ethnicity, tribe, nationality, civilization, or religion. The hopes and expectations of citizen pilgrims rest on the quest for a sustainable and spiritually fulfilling future for all in sustainable harmony with nature. In this respect, humanity is confronting, by a combination of unprecedented opportunity and danger, the practical and urgent imperative of fundamental change to meet existing threats and challenges and the prospect of catastrophic harm if a transition of sufficient magnitude does not occur in timely fashion.

This inquiry presupposes that transition of unprecedented scale is necessary, possible, and desirable, even though, at present, seemingly not feasible. Proposing with all seriousness what is possible, yet not widely seen as feasible, is one way of "thinking outside the box." This chapter explores two transitional paths to the future: (1) a revolutionary change in political consciousness that shapes a new planetary trajectory; and (2) statecraft that facilitates the pursuit of human and global interests. The first is actor-oriented, achieving transition without changing the structure of world order, whereas the second is system- or structure-oriented, insisting that needed behavioral changes will not happen without altering the institutional and ideational context within which public policies and practices are currently shaped. These two paths are not mutually exclusive. Indeed, long-term success will depend on a substantial convergence, if not their synthesis.

CITIZENS AND STATES

Our age is defined by the growing contrast between identities rooted in a state-centric conception of citizenship and the pressing need to address the main challenges confronting humanity as a whole. The horizons of citizenship for most persons on the planet generally coincide with the territorial boundaries of the state and reflect the related sovereignty-oriented ideology of nationalism.[3] Security for societies and individuals is mainly understood to be the responsibility of the governing authorities of states. Efforts to entrust international institutions with some of this responsibility have not been successful, especially for problems of global scope such as war and peace and managing the world economy.[4]

The historical transition underway entails a shift from structures and ideologies that serve the *part* to those that serve the *whole*, or humanity conceived of as a species. The political actors representing various parts include persons, corporations, NGOs, international institutions, religious organizations, and states.[5] Their outlook tends to be dominated by a fragmentary consciousness that seeks answers to various questions about "what is beneficial for the part," at best assuming this will be of benefit to the whole. Such actors do not generally waste their time on questions about "what is beneficial for the whole," which are most often dismissed as meaninglessly abstract or piously sentimental. Granted, the forces driving the emergence of a global polity do not all consider the good of the whole, either; various forms of oppressive centralized governance are also seeking historical relevance.[6]

Most people do not want or expect the perspective of the whole to be the basis of policy and action by decision-makers that represent the state, but are insistent that those who decide do their best to protect and promote what will most help the part whether it be country, corporation, religion, or group interests.[7] Citizenship is conferred by the state, which in return expects and demands loyalty, and even a readiness to sacrifice lives for the sake of the nation state, and certainly insists on the obligation to pay taxes and uphold laws. Citizenship, then, is very much bound up with ideas of a social contract between state and citizen, that is, an exchange of benefits and duties.

The citizen of a democratic state is a composite of juridical and psychological forms. The state confers citizenship through its laws, enabling participation in elections, issuing passports, and offering some protection abroad. Citizenship in this conventional sense is a *status* that varies from state to state in its particulars. Its essential function is to separate those who are included and those who are excluded. There are also legally grounded expectations of loyalty, the radical deviation from which can be the occasion for accusations of the capital crime of "treason." At the same time, the citizen of a constitutional democracy enjoys the right to dissent and to oppose unjust policies through the judicial process and through competitive elections. As such, the identity of a "citizen" contrasts with that of a "subject" of an absolute monarchy or autocracy where obedience is the paramount political norm.[8] A constitutional state struggles to maintain this delicate balance between the rights and duties of a citizen, especially in times of internal stress. One sign of a "successful" state is the existence of illegal or unwanted immigrants as a societal issue that often presupposes that citizenship is a privilege that the state can confer or withhold at its discretion.[9]

The second face of citizenship is psycho-political, the sense of loyalty as an existential reality, not a juridical category. When Palestinian citizens of Israel oppose the policies of their government toward the West Bank, East Jerusalem, and Gaza, they are reflecting a state of mind. Such sub-national identities and alienation from the nationality and orientation of the state is widespread in the world, the troubled realities of Kurds, Tamils, Basques, Kashmiris, and Western Saharans are illustrative, as are the numerous tribal loyalties throughout much of Africa or the marginalized identities of indigenous peoples in the Western Hemisphere and elsewhere. Many minorities feel alienated from the state of which they are citizens to varying degrees and collectively are, in effect, "captive nations" resident in states that do not command their loyalty. Treason and espionage vividly illustrate these issues. When Edward Snowden violated American security regulations by releasing many documents of the National Security Agency and disclosed its surveillance operations, he claimed to be acting on the basis of conscience, whereas the official leaders of the state viewed his actions as dangerous to the general well-being of society as determined by their interpretation of national security interests and existing laws. In a globalizing world, in which ethnicities and religions are mixed and interactive, the tensions between the juridical and existential demands of citizenship are intensifying. A poignant example is the plight of Mordechai Vanunu, a worker in the Israeli nuclear facility who many years ago confirmed the reality of Israel's suspected arsenal of nuclear weaponry and has since been treated both as an enemy of the state and a hero of humanity, serving eighteen years in prison, and even after being released, placed under a vindictive regime of house arrest in Israel.

What is new in these struggles between dissent and loyalty is that the issues now have an agenda and context that may exist within national boundaries (the Catalans and Scots, for example) as well as beyond the borders of the state. Some political innovations have acknowledged the latter, especially the idea of European citizenship superimposed on the citizenship conferred by European Union member states. So far, there is little evidence that those living in Europe are more likely to be loyal to their regional than to the traditional state affiliations, but at least this idea of European citizenship illustrates the layering of citizenship, enabling a person to be a legal and psychological participant in polities bigger (and smaller) than the territorial state that alone qualifies for membership in the United Nations and most international institutions. The layering of regional identities seems beneficial from the perspective of encouraging the development of the European Union as an instrument of cooperation and participation more effective than principally relying on intergovernmental patterns, but it does not meet the most urgent challenges of a planet in crisis.

GLOBAL CITIZENSHIP: NOT A REALITY, BUT AN ASPIRATION

Some years ago, I was chatting with a stranger on a long international flight. He was a businessman who traveled the world to find markets for his products. His home was in Copenhagen. He spoke very positively about the European Union's ability to overcome boundaries and national antagonisms. I asked him at that point in our conversation, "Does that make you feel like a European citizen?" His response was "Oh no, I am a world citizen." I asked him what he meant by that, and his reply was revealing: "Wherever I travel in the world I stay in the same kind of hotel. It makes no difference where I am, everywhere I go in the world seems the same to me."

Such an apolitical conception of world citizenship is a direct consequence of economic globalization and franchise capitalism. It is true that if you choose Westin or Intercontinental hotels in the main world cities you can travel the globe without ever leaving home, but this is a rather sterile view of the hopes and fears associated with the transition from a world of bounded nation-states absorbed by territorial concerns to a new world without boundaries. It surely leads to a weakening of the bonds of traditional citizenship without generating any new and broader sense of solidarity and community. It confuses the realities of the market with the realities of political community.

At the other extreme is the more familiar image of the world citizen as the idealist who experiences and celebrates the oneness of the planet and of humanity, overriding fragmented identities associated with the privileging of particular nations, ethnicities, religions, and civilizations. Like the businessman, the idealist is embracing an apolitical conception of citizenship, one which affirms identity on the basis of sentiment and evades the hard political work of overcoming the existential dominance of nationalism and state-centric world order. For such a world citizen, that which needs to be created is presupposed. The struggles of transition, as if by magic wand, are favorably resolved without encountering resistance.

These conceptions of what it means to be a "world citizen" possess an underdeveloped view as to the nature and value of citizenship. Being a proper citizen implies being an active participant in a democratic political community, extending loyalty, exhibiting approval and disapproval, voting, paying taxes, resonating to cultural expressions of unity by way of song, dance, and poetry, and having certain entitlements relating to reasonable expectations of human security. There is no possibility of having any of these attributes of citizenship fulfilled on a global scale given the way the world is currently governed. Prematurely proclaiming oneself a world citizen, if other than as an expression of aspiration, is an empty gesture that misleads more than it instructs.

To think of oneself as a European citizen is somewhat more meaningful, although still, on balance, more confusing than clarifying. To be sure, Europe has virtually abolished internal borders, war between European states verges on the unthinkable, the Euro acts a common currency for the entire continent, European institutions have broad authority to override national policies and laws under many circumstances, Europe has a regional framework setting forth binding human rights standards and a tribunal to resolve conflicts as to their interpretation, and finally, Europe has a parliament of its own that is now elected by direct votes of people. Yet Europe has still failed to establish a political community that elicits widespread loyalty or exhibits much unity under stress, except in relation to an external enemy. Most Europeans remain overwhelming nationalistic in their loyalties and want their national government to do what is best for their country, rather than what is best for Europe should the two clash. European citizenship, as conferred by the Maastricht Treaty, is at this point still an unfulfilled promise rather than a meaningful status in either a juridical or an existential sense.

The reality of citizenship is best displayed during periods of crisis, and the European recession has made people far more aware of the fragility of the regional experiment as it bears on the future of Europe. As the Mediterranean members of the EU succumbed to the economic crisis, the northern European states, especially Germany, began to exhibit discomfort and express condescension. Irritated Berliners were bemoaning why hardworking and prudent Germans should be helping lazy, indulgent Greeks live a decadent life beyond their means. In their turn, offended Greeks asked why they should forfeit their autonomy and mortgage their future to an anal retentive German fiscal policy that has learned none of the lessons of economic recovery from the experience of the Great Depression in the 1930s. The revival of European nationalism was even more pronounced in reaction to the migrant crisis of 2015 where borders were abruptly closed to halt the influx of unwanted refugees and asylum seekers, and the countries of Europe were resistant to adopting a regional approach to the humanitarian crisis.

In contrast, during the same experience of sharp recession in the United States, the debate centered on such issues as banks being too big to fail or why Wall Street rather than Main Street should alone receive bailout billions, rather than on the reckless-ness of Alabama as compared to, say, Connecticut. In the United States, despite its deep federal structure, there is an overriding sense of community at the national level. American citizenship is meaningful in ways that European citizenship falls short because of the abiding strength of national consciousness (despite the continuing divisiveness of American Civil War memories and a lingering sense of Southern separateness) as compared with the feeble bonds that bind Europeans together as Europeans.[10] In this sense, despite the success of the EU, there was a greater sense of Europeanness during the Cold War when the Soviet Union was perceived as a common threat than there is today. Anxieties about a perceived Soviet threat generated an unprecedented spirit of cooperation creating a community of fate in Europe.

In other words, some of the political preconditions for European citizenship are present but the most vital are still absent, while the political preconditions for world citizenship are almost totally missing. There are some good reasons to be confused about this latter reality. After all, the United Nations was established to prevent war among nations, and we indulge language games that allow us to talk about "the world community" as if there was one. A closer look at the way the world works makes us realize that the United Nations, despite the rhetorical pretensions of its Charter, is much more an instrument *of* statecraft than an *alternative* to it. Indeed, almost all governments continue to be led by political realists who view their role as serving short-term national inter-ests and are privately dismissive of any encroachment on these priorities that derive from notions of "world community," even if based on international law and morality.

Within this framing of global policy, the UN, international law (even international criminal law), and moralizing rhetoric are all instrumentally and selectively useful in the pursuit of foreign policy goals, especially if not applied consistently. The selective application of supposedly global norms makes transparent the state-centric and geopolitical underpinnings of world order. For instance, the double standards associated with the implementation of international criminal law suggest that up to now there is accountability for the weak and vulnerable and impunity for the strong, a pattern described as "victors' justice" after World War II. An International Criminal Court (ICC) has been established, which was a major achievement of its advocates, but a success tempered by the realization that the most dangerous political actors forego the option to join. The ICC pursues wrongdoers in Sudan and Libya, while turning a blind eye toward the United States, Russia, China, and the United Kingdom, and their closest allies. It is instructive to realize that the ICC came into being despite the resistance of the largest and most dangerous states in the world. The fact that a tribunal could be established in 2002 to assess the individual criminal responsibility of political and military leaders of sovereign states seemed like an encouraging move toward creating a global rule of law in relation to war/peace and human rights issues, and it was, although its performance has so far been uneven and often disappointing.

This clarifies the situation of global citizenship in two key ways. First, there is no effective enforcement of global norms relating to fundamental issues of human security, and therefore no bonds of community binding the individual to the world by way of citizenship based on a social contract. Second, major states manipulate the directives of the UN and international law to serve their own national interests, revealing the workings of a *geopolitical regime* of power rather than a *global rule of law regime* that would above all treat equals equally. Without a trusted system of laws, no sustainable community can be brought into being, and hence no genuine bonds of citizenship can be established.

Such a critique expresses the dilemmas of citizenship in this time of transition. The most fundamental missing element in this premature projection of world citizenship is *time*. It is possible to wish for, and even affirm, human solidarity, and to highlight the commonalities of the human species under conditions of heightened interaction and interdependence. Yet such feelings by themselves are incapable of creating the basis for acting collectively in response to urgent challenges of global scope. Such behavior requires the emergence on grassroots and elite levels of a widespread recognition that the only viable governance process for the planet is one that greatly enhances capabilities to serve human and global interests. This emergence is more likely to occur in an interactive sequence in which transnational grassroots activism precedes governmental shifts in priorities due to the obstacles posed by bureaucratic entrenchment that tends to resist fundamental changes of policy even when initially mandated by the citizenry. Only in the aftermath of a social movement that advances new demands are governing authorities likely to go along. The American civil rights movement is illustrative of these dynamics. The transition is about moving from the here of egoistic state-centrism to the there of humane geo-centrism, which implies a journey and a struggle against institutionalized social forces that are threatened by or opposed to such a transformation. In this undertaking, the citizen pilgrim combines the identity of a participant in a community and the acknowledgement that the desired community does not presently exist, that its essential nature is to bond with a community that is in the midst of a tortuous birth process.[11]

MATERIAL CONDITIONS OF URGENCY

Throughout human experience, there has always been a strong case for adopting the identity of "citizen pilgrim," and many spiritually motivated individuals have done so in their own ways under a variety of banners. What is historically unique about the present is that the challenge of transformation is rooted in fundamental material conditions resulting from human activities: the outcomes of technological innovations and earlier progress are now threatening the species and its natural habitat with apocalyptic blowback. In other words, it has always been true from an ethical perspective that there are far better ways for people to live together on the planet, especially under conditions of mutual respect, without collective violence, valuing human community, and in ways that reward achievement while caring for the poor and vulnerable. At times, the failure to adapt to challenges either from natural causes or from conflict has led to the collapse of communities or even entire civilizations, but never before has the species as such been confronted by challenges of global scale.[12] There have always been risks of planetary events such as collisions with giant meteors or an unexpected shift in the orbit of the sun that are beyond human agency, and could at some point doom the species. There have also been lethal pandemics that threatened to wipe out the human species resulting from diseases for which there was no known cure. Today, however, we see the accumulation of dangerous material conditions that have been generated by human agency and could be addressed in a manner that is beneficial for the survival, sustainability, wellbeing, and happiness of the species.

The two most dramatic examples of such realities are the dangers of nuclear war and climate change. These two sources of extreme danger both reflect the technological evolution of human society associated with modernity, scientific discovery, and the human search for wealth and dominion, and neither set of risks can be sufficiently reduced without significant progress with respect to the transition from state-centric to geo-centric world order. Addressing these threats requires a "new realism" informing the outlook of those with governing authority. Above all, this new realism involves a readiness to uphold commitments to serve human and global interests as necessary, even if it requires subordinating currently incompatible national interests and an array of private sector concerns.

This "new realism" can only be brought into being by drastic shifts in political consciousness that inform citizenship in such a manner that fosters the well-being of the species and restores a collaborative relationship between human activities and the surrounding environment. Such a relationship existed to an impressive degree in many pre-modern societies where there existed a sense of mutual dependence in relations between human activities and natural surroundings, as well as sensitivity to seven generations past and future, that is absent from the modernist sensibility that takes nature for granted. In this mindset, nature is valued either for its resources, as a sink for the free discharge of wastes, or as a retreat from the rigors of "civilization."[13] With resource scarcities, population growth, pollution, and climate change has come the realization that without a comprehensive post-modern equilibrium between human activity and the natural surroundings, the future prospects of the species are rather grim.[14] The unrepentant fantasies of modernity persist in the form of utopian geo-engineering schemes that represent efforts by the old realism to find technological solutions for the problems generated by technology, which is itself is revealing dangerous uncertainties and posing severe additional risks of its own.[15]

The imperatives of a transition to a safer, more sustainable world are resisted by the embedded assumptions of the old realism: that military capabilities and war-making are the keys to security, that GNP growth is the indispensable foundation of political stability and economic contentment, that technology and markets will find solutions for any challenges that arise before serious threats materialize, and that the correct role of governments of sovereign states is to manage this set of relationships on behalf of national political communities variously situated.[16] Such an orientation is not so much wrong as it is anachronistic and in need of fundamental adjustment. Further, such adjustment is much more likely to take place in a non-traumatic situation, that is, before catastrophe becomes a reality rather than a menacing possibility.

It would be a serious mistake to underestimate the obstacles that lie ahead and currently seem to lock societies into a civilizational orientation that falls far short of the bio-political potential and survival needs of the human species.[17] At present, governments seem unable to address the practical challenges posed by nuclear weaponry, climate change, poverty, political violence, and human security. Existing governance structures and ideological worldviews dominant among both officials and society seem stuck in past modes of problem-solving and are failing to meet expectations of the citizenry.[18] Such a failure is exhibited by widespread despair, denial, and alienation. Even when signs of active disaffection erupt unexpectedly as happened in the Middle East during the Arab Spring that produced a series of political upheavals and the Occupy Movement that briefly challenged the inequities generated by the machinations of Wall Street and the world economy, the embedded structures of governance and their societal allies have displayed an extraordinary capacity to resist such challenges, and restore a status quo that seemed earlier repudiated.

RECREATING POLITICAL COMMUNITY

The calling of the citizen pilgrim is not meant to be a lonely journey toward a better future. It is intended as a call for an engaged citizenry responsive to the need and desire for a reconstituted *future* as well as a repaired *present*. The commitment to navigating the transition entails the infusion of political leadership, the recreation of human community, and the invigoration of the electorate with the values and perceptions of the new realism. Transition can be achieved through a shift in governance structures such that state-centric world order is superseded by a humane geo-centric world order. Such a reorientation implies stronger globally oriented institutionalization by way of United Nations reform. Alternatively, a geo-centric world order could emerge as the self-conscious result of the establishment of a new framework for cooperative action capable of providing the world with the level of centralized governance that is required, while exhibiting sensitivity to ideas of subsidiarity, decentralization, dispersal of authority, checks and balances, even philosophical anarchism, and above all, a sense of global justice.[19]

In this respect, the engaged citizen pilgrim is devoted to the here and now of political action (as well as the pursuit of a visionary future), whether by way of exhibiting empathy and solidarity with the sufferings of those most vulnerable or by working toward innovative steps serving human and global interests. Such steps should, to the extent possible, reflect the interpretations and understandings of the new realism. Illustrative projects include the establishment of a global peoples parliament with an assigned mission of articulating interests from the perspective of people rather than of governments.[20] Another familiar proposal is a global tax of some kind, levied on currency transactions or international flights or casino and lottery profits, which could loosen the geopolitical and fiscal leash that now limit international institutions in their capacity to serve human and global interests. Along these lines would also be the establishment of an independent global emergency force capable of quick reactions to natural disasters and humanitarian catastrophes without being subject to funding by states or the veto power of the permanent members of the UN Security Council. These initiatives are not new, but their active promotion alongside avowals of citizen pilgrimages would manifest modes of participation in political life whose aim was to achieve humane global governance in accordance with the precepts of the new realist.[21]

Such innovations would help to overcome the design deficiencies of state-centric world order, given the current array of global challenges. Because of the still dominant influence of old realism, such innovations are vulnerable to various degrees of what might be called geopolitical cooption. The United Nations itself is undoubtedly the best example of an institutional innovation with a geo-centric mandate that has gone awry almost from its inception, with its deference to both sovereign states and hegemonic actors (via the Security Council veto) it seems clear that the architects of the UN saw the future through a multi-state and hegemonic optic, and hence the incapacity to address problems of truly global scope was part of the organizational matrix, and should not occasion surprise or disappointment. The UN has been geopolitically coopted over the period of its existence in such fundamental respects that its defining role has been stabilizing state-centric and hegemonic patterns of world order rather than preventing war and facilitating transition to a geo-centric future. This assessment is most evident in the double standards evident in the pattern of UN responses to emergency situations, for instance, in the diplomacy surrounding the application of the Responsibility to Protect (R2P) norm or in relation to the management of nuclear weaponry as between the nuclear weapons states and non-nuclear states.

As earlier mentioned, the potentially valuable contributions of the ICC have so far been marred by the same double standards that infuse the entire edifice of state-centric world order, resulting in a pattern of impunity for the West and accountability for leaders in the South. As such, the ICC is ambivalent in its contributions to peace and justice; still, it may yet become more attuned to human and global interests. It is that attunement that distinguishes the citizen pilgrim from what might be called "a liberal internationalist" who favors stronger global governance capacity, but lives within a bubble of the old realism and its questionable reconciliation of global reform and geopolitics. In this gradualist view of global reform, state-centric logic and national interests are taken for granted as the prism through which foreign policy is shaped, but to the extent feasible, the liberal internationalist favors more international cooperation along with the pursuit of a range of mutual interests, and favors greater funding for international institutions and more responsiveness to humanitarian needs. The realist nature of the perspective is expressed by limiting responsible discussion of global policy to that which is deemed "feasible" from the perspectives of the leadership of sovereign states, political actors of last resort, and their entourage of governing elites.

CITIZEN PILGRIMS AS NONVIOLENT WARRIORS OF THE GREAT TRANSITION

Prospects for the future depend on altering the outlook and performance of governments representing states so that they truly align with broad-based citizen, not special, interests. This is particularly true for constitutional democracies where public policy seems increasingly under the sway of strong private sector interest groups. Authoritarian states, especially with control over the economic infrastructure, do not require the consent of the governed to nearly the same extent, and can act or not more freely for better and worse to take account of rapidly changing perceptions. In constitutional democracies, the relationship of leadership to the citizenry is very direct, though often muted or corrupted by the influence of powerful special interests. Lobbying, extensive secrecy and surveillance, and corporatized media all deflect government from a rational calculation of equitably conceived national interests and tend to obstruct policy deference to long-term human and global interests. The "military-industrial-think tank-media complex" has over the decades protected the nuclear weapons establishment from disarmament advocacy, and the campaigns of the fossil fuel industry have lent a measure of credibility to climate skepticism despite its rejection by 97 per cent of climate experts.

Experience confirms that government policy will not shift against such entrenched interests without a popular mobilization that alters the political climate sufficiently to allow deep change to happen. In the 1980s, this happened in the United States and the United Kingdom in relation to apartheid South Africa. In this case, the ethical repudiation of official racism provided the basis for altering the political climate to such an extent that Ronald Reagan and Margaret Thatcher, both conservative leaders who valued strategic and economic cooperation with apartheid South Africa, were led to endorse sanctions that contributed significantly to the eventual success of the anti-apartheid campaign.

Nuclear weaponry does pose a profound ethical challenge, but its main challenge is a prudential one of resting the security of major states and their friends on a conditional commitment to destroy tens of millions of innocent persons in a global setting (what was called Mutually Assured Destruction or MAD in the Cold War discourse) where conflict and irrational behavior have been recurrent features. It would thus appear to be the case that both ethics and rationality favor phased and verified nuclear disarmament as had been legally stipulated by the nuclear weapons states in the Nonproliferation Treaty of 1968.[22] This prudential case has been reformulated in a post-Cold War setting by research calling attention to the dire consequences for the whole earth due to the prospects of a "nuclear famine" in the event of moderate usage of nuclear weaponry in a limited regional war.[23]

The global challenge of climate change is more complex and, in some ways, exposes more directly the limits of *globally* oriented problem-solving in a state-centric framework. Unlike the case of disarmament, there is strong intergovernmental support for the scientific consensus as to the need for mandatory regulations to reduce greenhouse gas (especially carbon) emissions so as to prevent further harmful climate disruption. For the past twenty years, the UN has sponsored annual conferences that bring together most governments in the world to move toward implementing the scientific consensus, and yet so far little happens. Rationality gives way to special interests, and short-term calculations of advantage are given precedence in the policy arenas of government, producing inevitable and intractable stalemates that cancel out the diplomatic rhetoric that seems to grasp the gravity of the situation and the need for drastic and timely action. The state system seems stuck, and the old realism seems set to shape human destiny in adverse ways for the foreseeable future.

In such settings, the citizen pilgrim offers society a voice of sanity that speaks from the liberated isolation of the wilderness.

It envisions a future responsive to the long-term survival of the human species and the goals of maximizing its wellbeing and pursuing global justice. Some citizen pilgrims may be seeking radical revisions of the worldview of the national leadership cadres of society in the form of the embrace of the new realism of human and global interests, pursued within an enlarged sphere of temporal accountability. Other citizen pilgrims may be thinking of a political community that is planetary in scope that organizes its activities to serve all peoples on the basis of individual and collective human dignity and envisions the replacement of a world of sovereign states with a democratically constituted geo-centric framework of governance – norms, institutions, procedures, and actors.

The citizen pilgrim is not primarily motivated by averting danger and mitigating injustice on a global scale, although such concerns occupy the foreground of her political consciousness. The most basic drive is spiritual, to pursue what is desired even if unattainable, to affirm as a goal the perfection of the human experience within the diverse settings present in the world. As Goethe said, "him who strives he we may save." By striving, the sense of time comes alive in citizenship and political participation, as it must, if the Mount Everest challenges of global transition are to be successfully traversed.

13

DOES THE HUMAN SPECIES WISH TO SURVIVE?

The question is deliberately provocative, yet relevant to reflections on the future of humanity. The question is framed to encourage inquiry into whether the human species as a species has the collective will needed to overcome several global challenges that confront humanity before the onset of catastrophic havoc. Such framing can be labeled as "prudent alarmism" given the risks arising from global warming trends and the continued possession, deployment, and development of nuclear weapons amid a politically fragmented global arrangements that continues to be embedded in a war system.

Apocalyptic thinking has acquired a deservedly bad name, a kind of cosmic "crying wolf." In public consciousness ultimate warnings are primarily associated with crazed religious cults that point to a particular date as the biblically designated end of the world, and when the date passes without anything happening, there is a shrug of the shoulders among true believers, reassuring words from the leader, and a resumption of business as usual.

Science fiction writers long preoccupied with real-world problems, especially the persistence of war, have developed a variety of apocalyptic and post-apocalyptic scenarios that at their best stretch our imaginative faculties. Such fiction usually entertains far more than it influences public perceptions, thrilling exploits of the imagination, but not to be taken seriously by the arbiters of power. There are occasional exceptions such as H.G. Wells' *War of the Worlds* and Aldous Huxley's *Brave New World*, but even such classics have a cultural rather than a political impact.

IMAGINING THREATS TO THE PLANET

One common theme encountered in science fiction literature does illuminate the failure to deal with common global problems through effective cooperation among sovereign states. The scenario is narrated as follows: a condition of intense fear on the part of political leaders is generated by confirmed reports of an impending attack on earth from a hostile advanced species located somewhere in the galaxy. The threat has been verified by the leading intelligence agencies of the world prompting an emergency global convention of political leaders to plan a unified defense. To ensure an effective defense of the planet persuades national leaders that it is expedient to establish a world government. In other words, the collective will to defend the peoples of the planet forges a planetary alliance preparing to wage a war of survival against threats of annihilation posed by alien intruders overcomes the political fragmentation that currently inhibits the protection of the human interest.

Such a scenario seems realistic if the credibility of the threat is accepted, although reactions could cover a wide range of responses. Political communities, whether tribal or national or even civilizational, have throughout history displayed a capacity for greatly heightened forms of cooperation, including extraordinary sacrifices of blood and treasure, if threatened by a common enemy. This experience of achieving exceptional cooperation rests on mobilizing the political will of existing communities. It relies on the logic of the war system as operating within a fragmented world order consisting of sovereign states, and presupposes an enemy. Without the menace created by an enemy, the record of cooperation for the sake of the human interest is not impressive. A prime example of both such expedient cooperation under conditions of perceived necessity and its fragility if the perception no longer exists is provided by the cooperation between the liberal democracies of the West during World War II and communist Soviet Union, and the onset of the Cold War shortly after the fall of fascism.

From religious visions of end time to science fiction depictions of inter-planetary warfare, we come to a contemporary secular envisioning of the end of human civilization in its most modern forms. The atomic attacks on Hiroshima and Nagasaki in 1945 created a widespread anxiety about what the future would bring if there was ever a third world war. Many dire warnings were made, perhaps most memorably by Albert Einstein: "I know not with what weapons World War III will be fought, but World War IV will be fought with sticks and stones." There were also artistic renderings in film and fiction that shared a sense that the species would likely survive a nuclear war, but in degraded forms identified with urban barbarism and "bare survival." One of the most rending portrayals of such a post-apocalyptic landscape is found in Cormac McCarthy's The Road.[1] The "lucky" survivors formed violent gangs of foragers that roam the countryside searching for scraps of food and sips of water. Such marauders are themselves never more than minutes away from rival predators also desperately seeking the necessities of life. These accounts of a post-apocalyptic future rest on the premise that the species would survive, but in dramatically diminished life circumstances dominated by anarchic violence, without governing institutions and procedures, and lacking any pretensions of civic community life.

PREVENTING HUMAN CATASTROPHE

What is missing from these accounts is some inquiry into what might have prevented the catastrophe from happening in the first place. I believe adopting such a focus is a necessary first step in meeting the global challenges. Humanity is in the midst of enduring unsustainable trends that increase the risk of a catastrophic future that can be avoided, but only by way of a collective response that draws strength from species identity. Perhaps, the most severe danger is not the threat of bare survival of the kind we associated with life in Nazi death camps or in a social setting dominated by anarchic gangs running wild in the city and countryside. The greatest hazard is better understood as directed at humane modes of existence that have in modern times steadily extended life expectancy, provided empowering technologies, raised materialist expectations, and eased the burdens of daily labor for many earthlings. That is, what is likely to be lost is what was long thought to have been the gains of modernity fueling illusions of inevitable progress thanks to the achievements of science and technology.

The experience with nuclear weapons illustrates vividly the inability of humanity to act like a *species* rather than as an antagonistic amalgam of *sub-species* communities, bounded in space and consciousness to identities of nation, race, ethnicity, religion, class, gender, and civilization. Expressed differently, to eliminate nuclear weapons, and other weapons of mass destruction, requires a strong dedication to the wellbeing of the *whole* that is absent from the collective consciousness of human societies and unsupported by the structures of either the world economy or the state system. The world continues to be organized and authority structured so as to give the highest and ultimate priority to the wellbeing and survival of the *part*. Some feel reassured that there has been no use of a nuclear weapon since 1945, but a more careful scrutiny of this period would suggest that the world escaped nuclear war on several occasions by the narrowest of margins. Recent research suggests that even a limited regional nuclear war would likely induce a global famine of ten years' duration that would cause an almost total collapse of organized life on the planet.

After World War II, beneath the shadows cast by the recent massive devastation of the just concluded conflict and forebodings about the nature of major future wars, the United Nations was brought into being. The primary pledge of the UN "to save succeeding generations from the scourge of war" was from the outset a meaningless gesture of aspiration. The requisite political will to address the scourge of war was missing. Even the capabilities and independence needed by the UN to implement the promise and potential of collective security were not forthcoming. And the more modest task of ridding the world of the specter of a future nuclear war turned out to be beyond the reach of global reformers and inconsistent with the political will of world leaders.

There were some early initiatives taken by the United States to achieve nuclear disarmament, but always in a manner designed to ensure American dominance should any future rearmament process occur if the arrangement broke down. Besides, there was no indication that the Soviet Union, although lacking the bomb, was itself willing to trust its ideological and geopolitical adversary before it too had the comparable weaponry. And so a costly and dangerous arms race unfolded rather than a demilitarizing disarmament process. The path of hard power security was chosen while the path of soft power security was not chosen.

The realism and consciousness of sub-species leaders of governments remained paramount. There were important grassroots initiatives in Western democratic societies throughout the Cold War exhibiting widespread fear of nuclear war and related expressions of ethical disgust about basing security on the threat of retaliatory omnicide. Despite this, the geopolitical rivalry between the two superpowers and their allies dominated the global stage. Significantly, the United Kingdom, France, and China each decided that their security would be more enhanced by possessing their own separate arsenal of nuclear weapons than by foregoing the option. Security based on deterrence, seeking to offset the omnicidal threats of adversaries by mounting counter-threats, was preferred to security based on disarmament. Additionally, the hierarchical side of world order was underscored by the nonproliferation approach, which rested on the perverse proposition that the main danger to world peace came from the countries that did *not* possess nuclear weapons rather than from those that possessed, deployed, and were continuing to develop this weaponry.

THE PERSISTENCE OF STATISM

What is evident in this process is that the UN as an institutional framework was structured around the idea that sovereign states, and only states, deserved to be treated as full members of international society. Even more revealingly, the most powerful (and dangerous) states were constitutionally exempted from any obligation to adhere to international law and the UN Charter. This exemption took the form of giving the five winners in World War II a veto power that was a guaranty that a valid UN decision would never override what the government of any one of these states decreed to be in its national interest. My point is to suggest that the menace of nuclear weapons could not be addressed in a manner consistent with the human interest given the primacy of sub-species identity that was deliberately embedded in the structure and operations of the UN since its establishment. As a result, the treatment of nuclear weapons has been "normalized" in ways that resemble earlier weapons innovations that were not threatening to the civilizational circumstance of the human species as a whole, but deemed useful and relevant to the security goals of states. In that spirit, chemical weapons were effectively banned despite their battlefield potency because the leading governments did not require them, and their low cost and simple technology would mean that even far weaker societies could develop capabilities to challenge global power hierarchies.

This same dynamic is evident in relation to climate change, but in an even starker form. At least with nuclear weapons, there is the possibility, however remote, that their use can be indefinitely avoided by prudence and deterrence, and luck. With global warming there is no such possibility. Scientists have been warning us in constantly shriller tones that if we go on as we have been since the industrial revolution disaster awaits us in coming decades. Already the telltale signs of global warming such as the frequency of extreme weather, melting glaciers, desertification, water and food scarcities abound. And there is no sign whatsoever that governments are prepared even to consider abandoning the iron law of growth or taxing carbon emissions or discouraging consumerism or restricting human fertility. That is, the main decentralized political units, sovereign states, are not able to summon the political will to respond responsibly to the near-scientific certainty that a terrible future awaits coming generations. True, the rich and sophisticated countries will be able to adapt better, and stave off many of the worst consequences anticipated by climate scientists, but only for an undetermined length of time, and during a period when less well endowed countries become a new type of "failed state," sending waves of migrants across their borders in search of safety and livelihood. The mass of migrants seeking refuge from war-torn countries in the Middle East and sub-Saharan Africa have produced a variety of reactions that exhibit both the best and the worst in human traditions of hospitality to strangers in need.

This overall assessment is shared by a consensus of expert observers, perhaps most persuasively by Clive Hamilton in two recent books: *Requiem for a Species: Why We Resist the Truth About Climate Change* (2010) and *Earthmasters* (2013). As with such other sages of our time as Richard Tarnas and Slavoj Žižek, Hamilton places his hopes on a transformed consciousness that will find a way forward by overcoming the modern idea that human activity best progresses by thinking of the environment, and nature more generally, as there to be managed, exploited, and dominated for human benefit.[2] The stress is placed on recognition of the danger, and then a resolve to act to overcome the radical disenchantment of human interactions with its environment that is the only home the human species can ever hope to have. I share completely this plea for active engagement in achieving this transformational shift in human consciousness, but it is not enough to rescue the species from impending doom.

CAN THE HUMAN SPECIES LEARN TO SURVIVE?

I would call attention to two additional sets of fundamental concerns. First of all, the bio-political character of human nature as it has evolved over the centuries, and in diverse social and cultural settings. The simple question raised is whether there exists a sufficiently evolved species identity as compared to less encompassing collective realities as family, neighborhood, nation. As far as I can tell there is no evidence that a collective will of meaningful strength at the species level exists. Even nuclear weapons survival threats were generally treated as threats to such existential levels of community, especially to individual, family, and national survival, and at most, to civilizational survival.

The second concern relates to those features of human behavior that facilitate survival in the face of severe challenges. Jared Diamond has explored survival success and failure from a civilizational perspective in his fine book, Collapse: How Societies Choose to Fail or Succeed (2005). In a later book Diamond investigates how we can learn and adapt survival skills from pre-modern societies.[3] Put differently, until the middle of the last century, *human* survival was never really challenged except by religious prophesy, science fiction and ominous fears prompted by pandemics posing unlimited threats to the health of the species.

Related to this lack of species experience with meeting collective challenges is the fragmented structure of world order as discussed earlier. The challenges of modernity did not require exceptional levels of cooperation to serve human interests. Governments could be induced to cooperate to the extent necessary for mutual benefit as in establishing secure international navigation and communication or for the general wellbeing if no great sacrifice of self-interest was entailed, as with establishing a system of governance for the oceans or Antarctica. When wealth, economic growth, and energy use is at issue diverse national and class interests along with corporate greed prevent cooperative solutions. This limit on cooperative solutions is accentuated by the extremely uneven resource endowments and technological capabilities of distinct political communities. The potential wealth of deep sea minerals was big enough to make powerful governments resist the effort of smaller states to treat such resources communally as belonging to and for the benefit of "the common heritage of mankind."

Responding to global challenges on the basis of species wellbeing will require taking account not only of the alienated consciousness that derives in the West from the Enlightenment, separating human activity from nature in destructive and misleading ways. It must also appreciate the problems that arise due to the lack of bio-political experience in dealing with challenges to *human* wellbeing associated with issues of truly global scope. Finally, there is the need to recognize that world order continues to rest on the primacy of sub-species identities as embodied in sovereign states, and that the UN is a failure if conceived of as a project to serve the human interest. The UN merely reproduces sub-species identities in both of these destructive forms without creating a global community in even a rudimentary form, that is, the sovereign state as the main agent of identity formation and the geopolitical super state remains the principal managerial and organizational force that manipulates global concerns to conserve and promote its dominant position.

For a more hopeful human future we as species need urgently to affirm the imperative of serving human interests and to recognize that this can only begin to occur if people are able to create a vibrant global political community that embraces the whole of humanity. Such a transformed identity does not imply the loss of more specific identities, but it does require their transcendence for the public common good when and as the need arises. The determination of this need and effective responses does seem to require much stronger global structures of authority than exist currently, and how this comes about given the resilience of sub-species identities and uneven material endowments is beyond the current outer limits of the politically attainable. Hence, we drift mindlessly toward a condition of more and more serious species jeopardy.

NOTES

2. THE POST-SECULAR DIVIDE

1 I have tried to explore this question in previous writing, especially Richard Falk, *Religion and Humane Global Governance* (New York: Palgrave, 2001), esp. 35–59.

2 Among the first prominent scholar/statesman to articulate this notion was Zbigniew Brzezinski, *The Grand Chessboard: American Primacy and Its Geostrategic Imperatives* (New York: Basic Books, 1997); a partial explanation of the failure to grasp the insufficiency of the secularist comprehension of world politics is the degree to which its preoccupations were constrained by its Western provincial orientation. With a less confined outlook the division of India into dominant Hindu and Muslim states at the moment of independence should have signaled the great importance of religious identity in the non-Western societies of the world.

3 See Tu Weiming, *The Global Significance of Concrete Humanity: Essays on the Confucian Discourse in Cultural China* (New Delhi, India: Centre for the Studies in Civilizations, 2010); Zhang Weiwei, *The China Wave: Rise of a Civilizational State* (Hackensack, NJ: World Century, 2012); Fred Dallmayr, *Being in the World: Dialogue and Cosmopolis* (Lexington, Kentucky: University of Kentucky Press, 2013).

4 See the approach taken by the influential Catholic theologian Hans Küng, in *A Global Ethic for Global Politics and Economics* (New York: Oxford, 1997); for a noninstitutionalized emphasis on spiritual transformation, see Richard Tarnas, *Cosmos and Psyche: Intimations of a New World Order* (New York: Viking, 2006); for a radical critique of West-centric world order that is not inclined toward the postsecular, see Stephen Gill (ed.), *Global Crises and the Crisis of Global Leadership* (Cambridge, UK: Cambridge University Press, 2012); Terrence E. Paupp, *Exodus from Empire: The Fall of America's Empire and the Rise of the Global Community* (London: Pluto, 2007).

5 In important respects it is misleading to oppose science to religion. The opposition is accurate in relation to the mechanistic premise of Cartesian dualisms that bifurcate reality, but there are religious traditions, even in the West, that are compatible with an organic worldview of the sort developed by Alfred North Whitehead. See, e.g.,

Whitehead's *Science in the Modern World* (Cambridge, UK: Cambridge University Press, 1930); and *Process and Reality: An Essay in Cosmology* (New York: Macmillan, 1960).

6 For a sensitive awareness of the challenges mounted towards secularism and its twin, modernity, see Octavio Paz, *The Other Voice: Essays on Modern Poetry* (New York: Harcourt Brace, 1990), 3.

7 For influential expression of the Western paradigm of world order as providing a universal template for politics and economics after the collapse of the Soviet Union and the end of the Cold War, see Francis Fukuyama, *The End of History and the Last Man* (New York: Free Press, 1992); and refutation from a Chinese perspective in Weiwei, Note 3, 139–175.

8 For instance, see Tariq Ali, *The Clash of Fundamentalisms: Crusades, Jihads and Modernity* (London: Verso, 2002); compare the secularism of Hans Morgenthau or Henry Kissinger, or even their antecedents such as Machiavelli and Thucydides.

9 See John Rawls, *The Law of Peoples* (Cambridge, MA: Harvard University Press, 1999).

10 For a survey of this evolution, see Micheline R. Ishay (ed.), *The History of Human Rights: From Ancient Times to the Globalization Era* (Berkeley, CA: University of California, 2004), 15–61.

11 See Samuel Huntington, later elaborated, yet altered, in a book, *Clash of Civilizations and the Remaking of World Order* (New York: Simon & Schuster, 1996); see also Salim Rashid (ed.), *The Clash of Civilizations? Asian Responses* (New York: Oxford, 1997).

12 See William Ebenstein and Alan O. Ebenstein, *Today's Isms: Socialism, Capitalism, Fascism, Communism, Libertarianism* (Upper Saddle River, NJ: Prentice Hall, 2000).

13 For example, see Cemil Aydin's insightful comparisons of Turkish and Japanese modernization as possessing distinctive elements that could not be assimilated to the Western template. *The Politics of Anti-Westernism in Asia: Visions of World Order in Pan-Islamic and Pan-Asian Thought* (New York: Columbia, 2007); on the rise and outlook of ISIS see Michael Weiss and Hassan Hassan, *ISIS:Inside the Army of Terror* (New York: Regan Arts, 2014).

14 For Derrida's text and a range of views, see Elisabeth Weber (ed.), *Living Together: Jacques Derrida's Communities of Violence and Peace* (New York: Fordham University Press, 2013), 18–41.

15 See Richard Falk, "Overcoming the Global Crisis: A Humanistic Standpoint," in *Global Trends: Law, Policy and Justice: Essays in Honor of Professor Giuliana Ziccardi Capaldo*, The Global Community Yearbook of International Law & Jurisprudence: Global Trends (New York: Ocean 2013), 413–425

16 A heuristic inquiry to the consequences and causes for the persisting refusal to respect limit conditions is set forth in Naormi Oreskes and

Erik M. Conway, "The Collapse of Western Civilization: A View from the Future," *Daedalus*, 142, 1 (2013): 40–58. Actually, their analysis applies, with adjustments, more or less to all civilizations. Suggestively, they believe that China has a better chance of weathering the storms unleashed by the failures in the present to constrain pressures on the ecosystem because it has more centralized control over the formation and implementation of global policy.

17 For an attempt to interpret the evolution of political life in Egypt since the Arab Spring, see Richard Falk, "Law and Revolution: The Unfolding of the Arab Spring" (unpublished manuscript).

18 Nader Hashemi and Danny Postel, eds., *The People Reloaded: The Green Movement and the Struggle for Iran's Future* (Brooklyn, NY: Melville, 2010), 189.

19 There are many variations on this pattern of state/society discrimination directed at the religious "other." For instance, there are continuing reports of vicious anti-Muslim violence fostered by Buddhist militant groups with government backing in Myanmar. See "Attacks on Muslims in Myanmar," *NY Times*, May 31, 2013.

20 And despite doubts as to the credibility of claims by Israel to represent "the Jewish people." See Shlomo Sand, *The Invention of the Jewish People* (London: Verso, 2010).

21 There is a reverse side to this process, which is a secular minority that is displaced from leadership roles by the outcome of free elections, yet is unwilling to acquiesce to the results, creating opposition that makes the state impossible to govern. Egypt as of 2013 is emblematic of this concern as both the Morsi leadership can be faulted for their lack of inclusiveness and the opposition is subject for criticism due to its generation of turmoil that has made the country ungovernable, and is pushing the economy toward collapse. See also discussion, Falk, Note 15.

22 This hierarchy has a civilizational and a geopolitical dimension. The civilizational dimension is the relationship between the West and non-West, especially during the epoch of European colonialism. The geopolitical dimension gives rise to patterns of leadership, force projection, and domination in the relations among juridically equal sovereign states. This feature of the way the world is governed has been given a constitutional status within the UN System by conferring on five states permanent membership in the Security Council with the right to veto any decision.

23 The jurisprudence of Hans Kelsen epitomizes this approach to law and society that reduces law to formal rules procedurally enacted by prescribed forms, and distinct from ethics and religious values. See Kelsen, *Pure Theory of Law* (Berkeley: University of California Press, 1967).

24 For instance, Sam Harris, *End of Faith: Religion, Terror, and the Future of Reason* (New York: Norton, 2005).

25 For text of the Obama May 23, 2013 speech on drones see www.
whitehouse.gov/the-press-office/2013/05/23/remarks-president-
national-defense-university.

3. WHY DRONES ARE MORE DANGEROUS

1   On the workings of the state-centric world order, see Hedley Bull,
The Anarchical Society: A study of order in world politics (Columbia
Univ. Press, 2nd edn, 1995); Robert O. Keohane, *After Hegemony:
Cooperation and discord in the world political economy* (Princeton Univ.
Press, 1984); the vertical axis of world order reflects the inequality of
states, and the special role played by dominant states; the horizontal
axis embodies the juridical logical of equality among states, that is the
foundation of the international rule of law. First order constraints would
entail the prohibition of nuclear weaponry and a phased and verified
disarmament process that eliminated nuclear weapons. For critiques of
the failures of diplomacy to achieve first-order constraints, see Richard
Falk and David Krieger, *The Path to Zero: Dialogues on nuclear dangers*
(Paradigm, 2012); Richard Falk and Robert Jay Lifton, *Indefensible
Weapons: The psychological and political case against nuclearism* (Basic
Books, 1982); Jonathan Schell, *The Fate of the Earth* (Knopf, 1982);
E.P. Thompson, *Beyond the Cold War: A new arms race and nuclear
annihilation* (Pantheon, 1982).

2   For standard rationale of deterrence doctrine that played a role during the
Cold War, even according to John Mearsheimer, preventing World War
III. For the worldview that endorses such extreme political realism, see
Mearsheimer, *The Tragedy of Great Power Politics* (Norton, 2001);
see also Mearsheimer, *Back to the Future*, International Security 15
(No. 1): 5–56 (1990). It is true that for certain isolated smaller and
medium states, nuclear weapons can operate as an equalizer and offset the
vertical dimension of world order. There is also a role played by nuclear
weapons in threat diplomacy that has been explored by many authors. See
Alexander George and Willima Simons, eds., *Limits of Coercive Diplomacy*
(Westview Press, 2nd edn, 1994). Other authors pushed rationality to
frightening extremes so as to find ways to take practical advantage of
American superiority in nuclear weaponry. See Henry Kissinger, *Nuclear
Weapons and Foreign Policy* (Doubleday, 1958); Herman Kahn, *On
Thermonuclear War* (Princeton University Press, 1960).

3   The arms control regime, despite its managerial rationale, has always
rejected any prohibition on first strike options, and thus casts doubt on
the morality and practical contributions of such second order constraints.

4   The nonproliferation regime, embodied in the Nuclear Nonproliferation
Treaty (NPT) (729 U.N.T.S. 10485), is a prime instance of a vertical
arrangement, allowing only the dominant states to retain nuclear

weapons, and is the main form that second order constraints have taken. It is relevant to note that the International Court of Justice in its important Advisory Opinion of 1996 offered the view in its majority opinion that a use of nuclear weapons might be lawful, but only if the survival of the state was credibly at stake. In what seems a futile gesture the judges were united in their belief that the nuclear weapons states had a clear legal obligation in Art VI of the NPT to engage in good faith disarmament negotiations, suggesting a legalistic horizontal element that is likely to have no behavioral impacts. The nuclear weapons states, above all the United States, have treated this authoritative statement of the bearing of international law as essentially irrelevant to their attitude toward the role of nuclear weapons in national security policy.

5 President Obama early in his presidency gave hope to those who had long sought the elimination of nuclear weapons when he spoke in favor of a world without nuclear weapons, but hedged his visionary statement with subtle qualifications that made it unlikely to proceed very far. See President Barack Obama, "Remarks by President Barack Obama in Prague," April 5, 2009 (www.whitehouse.gov/the-press-office/remarks-president-barack-obama-prague-delivered); the liberal realist view insists that nuclear disarmament is a desirable goal, but must not occur in the face of unresolved international conflicts. It is never made clear when the time will be right, which has the quality of a utopian precondition that precludes the morally, legally, and political compelling arguments for nuclear disarmament. For a typical statement of such mainstream liberal outlook, see Michael O'Hanlon, *Skeptic's Case for Nuclear Disarmament* (Brookings, 2010).

6 Among others, see Robert Jay Lifton, *Superpower Syndrome: America's apocalyptic confrontation with the world* (Nation Books, 2002); for a reluctant endorsement of the nuclear weapons status quo, see Joseph Nye, *Nuclear Ethics* (Free Press, 1986).

7 There are two extreme orientations toward normativity in world politics – the Kantian tradition of skepticism about international law, but affirmation of international morality, versus the Machiavellian tradition of calculative and self-interested behavior that rejects moral as well as legal authority in the conduct of state politics. A contemporary master of the Machiavellian approach was Henry Kissinger, an approach proudly acknowledged in Kissinger, *Diplomacy* (Simon & Schuster, 1994).

8 Despite their increased participation in all aspects of international life, non-state actors remain on the outside of the circle of Westphalian political actors that limit membership in the United Nations and most international institutions to sovereign states.

9 For views that international humanitarian law and the law of war generally are dubious contributions to human wellbeing as they tend to make war an acceptable social institution, see Richard Wasserstrom, ed., *War and Morality* (Wadsworth, 1970); see also Raymond Aron, *Peace*

and War: A theory of international relations (Weidenfeld & Nicolson, 1966); Richard Falk, *Legal Order in a Violent World* (Princeton University Press, 1968).

10 Chiaroscuro is usually defined as the treatment of light and darkness in painting; in the sense used here it refers to the contrasts of light and dark in the perceptions of the American global role.

11 The political leadership of states is legitimized by free elections, law and order, development as measured by growth rates, and executive political skills, including communication with the public, and only secondarily by fidelity to law and morality. Such an observation is even more accurate when applied to foreign policy, and more so yet, if a state of war prevails.

12 For classic exposition, see Reinhold Niebuhr, *Children of Light and Children of Darkness* (Scribners, 1960).

13 See Kissinger and Kahn, Note 2, who, among others, contended in Cold War contexts that nuclear weapons were needed as an offset to the alleged conventional superiority of the Soviet Union in the defense of Europe, and that the human and physical costs of a regional nuclear war were an acceptable price to pay. This illustrates the extremes to which realist thinkers were prepared to go on behalf of strategic goals.

14 President Barack Obama, "Remarks by the President at the National Defense University", May 23, 2013 (www.whitehouse.gov/the-press-office/2013/05/23/remarks-president-national-defense-university).

15 Lisa Hajjar, *Anatomy of the US Targeted Killing Policy*, MERIP 264 (2012).

16 Obama, Note 14.

17 For instance, there is no consideration of the disruption of tribal society, as in Pakistan, through the use of drones or the "blowback" in countries such as Pakistan from what appear to the public to be flagrant violations of national sovereignty. For important depiction of impact of drone warfare on tribal societies, see Akbar Ahmed, *The Thistle and the Drone: How America's war on terror became a global war on tribal Islam* (Brookings Inst. Press, 2013); for general assessment of blowback costs of relying on drones, see Scahill, *Dirty Wars: The world as a battlefield* (Nation Books, 2013); along similar lines, see Mark Mazzetti, *The Way of the Knife: The CIA, a secret army, and a war at the ends of the earth* (Penguin, 2013).

18 Before Brennan, it was Harold Koh, legal advisor to the secretary of state, who set forth a legal rationale for reliance on drones in an address given at the American Society of International Law, March 25, 2010.

19 John Brennan, "Remarks of John O. Brennan, 'Strengthening our Security by Adhering to our Values and Laws'," September 16, 2011 (www.whitehouse.gov/the-press-office/2011/09/16/remarks-john-o-brennan-strengthening-our-security-adhering-our-values-an).

20 Obama, Note 14.

21 See Jeremy Scahill on the non-indictment of al-Awlaki, Note 17.

22 Obama, Note 14.

23 Brennan, Note 19.

24 *Meet the Press: Dick Cheney* (NBC television broadcast 16 September 2001), available at www.fromthewilderness.com/timeline/2001/meetthepress091601.html.

25 For texts and commentary on torture during the Bush presidency, see David Cole, ed., *The Torture Memos: Rationalizing the Unthinkable* (New Press, 2009).

26 See Scahill, Note 17, loc. 1551 (Kindle edition).

27 Jane Mayer, *The Dark Side* (Doubleday, 2008); see also Laleh Khalili, *Time in the Shadows: Confinement in counterinsurgencies* (Stanford University Press, 2013).

28 In this connection, it is worth noting that Richard Perle, the intellectual standout in the liliputian world of neocons was dubbed "the prince of darkness," which was treated in the media as part comedy, part opprobrium, and part honorific in view of his influence.

29 For an analysis along these lines, *see* Sheldon Wolin, *Democracy Incorporated: Managed Democracy and the Specter of Totalitarianism* (Princeton University Press, 2008).

30 For detailed documentation, see Ahmed, Note 17.

31 More accurately, reliance on a discretionary approach to war is to revert to the status of war in world politics prior to the adopt of the Kellogg-Briand Pact in 1928.

32 See David Cole, *A Secret License to Kill*, NYR Blog (19 September 2011, 5:30 PM), www.nybooks.com/blogs/nyrblog/2011/sep/19/secret-license-kill/.

33 For elaboration, see Richard Falk, "Torture, War, and the Limits of Liberal Legality", in *The United States and Torture: Interrogation, Incarceration, and Abuse* (Marjorie Cohn ed., NYU Press, 2011), 119.

34 For useful discussion and documentation, see Medea Benjamin, *Drone Warfare: Killing by remote control* (Verso, rev. edn, 2013).

4. CONTOURS OF NEW CONSTITUTIONALISM

1 See Stephen Gill and A. Claire Cutler, eds., "General Introduction" to *New Constitutionalism and World Order* (Cambridge: Cambridge University Press, 2014); for earlier Gill formulations see Gill, "New Constitutionalism, Democratisation and Global Political Economy," in *Pacifica Review: Peace Security and Global* Change, 10(1): 23–38, 1998, Gill, *Power and Resistance in the New World Order* (New York: Palgrave Macmillan, 2nd rev. edn, 2008) 161–176.

2 See Ronnie D. Lipschutz, *The Constitution of Imperium* (Boulder, CO: Paradigm, 2009).

3 The April 2012 expropriation by the Argentine's government of the Spanish company's interest in its oil company is an example of

ongoing efforts by countries in the South to retain control over national resources located within their own territories. Yet it also suggests that such resources, and increasingly those offshore energy deposits are becoming sites of struggle in a new cycle of resource conflict. The various overlapping and contentious island claims in the East and South China Seas and the Eastern Mediterranean are illustrative, as is the incipient tensions involving exploration and resources claims in the Arctic. Of course, there are links between the profitability of previously commercially unviable energy reserves, wasteful consumption patterns, energy subsidies, and the growing concerns generated by global warming.

4 Jeremy Scahill, *Blackwater: The Rise of the World's Most Powerful Mercenary Army* (New York: Nation Books, 2007).

5 Peter Dale Scott, *American War Machine: Deep Politics, the CIA Drug Connection, and the Road to Afghanistan* (Lanham, MD: Rowman & Littlefield, 2010).

6 David Orr, *Down to the Wire: Confronting Climate Collapse* (New York: Oxford University Press, 2009).

7 On U.S. global leadership see Michael Mandelbaum, *The Case for Goliath: How America Acts as the World's Government in the Twenty-first Century* (New York: Public Affairs, 2005); Robert Kagan, *The World America Made* (New York: Random House Digital, 2012); Zbigniew Brzezinski, *Strategic Vision: America and the Crisis of Global Power* (New York: Basic Books, 2012).

8 Richard Falk, *Predatory Globalization: A Critique* (Cambridge, UK: Polity Press, 1999).

9 See Richard Falk, Mark Jeurgensmeyer and Vesselin Popovski, eds., *Legality and Legitimacy in Global Affairs* (New York: Oxford University Press, 2012).

10 John Vincent, *Non-Intervention and International Order*, (Princeton, NJ: Princeton University Press, 1974); Nicholas Wheeler, *Saving Strangers: Humanitarian Intervention in International Society* (Oxford, UK: Oxford University Press, 2000).

11 See Upendra Baxi, "Public and insurgent reason: adjudicatory leadership in a hyper-globalizing world," in Stephen Gill, *Global Crises and the Crisis of Global Leadership* (Cambridge, UK: Cambridge University Press, 2012), 161–178, esp. 170–176.

12 See Independent International Commission on Kosovo, Ottawa, Canada: International Development Research Centre, *Kosovo Report* (Oxford, UK: Oxford University Press, 2000); Richard Holbrooke, *To End a War* (New York: Random House, 2004).

13 *The Responsibility to Protect*, International Commission on Intervention and State Sovereignty, 2001.

14 Noam Chomsky, *The New Military Humanism: Lessons from Kosovo* (Monroe, VT: Common Courage Press, 1999).

15 Ken Booth, "Human Wrongs in International Relations," *International Affairs,* 71(1): 103–26 (1995).

16 See President Barack Obama, "Remarks by the President in Address to the Nation on Libya," March 28, 2011 (www.whitehouse.gov/the-press-office/2011/03/28/remarks-president-address-nation-libya).

17 As per UN Security Council Resolution 1973, 2011.

18 The legitimacy factor can be treated as relevant in a different manner by according primacy to the logic of self-determination, invalidating all interventions that are not credibly associated with the prevention of genocide or massive crimes against humanity.

19 For such approving interpretation see Anne-Marie Slaughter, "Fiddling While Libya Burns," *New York Times,* March 13, 2011.

20 International Court of Justice Reports, 1986.

21 See Muge Sokman, ed., *The Iraq War Tribunal: Making the Case Against War* (Northampton, MA: Oliver Branch Press, 2008).

22 The New Haven School of International Law merged what is legal with a sociological sense of "reasonable expectations," thereby purporting to close the gap between law and geopolitics by linking law to effectiveness. See Myres S. McDougal and Florentino P. Feliciano, *Law and Minimum World Public Order* (New Have, CT : Yale University Press, 1961).

23 Upon victory over Saddam Hussein's military forces in 2003, the U.S. installed The Iraq Coalition Provisional Authority or CPA headed by L. Paul Bremer III, which then issued 88 Orders i.e. "binding instructions or directives to the Iraqi people that create penal consequences or have a direct bearing on the way Iraqis are regulated, including changes to Iraqi law." Most of these orders were designed to privatize and liberalize the Iraq economy and open it up to foreign investors, measures modeled precisely on neo liberal New Constitutionalist principles. See, for example, Order 39 on Foreign Investment: CPA/ORD/19 September 2003/39: iraqcoalition.org/regulations/~Foreign_Investment_.pdf.

24 Anne Orford, *Reading Humanitarian Intervention* (New York: Cambridge University Press, 2003).

25 Falk, Juergensmeyer, and Popovski, Note 9.

26 The celebrated German philosopher Karl Jaspers argued that Nuremberg could only become "just" if in the future those who sat in judgment when Nazi leaders were convicted would submit to the same kind of legal regime to assess their actions. See Jaspers, *The Future of Germany* (Chicago: University of Chicago Press, 1967).

27 It would be a useful exercise to compare the roles of law in Old Constitutionalism, New Constitutionalism, and what I am calling Just New Constitutionalism.

28 See David Cole and Jules Lobel, *Less Safe, Less Free: Why America is Losing the War on Terror* (New York: New Press, 2007); Benjamin

Wittes, *Law and the Long War: The Future of Justice* (New York: Penguin, 2008).

29 Shelden Wolin, *Democracy Incorporated: Managed Democracy and the Spector of Inverted Totalitarianism* (Princeton, NJ: Princeton University Press, 2008).

30 Lipschutz, Note 2, 92.

31 See G. John Ikenberry, *Liberal Leviathan: The Origin, Crisis, and Transformation of the American World Order* (Princeton, NJ: Princeton University Press, 2011).

32 See Falk, Note 8.

33 See Gill (2008), Note 1.

34 James Mittelman, *Hyperconflict: Globalization and Insecurity* (Palo Alto, CA: Stanford University Press, 2010).

35 It is important to distinguish two types of legitimacy: the first justifying various forms of otherwise unacceptable behavior in accord with New Constitutionalism by invoking "legitimacy" and the second, circumventing strict legal guidelines as with intellectual property rights to provide medicine and food to impoverished societies in accord with Just New Constitutionalism.

36 Balakrishnan Rajagopal, *International Law from Below: Development, Social Movements and Third World Resistance* (Cambridge: Cambridge University Press, 2003); Rajagopal, "Counter-hegemonic International Law: Rethinking Human Rights and Development as a Third World Strategy," in Richard Falk, Balakrishnan Rajagopal, and Jacqueline Stevens, eds., *International Law and the Third World* (Oxford, UK: Routledge Cavendish, 2008).

37 Rajagopal (2003, 2008), Note 36.

38 Richard Falk, *Achieving Human Rights* (New York: Routledge, 2009), 13–24.

5. HORIZONS OF GLOBAL GOVERNANCE

1 Ralph Waldo Emerson, *Essential Writings of Ralph Waldo Emerson* (New York: Randon House, 2000), 11.

2 See James Lovelock, *The Revenge of Gaia: Earth's Climate Change and the Fate of Humanity* (New York: Basic Books, 2006); James Hansen, *Storms of My Grandchildren: The Truth about the Coming Climate Change Catastrophe and Our Last Chance to Save Humanity* (New York: Bloomsbury, 2009); Clive Hamilton, *Requiem for a Species: Why We Resist the Truth about Climate Change* (London: Earthscan, 2010); on the wider ranges of challenges see J. H. Kunstler, *The Long Emergency: Surviving the End of Oil, Climate Change, and Other Converging Catastrophes of the 21st Century* (New York: Grove Press, 2005); see also the nuclear winter scenario from nucleardarkness.org

3 See Jared Diamond, *Collapse: How Societies Choose to Fail or Succeed* (New York: Viking, 2005) for a study of whether or not a particular social community identified the threat and was able to avoid or mitigate its impact.

4 Naomi Oreskes and E. Conway, *Merchants of Doubt: How a Handful of Scientists Obscured the Truth on Issues from Tobacco Smoke to Global Warming* (New York: Bloomsbury, 2010).

5 On the benefits of an early response see Nicholas Stern, *The Economics of Climate Change: The Stern Review* (Cambridge: Cambridge University Press, 2007).

6 See Charles Jencks, *Architecture of a Jumping Universe* (London: Academy Editions, 1995); Nassim Nicholas Taleb, *The Black Swan: The Impact of the Highly Improbably* (New York: Random House, 2007).

7 See Upendra Baxi, "Rethinking Progressive Global Governance: Some Reflections with Reference to the Judiciary and the Rule of Law," in Stephen Gill, ed., *Critical Perspectives on the Crisis of Global Governance: Reimagining the Future* (New York: Palgrave Macmillan, 2015).

8 See Taleb, Note 6.

9 For an important critique of thinking and deciding in relation to security see Ken Booth, *Theory of World Security* (Cambridge: Cambridge University Press, 2007).

10 Richard Falk, Mark Juergensmeyer, and Vesselin Popovski, eds., *Legality and Legitimacy in Global Affairs* (New York: Oxford University Press, 2012).

11 Henry Kissinger, *Diplomacy* (New York: Simon & Schuster, 1994); for later Kissinger outlook see Henry Kissinger, *World Order* (New York: Penguin, 2014); for assessment see Richard Falk, "Anarchism without Anarchism: Searching for a Progressive Politics in the 21st Century," *Millennium* 39(2): 381–398, 2012.

12 Richard Falk and Andrew Strauss, *A Global Parliament: Essays and Articles* (New York: Committee for a Democratic UN, 2011); Daniele Archibugi, M. Koenig-Archibugi, and R. Marchetti, eds., *Global Democracy: Normative and Empirical Perspectives*, Cambridge: Cambridge University Press, 2011; see also Luis Cabrera, ed., *Global Governance, Global Government: Institutional Visions for an Evolving Global System* (Albany, NY: SUNY Press, 2011); see also Global Government Research Network.

13 See Baxi, Note 7.

14 For discussions along these lines see Richard Falk and David Krieger, *The Path to Zero: Dialogues on Nuclear Dangers* (Boulder, CO: Paradigm, 2012).

15 There were earlier trials organized after World War I in response to the outcry arising from the massacres of Armenians in 1915 by the Ottoman government. For a presentation that deplored the failure of these trials to bring defendants to justice due to Turkish nationalist opposition, see

V. N. Dadrian and T. Akçam, *Judgmet at Istanbul: The Armenian Genocide Trials* (New York: Berghahn Books, 2011); for a broad overview, see Gary Jonathan Bass, *Stay the Hand of Vengeance: The Politics of War Crimes Tribunals* (Princeton, NJ: Princeton University Press, 2000).

16 See Karl Jaspers, *The Question of German Guilt* (New York: Capricorn, 1961).

17 The UN Security Council Resolution was endorsed by a vote of 10-5-0 with abstentions from five important countries (China, Russia, Germany, India, Brazil); four of the five are outside the Euro-American Orientalist consensus.

18 See for instance the positive spin given to the Libyan intervention in Ivo Daalder and J. Stavridis, "NATO's Triumph in Libya," *Foreign Affairs* 91(2): 2–7, 2012.

19 See Stephen Gill, ed., *Global Crises and the Crisis of Global Leadership* (Cambridge: Cambridge University Press, 2012).

20 The strength of neoliberal orthodoxy in the realms of public reason is underscored by the failure to act responsibly in view of the consensus among climate scientists as to the need to reduce drastically GHG emissions.

21 Along the lines of Stephen Gill's discussion of the Post-modern Prince in Stephen Gill, *Power and Resistance in the New World Order* (New York: Palgrave Macmillan, 2nd rev. edn, 2008); Michael Hardt and A. Negri, *Multitude* (New York: Penguin, 2004).

22 The still controversial compromise made to achieve this outcome in South Africa was to leave unchallenged the *economic* and *social* dimensions of the apartheid regime. We can even pose the provocative question, "Was the apartheid regime really ended, or was only its political dimensions terminated?"

6. RESPONDING TO THE GLOBAL CRISIS

1 See Jacques Derrida, "Avowing the Impossible: 'Returns,' Repentance, and Reconciliation," in Elisabeth Weber, *Living Togerther: Jacques Derrida's Communities of Violence* (New York: Fordham University Press, 2013).

2 For a positive interpretation of early human collective existence and an explanation for its later rejection see Stanley Diamond, *In Search of the Primitive: A Critique of Civilization* (New Brunswick, NJ: Transaction, 1974).

3 Plato's *Republic*; philosophical anarchism carries on the traditions of localized governance based on natural human communities.

4 Dante, *De Monarchia;* Cornelius Murphy, *Theories of World Governance: A Study in the History of Ideas* (Washington, D.C.: Catholic University of America Press, 1999).

5 See Grenville Clark and Louis B. Sohn, *World Peace Through World Law* (Cambridge, MA: Harvard University Press, 3rd edn, 1966); for a more restrained approach to political centralization, with more emphasis on subsidiarity, see Richard Falk, *A Study of Future Worlds* (New York: Free Press, 1975).

6 See such World Order Models Project (WOMP) studies from diverse perspectives as Rajni Kothari, *Footsteps to the Future: Diagnosis of the present world order and a design for an alternative* (New York: Free Press, 1975); Ali Mazrui, *World Federations of Cultures: An African Perspective* (New York: Free Press, 1976); Saul H. Mendlovitz, eds., *On the Creation of a Just World Order* (New York: Free Press, 1975); also Richard Falk, *On Humane Global Governance: Toward a New Global Politics* (Cambridge, UK: Polity, 1995).

7 Raymond Aron, *Peace and War: A theory of international relations* (London: Wiedenfeld & Nicolson, 1966); H. Bull, *The Anarchical Society: A Study of Order in World Politics* (New York: Columbia University Press, 1977); George F. Kennan, *American Diplomacy 1900-1960* (New York: New American Library, 1952).

8 Henry Kissinger, *Diplomacy* (New York: Simon & Schuster, 1994); Machiavelli, *The Prince.*

9 For endorsement and critique see Michael Doyle, *Liberal Peace: Selected Essays* (New York: Routledge, 2011).

10 E.P. Thompson, "Notes on Exterminism, The Last Stage of Civilisation," in *Beyond the Cold War: A New Approach to the Arms Race and Nuclear Annihilation* (New York: Pantheon, 1982), 41–79; Robert Jay Lifton and Richard Falk, *Indefensible Weapons: The Political and Psychological Case Against Nuclearism* (New York: Basic Books, 1982).

11 J. Schell, *The Fate of the Earth* (New York: Knopf, 1982); Richard Falk and David Krieger, *The Path to Zero: Dialogues on Nuclear Dangers* (Boulder, CO: Paradigm, 2012).

12 For alarmist assessments by informed authors see James Hansen, *Storms of my Grandchildren: The Truth about the Coming Climate Catastrophe and Our Last Chance to Save Humanity* (New York: Bloomsbury, 2009); James Lovelock, *The Revenge of Gaia: Earth's Climate Crisis & the Fate of Humanity* (New York: Basic Books, 2006); Clive Hamilton, *Requiem for a Species: Why We Resist the Truth about Climate Change* (London: Earthscan, 2010).

13 For a prominent example of such a normative inquiry drawing on religious, cultural, and ethical sources of guidance see Hans Kung, *Global Responsibility: In Search of a New World Ethic* (New York: Continuum, 1993).

14 For depiction and documentation see Jared Diamond, *Survival: How Societies Choose to Fail or Succeed* (New York: Viking, 2005).

15 See Roger Pielke, Jr., *The Climate Fix: What scientists and politicians won't tell you about global warming* (New York: Basic Books, 2010), esp.

191–216; see also the more polemical essay by the climate skeptic Bjorn Lomborg, "Environmental Alarmism, Then and Now," *Foreign Affairs* 91 (No. 4): 24–40; for devastating critique of Lomborg's deceptive methodology to dismiss climate change concerns see Howard Friel, *The Lomborg Deception: Setting the Record Straight About Global Warming* (New Haven, CT: Yale University Press, 2010).

16 See Hedley Bull's opposition to globalizing legal accountability in "The Grotian Conception of International Society," in Herbert Butterfield and Martin Wight, eds., *Diplomatic Investigations* (Cambridge, MA: Harvard University Press, 1968), 50–73.

17 On neoliberal globalization as illustrative of capital-driven global policy see Richard Falk, *Predatory Globalization: A Critique* (Cambridge, UK: Polity, 1999).

18 For a sense of the deep structures of dysfunction see William Ophuls, *Plato's Revenge: Politics in the Age of Ecology* (Boston: MIT Press, 2011).

19 For a suggestive depiction of an emerging alternative paradigm see Richard Tarnas, *Cosmos and Psyche: Intimations of a New World View* (New York: Viking, 2006).

20 See reasoning of the International Court of Justice that left a tiny opening for reliance on such weaponry, and compare it with the rationale of the defense that sought to preclude all claims under all conditions. "The Legality of the Threat or Use of Nuclear Weapons", Advisory Opinion and dissents, ICJ Reports, 1996.

21 See early advocacy along these lines by Robert C. Johansen, *The National Interest and the Human Interest: An Analysis of American Foreign Policy* (Princeton: Princeton University Press, 1980).

22 For a fuller exposition of "citizen pilgrim" see Richard Falk, *Achieving Human Rights* (New York: Routledge, 2009), 202–207.

23 Richard Falk and Andrew Strauss, *A Global Parliament: Essays and Articles* (Berlin: Committee for a Democratic UN, 2011).

24 Some non-conservative liberals have promoted such a conception, e.g. Michael Mandelbaum, *Case for Goliath: How America acts as the world's government in the twenty-first century* (New York: Public Affairs, 2005), not as a response to the global crisis but as a disseminator of positive values and sensible leadership positions.

25 For critique see Andrew J. Bacevic, *American Empire: The Realities and Consequences of U.S. Diplomacy* (Cambridge, MA: Harvard University Press, 2002); Chalmers Johnson, *The Sorrows of Empire: Militarism, Secrecy, and the End of the Republic* (New York: Metropolitan Books, 2004).

26 These horizons are more fully explored in Chapters 4 and 5.

27 For exposition see G. John Ikenberry, *After Victory: Institutions, strategic restraint, and the rebuilding of order after major wars* (Princeton: Princeton University Press, 2001).

28 For a path-breaking argument in support of cosmopolitan democracy, see Daniele Archibugi, *The Global Commonwealth of Citizens: Toward*

Cosmopolitan Democracy (Princeton: Princeton University Press, 2008); and the Manifesto for a Global Democracy, www.federalunion.org.uk/manifesto-for-a-global-democracy-27-June-2012/.

29 See the important study highlighting the potential positive world order contributions of regionalism by Terrence E. Paupp, *The Future of Global Relations: Crumbling Walls, Rising Regions* (New York: Palgrave, 2009).

30 See Philip Golub, *Power, Profit & Prestige: A History of American Imperial Expansion* (London: Pluto, 2010), esp. 125–154, on the benefits of multipolarity. This contrasts with the assumed hard power geopolitics that is anticipated in Robert Kagan, *The Return of History and the End of Dreams* (New York: Knopf, 2008).

31 Although see Tarnas, Note 19, for an approach that restates such a quest for humane governance on the basis of a radically different set of *cultural* possibilities, which imply a plausible convergence in the near future of horizons of feasibility and horizons of desire.

7. TOWARD A GLOBAL IMAGINARY

1 Mark Mazower, *Governing the World: The History of an Idea* (New York: Penguin, 2012), 427.

2 Nassim Talib, *Black Swan: The impact of the highly improbable* (New York: Random House, 2007).

3 See Tu Weiming, *The Global Significance of Concrete Humanity: Essays on the Confucian Discourse in Cultural China* (New Delhi, India: Centre for the Studies in Civilizations, 2010); Upendra Baxi, "Public and insurgent reason: adjudicatory leadership in a hyper-globalizing world," in Stephen Gill, *Global Crises and the Crisis of Global Leadership* (Cambridge, UK: Cambridge University Press, 2012), 161–178.

4 Also see Article IV of the Treaty on the obligations to share nuclear energy technology; for further consideration of these issues see Richard Falk and David Krieger, *The Path to Zero: Dialogues on Nuclear Dangers* (Boulder, CO: Paradigm, 2012).

5 The classic statement on the apocalyptic risks of the nuclear arms race can be found in Jonathan Schell's influential *The Fate of the Earth* (New York: Random House, 1982).

6 See Daniel Deudney, *Bounding Power: Republican Security Theory from the Polis to the Global Village* (Princeton, NJ: Princeton University Press, 2004).

7 See Robert Johansen, *The National Interest and the Human Interest: An analysis of U.S. foreign policy* (Princeton University Press, 1980).

8 Richard Falk, "Climate Change, Policy Knowledge, and the Temporal Imagination," in Paul Wapner and Hilal Elver, eds., *Reimagining Climate Change* (New York: Routledge, 2016).

9 Influentially argued by Mary Kaldor, *Global Civil Society: An Answer to War* (Cambridge, UK: Polity, 2003).

10 See Richard Falk and Andrew Strauss, *A Global Parliament: Essays and Articles* (Berlin, Germany: Committee for a Democratic UN, 2011).

11 For a conservative assessment of the shifting nature of global conflict see Philip Bobbitt, *Terror and Consent: The Wars for the Twenty-first Century* (New York: Knopf, 2008).

12 Richard Falk, *On Humane Global Governance: Toward a New Global Politics* (Cambridge, UK: Polity, 1995).

13 David Graeber, *Fragments of an Anarchist Anthropology* (Chicago: Prickly Paradigm Press, 2004), 10.

14 See various contributions in Luis Cabrera, ed., *Global Governance, Global Government* (Albany, NY: SUNY Press, 2011), esp. Alexander Wendt's contribution, "Why a World State is Inevitable," 27–63; perhaps, the most ambitious and comprehensive depiction of world government in the last seventy-five years is to be found in Grenville Clark and Louis B. Sohn, *World Peace Through World Law* (Cambridge, MA: Harvard University Press, 3rd edn, 1966).

15 Comprehensively, if uncritically, articulated by Michael Mandelbaum, *The Case for Goliath: How America acts as the world's government in the twenty-first century* (New York: Public Affairs, 2005).

16 For opposing prescriptions relating to such a vision see Stephen Gill, *Power and Resistance in the New World Order* (New York: Palgrave Macmillan, 2nd rev. edn, 2008); Thomas P.M. Barnett, *Blueprint for Action: A Future Worth Creating* (New York: G.P. Putnam's, 2005).

17 The positive potentials of world order regionalism have been best explicated in Terrence Paupp, *The Future of Global Relations: Crumbling Walls, Rising Regions* (New York: Palgrave Macmillan, 2009).

18 For broader assessment from such an outlook, see Michael Hardt and Antonio Negri, *Multitude: War and Democracy in the Age of Empire* (New York: Penguin, 2004).

19 W. S. De Piero, "Mickey Rourke and the Bluebird of Happiness: A Notebook," *Poetry*, Feb. 2013, 585–592, at 588.

8. FRAMING AN INQUIRY

1 Joel S. Migdal, *Strong Societies and Weak States: State–Society Relations and State Capabilities in the Third World* (Princeton, NJ: Princeton University Press, 1988).

2 See Deepak Tripathi, *Breeding Ground: Afghanistan and the Origins of Islamist Terrorism* (Washington, DC: Potomac Books, 2011).

3 See Mary Kaldor, *New and Old Wars: Organized Violence in a Global Era* (Cambridge: Polity Press, 3rd edn, 2012).

4 Jonathan Schell, *The Unconquerable World: Power, UN, and the Will of the People* (New York: Metropolitan Books, 2003).

5 See Farhad Khosrokhavar, *The New Arab Revolutions that Shook the World* (Boulder, CO: Paradigm, 2012).

6 See Anne-Marie Slaughter, *A New World Order* (Princeton, NJ: Princeton University Press, 2004); Mark Mazower, *The Governing of the World* (New York: Penguin, 2012); Luis Cabrera, ed., *Global Governance, Global Government: Institutional Visions for an Evolving World System* (Albany, NY: SUNY Press, 2011).

9. DISRUPTIVE LEGACIES OF WORLD WAR I

1 See Hannah Arendt, *The Origins of Totalitarianism* (New York: Harcourt, Brace, 1951), 267.

2 See Francis Fukuyama, *The End of History and the Last Man* (New York: Free Press, 1992).

3 See Richard Falk, *Predatory Globalization: A Critique* (Cambridge, UK: Polity Press, 1999).

4 Richard Falk, *On Humane Global Governance: Toward a New Global Politics* (Cambridge, UK: Polity Press, 1995)

5 Richard Crossman, ed., *The God that Failed* (London, Hamilton, 1950).

6 Richard Minear *Victors' Justice: The Tokyo War Crimes Trial* (Princeton, NJ: Princeton University Press, 1971).

7 Mark Mazower *Governing the World: The History of an Idea* (New York: Penguin, 2012).

8 Mohammed Ayoob, *Will the Middle East Implode?* (Cambridge, UK: Polity Press, 2014).

9 See "Pakistan's parallel justice system proves Taliban are 'out-governing' the state," www.theguardian.com/world/2014/jun/16/pakistan-parallel-justice-system-waziristan-taliban-outgoverning-state

10 Raymond Aron, *The Century of Total War* (Garden City, NY: Doubleday, 1954), 27.

11 Gabriel Kolko, *A Century of War: politics, conflict, and society* (New York: New Press, 1994).

12 453.

13 Both quotes, at 454.

11. QUESTIONING PERPETUAL WAR

1 President Barack Obama "Remarks by the President at the National Defense University," May 23, 2013.

2 The idea of the United States as a "global state" calls attention to the projection of American power to the furthest reaches of the planet in ways that are detached from traditional Westphalian ideas of territorial sovereignty. The network of foreign military bases and the deployment of navies in all oceans is expressive of this globalization of American ideas of what continues to be called national security. Some other

states have varying claims of extra-national, sub-regional, and regional security, but none other than the United States makes global claims.

3   This idea of exceptionalism is affirmed in different ways by Michael Ignatieff, ed., *American Exceptionalism and Human Rights* (Princeton, NJ: Princeton University Press, 2005); also Ignatieff, *The Lesser Evil: Political Ethics in an Age of Terror* (Princeton, NJ: Princeton University Press, 2004); and Michael Mandelbaum, *The Case for Goliath: How America Acts as the World Government in the 21st Century* (New York: Public Affairs, 2005).

4   Important expressions of this American claim related to recourse to force in the Kosovo War (1999) without seeking Security Council approval due to an anticipated Russian veto and the attack on Iraq in 2003 when an appeal to the Security Council for authorization failed.

5   Such a comment refers to Obama's foreign policy record during the first six years of his presidency that was dominated by disappointment. In the last two years, with the normalization initiatives undertaken toward Cuba and even more so, by the diplomacy associated with achieving an agreement on Iran's nuclear program, the record looks better.

6   Of course, part of the explanation is associated with the compression of time and space resulting from technological and tactical innovations in war making. The Pearl Harbor was a dramatic reminder to America that oceanic distance is no longer a security cushion. In the age of emerging cyber warfare, this compression has reached an Omega Point.

7   And no recognition of the opposition to "standing armies" on the part of some early advocates of a federalist constitution who were worried about the spillover of military institutions onto civilian domains of governance, believing that accountable government based on the rule of law depended on civilian supremacy.

8   This embrace of a war discourse and scenario after 9/11 was a costly mistake made by American leadership with many adverse reverberations, which are continuing without an end in sight. For an early assessment see Richard Falk, *The Great Terror War* (Northampton, MA: Olive Branch Press, 2003).

9   See Chapter 3.

12. CHANGING THE POLITICAL CLIMATE

1   The writings of James Lovelock on the Gaia balances of the earth are relevant, as are the speculations that human activities are undermining the equilibrium that has for many centuries allowed plants and animals to live comfortably on the planet. It is the dawn of the age of the Anthropocene that is threatening to disrupt this balance that has facilitated biological evolution since the first glimmers of habitation on planet earth. *Revenge of Gaia: Earth's Climate in Crisis and the Fate of Humanity* (New York: Basic Books, 2006).

2 See Robert C. Johansen's breakthrough contribution seeking to overcome the tension and destructive dualism between the national interest and the human interest. See *National and the Human Interest: An Analysis of U.S. Foreign Policy* (Princeton, NJ: Princeton University Press, 1980).

3 This merger of state and nation is coherent if limited to impersonal juridical notions of identity and application of law, but it is very misleading if it is understood psychopolitically as there exist a whole spectrum of identities reaching from unconditional loyalty and identification with the state to extreme alienation and hostile attitudes toward the state, including giving priority to alternative configurations of "nation" based on historical, cultural, and ethnic considerations rather than by reference to the state.

4 For one view of how the state is "disaggregating" in ways that enable it to cope with the challenges of an increasingly interactive world, see Anne-Marie Slaughter, *The New World Order* (Princeton, NJ: Princeton University Press, 2004); there are also many instances of cooperation among states for the sake of mutual benefit, especially in relation to the management of the global commons.

5 See *Revenge of Gaia: Earth's Climate in Crisis and the Fate of Humanity* (New York: Basic Books, 2006).

6 I would include here various anti-democratic forms of imperial and hegemonic governance. See, among others, Andrew Bacevich, *American Empire: The Reality and Consequences of U.S. Diplomacy* (Cambridge, MA: Harvard University Press, 2002; and especially Michael Mandelbaum's *Case for Goliath: How America Acts as the World's Government in the Twenty-first century* (New York: Public Affairs, 2005).

7 Of course, realistically, governments and other fragmented actor perspectives, generally seek to serve the part of the part, a fraction or faction of the fragment. This is especially true of such actors as governments or international institutions that are oriented toward serving class, ethnic, and economic elites.

8 For wide-ranging defense of democracy along these lines, see Daniele Archibugi's important study *Global Commonwealth of Citizens: Toward Cosmopolitan Democracy* (Princeton, NJ: Princeton University Press, 2008).

9 Such a struggle has been evident in the United States in the period since the 9/11 attacks. For a critical account of the mismanagement of the balance see David Cole and Jules Lobel, *Less Secure, Less Free: Why America is Losing the War on Terror* (New York: New Press, 2007).

10 But see California chapter in John Micklethlwait and Adrian Woolridge, *The Fourth Revolution: The Global Race to Reinvent the State* (New York: Penguin, 2014) for an attempt to "federalize" their critique of what has gone wrong with governance in the United States.

11 The idea of "citizen pilgrim" is inspired by Saint Paul's Letter to the Hebrews in which he talks of the pilgrim as someone animated by faith

in that which is not seen, and does not exist as yet, and yet embarks on a journey dedicated to a better future in which that vision will be realized, not as an earthly city but as a heavenly city.

12 The issue of civilizational collapse, and its avoidance, has been influentially explored in Jared Diamond, *Collapse: How societies choose to fail or succeed* (New York: Viking, 2005); see also Diamond, *World Until Yesterday: What can we learn from traditional societies?* (New York: Viking, 2012); the question of the risks to the species arising from human activities is addressed in Clive Hamilton, *Requiem for a Species: Why We Resist the Truth about Climate Change* (London: Pluto, 2004); see also Elizabeth Kolbert, *The Sixth Extinction: An Unnatural History* (New York: Henry Holt, 2014).

13 See Richard Falk, *This Endangered Planet: Prospects and Proposals for Human Survival* (New York: Random House, 1972); on the orientation of indigenous peoples, thinking ahead and looking back seven generations, see Maivan Lam, *At the Edge of the State: Indigenous Peoples and Self-Determination* (Ardsley, NY: Transnational, 2000).

14 Sensitive interpretations of the approaching limits of modernity as a legacy of the Enlightenment and Industrial Revolution in Bruno Latour, *We Have Never Been Modern* (Cambridge, MA: Harvard University Press, 1993); Weiming Tu, *The Global Significance of Concrete Humanity* (New Delhi: New Studies in Civilizations, distrib. Munshrivam Manoharial Publishers, 2010).

15 Clive Hamilton critically explores this search for a technological escape via geo-engineering from the dilemmas posed by adherence "the iron law of growth," population increase, and continuously rising living standards. In Hamilton, *Earthmasters: The Dawn of the Age of Climate Engineering* (New Haven: Yale University Press, 2013).

16 Such formulations overlook hierarchies of privilege and status that bias behavior by those representing sovereign states in international and global venues.

17 Chapter 13.

18 In *The Fourth Revolution*, Micklethwait and Woolridge, note 10, are persuasive that national governments are generating widespread dissatisfaction among their citizens, although their focus is upon issues of efficiency and scale as the source of this public mood of alienation.

19 Some suggestions along these lines are contained in Richard Falk, "Anarchism without 'Anarchism': Searching for Progressive Politics in the Early 21st Century," *Millennium – Journal of International Studies* 39, no. 2 (December 2010): 381–398.

20 See Richard Falk and Andrew Strauss, *A Global Parliament: essays and articles* (Berlin: Committee for a Democratic UN, 2011).

21 For elaboration see Richard Falk, *On Humane Global Governance* (Cambridge, UK: Polity Press, 1995).

22 See for development of these themes Richard Falk and David Krieger, *The Path to Zero: Dialogues on Nuclear Dangers* (Boulder, CO: Paradigm, 2012); but see Joseph S. Nye, Jr., *Nuclear Ethics* (New York: Free Press, 1986) for a contrary view. See also Geoffrey Darnton, ed., *Nuclear Weapons and International Law: from the London Nuclear Warfare Tribunal via the International Court of Justice* (Bournemouth, UK: Requirements Analytics, 2015).

23 For important research on the devastating effects upon the entire planet of even a limited regional war fought with nuclear weapons see the report of research in the "nuclear famine" project of Michael Mills and others. http://acd.ucar.edu/~mmills/pubs/201

13. DOES THE HUMAN SPECIES WISH TO SURVIVE?

1 McCarthy, *The Road* (New York: Knopf, 2006).

2 Clive Hamilton, *Requiem for a Species: Why We Resist the Truth about Climate Change* (Abingdon, UK: Earthscan, 2010); Hamilton, *Earthmasters: The Dawn of the Age of Climate Engineering* (New Haven, CT: Yale University Press, 2013); see also Richard Tarnas, *Cosmos and Psyche: Intimations of a New World View* (New York: Penguin, 2006); Slavoj Žižek, *Living in the End Times* (London: Verso, 2010).

3 Jared Diamond, *The World Until Yesterday: What We Can Learn from Traditional Societies?* (New York: Penguin, 2012); also Diamond, *Collapse: How Societies Choose to Fail or Succeed* (New York: Penguin, rev. edn, 2011).

INDEX

desperation: horizons of, 110;
societal mood, 109
deterrence, idea of, 46
Deudney, Daniel, 157
dialogue, politics of, 9-10
Diamond, Jared, 163, 261
diplomacy: colonialist, 205; Obama
bent for, 17
diverse religions, American concern
for, 37
Doyle, Michael, 131
drones, attack and surveillance
use, 44, 55, 59, 227: accelerated
reliance on, 50, 56, 60; advent
of, 179; atomic weapons
comparison, 49; debate on, *see
below*; community anxiety creation,
64; international law damage,
51, 61, 65, 71; global possession
of, 230; killing justifications, 92;
Langley HQ, 229; liberal critics,
226; Obama abstractions, 52;
political attractiveness of, 47-8, 63;
precedents created, 71; Predator,
43; regulation difficulty, 47;
technology of, 61, 69-70, 138, 143
drone use debate: American
exceptionalism assumed, 67;
substance avoided, 60, 62, 70

East Europe, Communist bloc
disintegration, 195; soft
revolutions, 172
economic recession, European
impact, 240
extra-judicial executions, 65
Egypt, 127, 174, 181; bloody coup
2013, 29; conservative society, 31;
Coptic minority, 33; Mubarak fall,
126; Mubarak regime, 182; Nasser
era, 188; political future debate, 38;
post-2011 experience, 173; second
rising 2013, 183; 2013 coup, 31
Einstein, Albert255
Eisenhower, Dwight, 225
El-Sisi, General Abdel Fattah, 31, 173
electricity provision, 148
elites, Western world, 9
emergency situations, UN response
to, 248

Emerson, Ralph Waldo, 101
English cities German rockets fired
at, 64
Enlightenment tradition, 21
environment, the, religious authority
rise, 146
Erdogan, Recep Tayyip, 34-5, 37;
Egypt comments, 29, 31; Kemalist
suspicion of, 30; secularism
advocacy, 32-3
Europe: citizenship, 237, 239;
colonialism of, 217; colonies loss,
156, 192; migrant crisis, 220,
240; military technology historic
superiority, 180
European Union, 148, 202, 238;
achievements of, 17; confidence
loss, 152; fragility, 240; Parliament,
240
events, unpredicted transformative,
104
extra-judicial executions, 93
extraordinary rendition, 58
extremist, suicidal, 42

"failed states", 150, 260
fascism, European, 25, 205
feasibility, trapped horizons of, 105,
107, 144-5; necessity gap, 109,
146-7, 154-5, 157
financial meltdown 2008, 104
First World War, *see* World War I
"fixes", 138
foreign domination, indigenous
resistance to, 6
Fort Hood shooting, 55
fossil fuels, dangerous innovations,
146
France, 66: Arab betrayal, 206;
colonial ambitions disguise, 203;
Middle East colonialism, 207;
nuclear arsenal, 258
"Freedom flotillas", 125
French Revolution, 41
Frost, Robert, 199
Fukushima reactor, meltdown, 146
Fukuyama, Francis, triumphalism,
195; hubris of, 25
fundamentalism/ists, market, 28;
religion rise, 155; secular, 42